D0769986

LOOKING FOR

Carrascolendas

LOOKING FOR
Carras

colendas

From a Child's World to

Award-Winning Television

AIDA BARRERA

Austin ⫸ University of Texas Press

Copyright © 2001 by the University of Texas Press
All rights reserved
Printed in the United States of America
First edition, 2001

Requests for permission to reproduce material from this work should be sent to
Permissions, University of Texas Press, P.O. Box 7819, Austin, TX 78713-7819.

♾ The paper used in this book meets the minimum requirements of ANSI/NISO
Z39.48-1992 (R1997) (Permanence of Paper).

Library of Congress Cataloging-in-Publication Data
Barrera, Aida.
    Looking for Carrascolendas : from a child's world to award-winning television /
Aida Barrera.—1st ed.
        p.   cm. — (Louann Atkins Temple women and culture series)
    Includes bibliographical references.
    ISBN 0-292-70891-2 (cloth : alk. paper)—ISBN 0-292-70892-0 (pbk. : alk. paper)
    1. Carrascolendas (Television program)   I. Title.   II. Series.

PN1992.77.C33 B37   2001
791.45 72—dc21   00-061605

This book inaugurates the

Louann Atkins Temple
Women & Culture Series

Books on women and families,

and their changing role in society

The Louann Atkins Temple Women & Culture Series
is supported by Allison, Doug, Taylor, and Andy Bacon;
Margaret, Lawrence, Will, John, and Annie Temple;
Larry Temple; the Temple-Inland Foundation;
and the National Endowment for the Humanities.

For the children of

Carrascolendas

and for my mother

who was the inspiration

Contents

Acknowledgments

I WANT TO THANK the following persons, whose conversations inspired and informed me as I wrote this account: Mary Ches Applewhite, David Arroyo, Alma Barrera, Tadeo Barrera, Cynthia Bebon, Lesbia Bebon, Dave Berkman, Olivia Alamia Besteiro, Amparo Buitron, José L. Cantú, Consuelo Longoria Carrales, Malcolm Davis, Ramiro de la Garza, Ada Garza Pewitt, Emma Garza, Emma Garza Brann, Filemon Garza, Higinio Fernando Garza, Lauro Garza, Severo Gomez, Leticia Green, Virginia Green, Vilma Gorena Guinn, Nancy Hagen, Raul Hernandez, Dorothy MacInerney, Imelda Muñoz, Mary Pilon, Manuel Ramirez Jr., Rosa Hernandez Salinas, Shiree Salinas, Irma Deane Soward, Baudilia Dreumont Stillwell, José Villarreal, and Frederick Williams. I want to express a special note of gratitude to William H. Goetzmann, who first encouraged me in the effort to do this book. I also want to acknowledge the valuable conversations I had with the following people, who have since died: Minerva Barbosa, Jovita González, Raoul González, Américo Paredes, and Hortencia Ramirez.

The photographs of television productions in this book were taken by David Eberhard and Gabriel Suazo, as well as other staff photographers at KLRN-TV.

Rose Craig ("Rosa Crehg"), Aida's maternal grandmother, and Rosa's sister
Mary (left), in Rio Grande City, circa 1905.

Enrique Barrera Guerra, Aida's paternal grandfather (extreme right), shown with Venustiano Carranza (second from right) and other officers of the north during the Mexican Revolution of 1910.

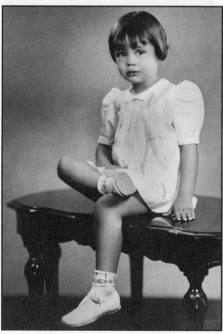

Aida during a visit to Monterrey, Mexico, to visit Tío Abrahán Hinojosa, her paternal grandmother's brother.

Aida as a first grader at an Incarnate Word Academy operetta in Brownsville.

Dorothy Rogers, shown in Aida's angel costume, during Father Phil J. Kennedy's silver jubilee celebration. Father Kennedy (center) and the rest of the Anglo congregation are pictured in front of the Sacred Heart Church in Edinburg.

Alma Barrera (front row, third from left) at her eighth-grade graduation from St. Joseph School in Edinburg. Father Sebastian Mozos, the pastor for the Mexican congregation at Sacred Heart Church, is in the front row, extreme right, and Sister Helena, the teacher for the fifth through the eighth grades, is in the back row, extreme left.

Aida at seventeen as Woman's Editor of *The Edinburg Daily Review*.

Señorita Barrera celebrates Ricardín's birthday in 1962 surrounded by the almost one thousand birthday cards and letters viewers sent during a one-week period.

The set, with the one-dimensional house facade, used in the production of the Spanish–English programs broadcast from 1962 to 1968.

Carrascolendas goes on the air in 1970. Shown from left are Señorita Barrera, Berta (Natalia "Berta Cruz" Dowd), Agapito (Harry Porter), and puppets Manolín and Ruperto.

Señorita Barrera plays the stern teacher in a comedy routine with Juana, La Loca (Dyana Elizondo).

Señorita Barrera is startled by a stranger (David McKenna) while doing cleaning chores.

The frilly costumes of the dolls, left to right, Berta (Natalia "Berta Cruz" Dowd) and Dyana (Dyana Elizondo) elicited some negative comments.

Cast members prepare to break into song. Señor Villarreal (José Villarreal) at the piano. Left to right, Caracoles (Pete Leal), Señorita Barrera, Agapito (Harry Porter), and Campamocha (Mike Gómez). Caracoles and Campamocha are shown in their original *pícaro* (picaresque) costumes, before they cleaned up their act and obtained jobs.

Uncle Andy (Joe Bill Hogan), Señorita Barrera, and Cuca (Graciela Rogerio) discuss the options of eating *cuchifritos* in a Puerto Rican restaurant in New York.

Agapito (Harry Porter) gives Señorita Barrera a lionly hug.

Doña Paquita (Eloise Campos), the grandmother, gives Agapito (Harry Porter) one of her baked delicacies.

Schoolchildren enjoy a visit to Carrascolendas. Shown in front, left to right, Uncle Andy (Joe Bill Hogan), Señorita Barrera, Agapito (Harry Porter), and Cuca (Graciela Rogerio). Descending from stairway, Caracoles (Pete Leal), Campamocha (Mike Gómez), Tío Cheo (Armando Roblán), Dyana (Dyana Elizondo), composer Raoul González, and Berta (Natalia "Berta Cruz" Dowd).

Carrascolendas cast members take to the high seas in a special pirate sequence.

Agapito (Harry Porter) takes over from Caracoles (Pete Leal), the ringmaster, in a scene at the circus to the applause of *Carrascolendas* children.

The *Carrascolendas* kids suspend their rules of "*solo para niños*" (for kids only) to permit a visit from Señorita Barrera.

Tío Cheo (Armando Roblán), Berta (Natalia "Berta Cruz" Dowd), Dyana (Dyana Elizondo), Señorita Barrera, and Uncle Andy (Joe Bill Hogan) pose for the camera.

Campamocha (Mike Gómez), Caracoles (Pete Leal), Señorita Barrera, Agapito (Harry Porter), and Señorita Hernández (Camille Carrión), a teacher, in front of "El Nopal" restaurant.

Above and right: The *Carrascolendas* set in the fifty-four-hundred-square-foot studio at KLRN-TV in Austin.

Carrascolendas children teach characters Iraida (Iraida Polanco), Caracoles (Pete Leal), Dyana (Dyana Elizondo), and Campamocha (Mike Gómez) how to make paper cutouts.

Chuchín (Ray Ramirez), Caracoles (Pete Leal), and Iraida (Iraida Polanco), the vendor, share dish-washing chores.

LOOKING FOR

Carrascolendas

■ Spiders

WHEN I ENTERED the classroom, the kindergartners were scraping the rows of small desks and chairs closer to the front. They stopped in mid-motion, their eyes widening as they looked at me in disbelief. No one said a word. I hurried to the front of the room and without pausing said, "*Buenos días, niños.*" The familiar words interrupted the silence and the children's self-imposed composure. Responding with an array of smiles, they chorused back, "*Buenos días*, Señorita Barrera."

I had never been in this classroom, nor had the children ever seen me in person. Yet, the routine was familiar. Their pronunciation in Spanish was impeccable. No one hesitated to voice the greeting even though I knew from talking to school administrators the mix of students in the class included some children who spoke Spanish, others who knew a little, while the majority had never spoken the language.

The children were in San Antonio, Texas, close to my home base of Austin. They knew who I was. I was their teacher at a distance in the earliest experiment with bilingual television programming done on PBS.

If the faces of the kindergartners in front of me were unfamiliar, my visit and everything connected with it were part of a procedure I knew well. What had been a mild, drizzly morning outside had quickly turned into the near-noon slow bake common inside many Texas schools in September. The glare from the open windows made it seem hotter than it actually was, but the assembly of youngsters paid little attention to the weather. Their eyes were filled with the freshness that always seems in continual supply with young children.

The class, like the others I visited later that day, focused its concentration on the preparations for the special event. My visit had been scheduled a month in advance, and the elementary school teachers and students in San Antonio had worked hard for this moment. Last-minute arrangements were in progress when I arrived, and it was obvious from the half gestures the teacher made and the knowing responses from the students that everyone had practiced what to do.

As predictable as these visits were, I never tired of being the recipient of so much childhood attention. Art covered the wall space around the room. Taped across the chalkboard at the front were layers of butcher paper sheeting showing the artistic renditions of the members of the class. The uneven lettering of the word "Carrascolendas," a childlike imitation of the opening titles of the program the children saw as part of their morning educational broadcasts, ran the entire length at the top of the display.

The mythical television village of Carrascolendas, the namesake of the children's series I had created and was directing, appeared below. Broad strokes of primary reds, yellows, and blues filled the flat two-dimensional space. The vibrancy of the renditions reflected from the windows and crisscrossed in a rainbow of hues around the room. The drawings were a whimsical combination of what the students watched during their weekly fare of programs such as *Sesame Street* and *Mr. Rogers' Neighborhood*, which carried educational messages into homes and classrooms in the late 1960s and early 1970s.

I had been a regular visitor to Central Texas classrooms since 1962 as part of the Spanish and English programs I produced for the San Antonio–Austin educational television station, so these excursions to meet with my audience of students were a vital follow-up of the production process. Eventually, I had used the local productions to attract substantial budgets leading to a national program. I had called that program *Carrascolendas*, the common usage of the original historical name of the town in South Texas where I was born. This new generation of kindergartners in the San Antonio classroom, like thousands of other elementary school-age children who would later join them throughout the country, had become *Carrascolendas* viewers.

The fanciful characters of *Carrascolendas*, the impossibly hard-to-pronounce name for English-speaking adults but whose syllables easily rolled off the tongues of young children, occupied a place of honor on the makeshift mural. The students' abilities in pronunciation did not necessarily translate into artistic dexterity, but they more than made up for it in the creative imagination which they had used in their sketches.

Agapito, the bombastic humanoid lion, occupied the lead position in the classroom poster, befitting his starring role in *Carrascolendas*. His overblown costume and the rubbery, real face he used to go from one language to another were rendered in comic detail bursting out of a giant television set. I could almost hear Agapito as he lumbered from one bilingual escapade to another, punctuating a broad range of emotions with lion-like roars needing no translation in any language.

On the other side of the television monitor stood the stick figure of my television teacher/host persona, Señorita Barrera, complete with familiar bangs across the forehead and upswept knot of black hair. As a young child had said in a previous classroom visit, the kindergartners had used the "magic lamp" to take me out of the television set and with the "magic" of their young minds had placed me on the wall in their very own classroom.

The other characters in the program followed in marquee fashion. The life-size dolls of Berta and Dyana, with their circles of red rouge, swooping lashes, ruffled bloomers, and pinafore dresses, were placed on top of giant alphabet blocks. The classroom of young viewers was oblivious to the consternation the dolls' costumes and makeup had caused to the feminist sensibilities of the non-Hispanic, college-age women who worked in our studio crew at the Communications Center of the University of Texas at Austin, where we spent six years, from 1970 to 1976, producing the six-million-dollar series of programs.

Children of different sizes, genders and ethnic and racial backgrounds surrounded Campamocha, the fix-it man; Caracoles, the restaurant owner; and the English-speaking Uncle Andy, the seller and repairer of shoes. At first, I thought the children in the mural represented the children who appeared on the television program, but then I realized the names labeling each of the children in the drawing corresponded to the names of the children in the classroom.

The youngsters had placed themselves in the midst of their artistic representation of the television program. In the curious way television interacts with us and alters our perception of how we look at the world, the children in the classroom were responding by inserting their own variety of linguistic and cultural viewpoints in the middle of the program. If indeed the program was affecting the way they saw language and the people who spoke that language, they, in turn, in their creative recreation were becoming active participants in the cultural and linguistic exchange.

Given the spatial limitations of television, I had envisioned the program as having certain inherent and insurmountable restrictions. The narrowness of the audience was one of these considerations, a fact pointed out by officials within PBS itself. But even in this beginning period, *Carrascolendas* went beyond the conceptualization of a program for only certain groups of children. Initially planned for young Mexican American viewers in the Central Texas area, *Carrascolendas* soon extended its reach from its first broadcast date in 1970, a few months after *Sesame Street* went on the air. It became the first network bilingual television program in the United States to address the needs of Hispanic children and one of the earliest programs to do so within a multicultural context.

At the height of its popularity in 1975, *Carrascolendas* was broadcast by some 200 out of 243, or 82 percent, of the public television stations in the country. The program received regional, national, and international awards, becoming the first American program to win the UNICEF prize in Japan, given for its contributions to cross-cultural understanding.

Such projections were not part of *Carrascolendas* during those early production years. The accolades and the impact the program would have on the children viewers as they grew to adulthood in the subsequent decades were not part of the scene I was witnessing in San Antonio. Uppermost in my mind that September morning were the children who were responding to the program I had produced. They, like me, had scant awareness of what the future would bring. Their thoughts were of the present. Mine co-mingled the present with the past, resulting at times in a cacophony of layers which pulled me in directions over which I had little control.

I was sure of some things. I identified with those children in San Antonio, not necessarily because I was producing a program they watched but because of events which had occurred nearly thirty years earlier. The program I was now doing had its genesis some six hundred miles directly south, in the towns dotting the Texas side of the Mexican border, across the Rio Grande River and beyond, to the two-hundred-mile stretch making up the northern part of the states of Tamaulipas and Nuevo Leon in Mexico.

In places with names like Mier, San Pedro, Monterrey, Rio Grande, Roma, Brownsville, and Edinburg, where border distinctions sometimes blurred, I was a young child, like the ones I was seeing before me. I, too, had taken my "magic lamp" and created a personal and cultural mythology from the things I saw and heard. And out of this complex imagery, I had eventually created a children's imaginary mosaic which I called *Carrascolendas*.

Although I had no idea that those early events would prove to be so critical to my later professional pursuits, the days I spent as an anxious, energetic child in South Texas schools left an indelible mark on me and the work I later did for young children. In a way, I carried *Carrascolendas* in my own imagination from the beginning.

It began with the Spiders story, but in a very different kind of classroom, at a time when I had no consciousness of what would come to pass in the future.

The morning had started out warm and clammy, with the deceptive stillness that days in early January have in the Rio Grande Valley. The Valley, as those of us who grew up there call the area, is made up of the southernmost strip of small towns hugging the Texas side of the Texas–Mexico border.

Sparsely dotted with palm trees and bougainvillea shrubs in brilliant fuchsias and corals, the terrain makes a hearty plea for being semi-tropical. Some people say calling it "the Valley" is a euphemism.

While they concede it is an agricultural region, they counter with the fact that it is the back-breaking labor of the people who have transformed the land into productivity. They smile and, with a mixture of pride and cynicism, say the Valley missed the "tropical" and translated the "semi" into mostly mesquite and scrub brush. The Valley I remember was mostly brown, interrupted by the places where people could afford to water their yards or the citrus and vegetable fields where growers relied on artificial systems of irrigation called canals.

By noon on that January day, the norther had blown in, sending us chasing through satchels for forgotten hand-me-down sweaters. As we rolled up sleeves that were too long and hand pressed the more obvious wrinkles, those of us making up the count of the fifth, sixth, seventh, and eighth grades sat trying to pull as much warmth as possible from the one space heater at the front of the room.

Sister Helena was the lone teacher for all four grades. In rote formation, our eyes followed the slim figure who acted as our scholarly mentor, spiritual guide, and general keeper of the one defining document in our young lives, the class grade book.

Sister Helena was friendly enough, a tall, graceful woman whose long flowing black robes rustled softly as she moved between the rows of desks. Her face was framed in the familiar white starch, and her most visible feature was a pair of rimless glasses held in place by a large, slender nose which I could see clearly from the back row.

Sister Helena's face was always composed, as if her mind had arranged the folds in her skin to show the peaceful alliance she had with the physical world; but once satisfied that all things material were resolved, the mind went off to a distant place. This was especially true when Sister Helena led us in prayer, which in our grade-school impatience, seemed to occur all the time.

In fact, we prayed eight times during the school day. At the beginning of class, before morning recess, after morning recess, before lunch, after lunch, before afternoon recess, after afternoon recess, and finally at the end of class.

Up we stood, as if on theatrical cue, eyes trained on the unvarnished wooden floor, open palms clasped together firmly at our chests in the position we all knew must be assumed when we talked to God or anyone related to him.

"Hail Mary, full of grace . . ."
"Our Father, who art in heaven . . ."
"We believe in God, Father Almighty . . ."

The echo of our prayers stretched as far as the Texas sky, convincing each and every one of us the infinity of sounds would surely take us up to the heavens above, assuring us of eternal salvation and taking us beyond the realm of mere mortals. Our prayers punctuated our days with the same steadfastness with which Sister Helena walked among us.

In those brief moments, the repetition of words insulated us from the reality of the outside world as surely as Sister Helena's robes separated her from the day-to-day world we knew. Although we were sure our minds were stuck inside our heads and had not gone off somewhere like Sister Helena's, our prayers were firm reminders that our minds could take us anyplace we wanted to go.

Prayer was the one identifiable link between St. Joseph, where I now found myself, and Incarnate Word, the school I had just left. But everything else about the two settings was different. This was my first week at St. Joseph and already there was trouble. I was supposed to be in the fourth grade but had stayed in that class exactly two days.

St. Joseph was in Edinburg, less than twenty miles from the border, and Incarnate Word was in Brownsville, nearly sixty miles away at the tip of Texas right before you cross the Rio Grande River into Mexico. Today people go from one Valley town to another as fast as local law enforcement will allow, but in the 1940s and early 1950s, travel was limited to the affluent families who had cars or to those lucky enough to have relatives who did. My own family's predicament was measured by my father's sporadic jobs, which made no allowances for car purchases, and my mother's recurring inventiveness in convincing relatives to transport us from one place to another.

If prayer connected us to the world of our imagination, then our frequent moves from one house to another, one town to another, or even one state to another, gave us the wherewithal to become quick-change artists, adapting ourselves to the dictates of the passing scenery. When the upheavals elicited reluctance, my mother's Mexican aphoristic admonitions soon brought us into line.

"*Cuando una puerta se cierra, otra se abre*," she said on numerous occasions. "When one door closes, another one opens."

"*No hay mal que por bien no venga*," was the constant refrain. "There is no ill that doesn't come because of some good."

If prayers led us by the hand, then the *dichos* or sayings wrapped us with the warmth of a good hug, telling us we had inherited more than the words of those who had come before us.

Moving from Brownsville to Edinburg during the Christmas holidays was not easy. But my mother's second cousin Tío Cheo, who lived in nearby Weslaco, once again came to our rescue with his family's flatbed truck. This was the same truck that had taken us a few years before from Rio Grande City, where we were all born and where we lived at the time, to Las Cruces in New Mexico. And this was the same truck that less than a year later had brought us back to Texas. This time, however, my father had decided to try his luck with jobs in Brownsville, so we had gone there and lived with my Tía Tencha, a cousin-sister of my mother's, while we waited for my father to find work.

When not helping extended relatives like us, Tío Cheo used his truck to transport fruits and vegetables from the Valley to places in the North. Sometimes he took entire families to pick crops in other states. Our family never did this. We did not go to pick anything in Las Cruces. My father, who did clearing of land with big yellow Caterpillar tractors, had gone to do some work in New Mexico. But the work had not lasted long.

I was happy to come back to Texas. I liked the thought of being in one place and staying there. Leaving a town or a house filled me with an overwhelming sadness. I had the sensation that if I left something it would be gone from me forever. I would never be able to return no matter how much I wanted it. When we went to New Mexico, I did not want to leave Texas. I wanted to stay in Rio Grande City and felt in some strange way the town belonged to me and I to it.

I actually lived in Rio Grande City for less than four years. These were the first years of my life, so it seems I wouldn't remember much about it. Even those four years were interrupted because before going to New Mexico, we lived in nearby Roma for a time. After that, we returned to Rio Grande City and then left again.

If we counted the days on the calendar we lived in Rio Grande City, then we really weren't from there; but if we counted the days in our minds, we couldn't be from anywhere else. Although we visited the town only a few times after we moved away, we lived with daily reminders we were from there. With the exception of my father, who had been born in La Guajolota, a ranch a few miles away, everyone in my family had been born in Rio Grande City. But being born there did not begin to describe the complex set of meanings Rio Grande City had for us. At a very fundamental level, Rio Grande City, or Rio Grande as we called it, was a place like no other. This probably was because of the stories.

Rio Grande had an inexhaustible supply of stories. No other town I have ever known or lived in had more stories than Rio Grande. The stories did not come as an intentional, formal collection, put in books and placed on shelves. Rather they appeared in casual bits of talk, thrown in here, said in an aside there. They traveled along the surface, multiplied, and became part of a larger narrative.

The principal teller of these stories was my mother, although my father told plenty of his own. Joining the chorus with their particular versions were an assortment of uncles, aunts, and cousins who were either blood relatives or whose close relationship with our family had gone on for so many generations people forgot who was related and who wasn't and assumed it was better to treat all of them as if they were.

Practically everyone we knew had a direct or an indirect connection with Rio Grande. People were always coming from there, going there, had been born there or were going to be buried there after they died.

Rio Grande existed in the telling, and something happened in the process that was difficult to explain. Each teller had a unique vision of Rio Grande, and each teller provided an embroidery of embellishments that gave the stories shape and form. We, the listeners, did the same, providing our own dimensions and changing the contours to satisfy our own needs.

If the stories lived in one way as they left the lips of the teller, they lived in another way once they were placed in our minds. This was vital to what happened to Rio Grande as it was created in my own imagination. The same thing happened to Carrascolendas, because Carrascolendas and Rio Grande were one and the same.

Although there was a general narrative, and we all shared in that narrative, the stories as they lived for me took their own unique shape. The new creations, repeated over and over as I thought and rethought about them throughout the years of my childhood, made the central narrative more real than if I had actually lived it.

In these larger stories, I could be like I could not be in any other place.

"The move to Edinburg," my father said, "will be the last one we make."

I didn't believe him, but as it turned out we lived in Edinburg during my entire youth, adolescence, and early adulthood. This was a strange prediction for my father to make, given his liking for taking chances and going places. My Tía Tencha called him an *ambulante*. That meant he liked to move around and do things. But something happened to him when we went to Edinburg. I always felt that the harshness of the reality surrounding him and the job setbacks facing him finally convinced him possibilities in life were limited.

"People in hell want ice water, and they can't have it," he told us, more as a way of convincing himself rather than convincing us.

As a young man, my father had lost a lung due to the accidental firing of one of his guns. Dr. L. J. Montague, who was credited with saving his life, told him the only way to strengthen the one lung he had left was to give up his office job and go work in the open air. My father left his job working at the Hidalgo County Courthouse in Edinburg and took up clearing brush from land to get it ready for development, whether the creation of a town, a farm, or a ranch. Obviously driving a tractor in the dust was healthier than sitting behind a desk because my father lived until he was eighty-four years old.

Clearing land was an off-and-on job. Contracts began and ended, with the inevitable wait for the next contract to begin. Whenever there was rain, there was no work. And when there was no work, there was no pay. There were no benefits and no paid vacations. And anyone who was fired left with no explanation and no severance pay. Evidently my father was good at what he did because this never happened to him.

During World War II, while we were still living in Brownsville, my father was in the group of men in the Valley who volunteered and joined the Air Force. Although the recruitment personnel told him he was too old and didn't have to serve, he insisted so much they took him anyway. He said the officers in Waco where he was stationed told him they wished there were more men like him.

The war changed the way we lived. My father joined the Air Force out of patriotism, but it turned out that being in the Air Force gave him status he had not had before. It also gave him a steady job and a steady paycheck. The government checks were sometimes delayed in getting to us, but we still had the assurance that the money would be there. When the check was late, my mother ran around "*poniéndose cara de vaqueta*" (putting on a leather face)—asking the landlord for an extension on the rent; asking Doña Albina, who owned the corner grocery store, to extend our credit; or bartering ration coupons in exchange for coffee so Tío Daniel, our great-uncle who lived with us, wouldn't get headaches.

Doña Albina was memorable, or so the neighborhood story went, because when she crossed the border to come to Brownsville, she took her money and hid it in her bosom. We never knew whether or not the story was true, but we thought the story was so sensational, I made up a set of lyrics to dramatize the event. Placing our hands in the exact spot Doña Albina had hidden the money, we'd chant our way past the store.

Doña Albina, Doña Albina,
Aquí mero, aquí mero,
Pasó el dinero, pasó el dinero,
Doña Albina, Doña Albina.

Doña Albina, Doña Albina,
Right here, right here,
She passed the money, she passed the money,
Doña Albina, Doña Albina.

The war changed the intensity of our prayers. My mother prayed every night, not silently but aloud, and, as children, we were included in these sessions. The ritual was always the same. If the prayers were going to be short, we knelt, but if the prayers were long, like when my mother said the rosary, we sat beside her on the bed. At the end, or if we were sick, my mother said prayers over us before tucking us into bed. She did this with her right thumb and forefinger folded over into a little cross like the priest did at church, moving her hand rapidly over our entire body. If one of us sprained an ankle or broke an arm, which seemed to happen often in our family, she concentrated the motions on the part that most needed it.

Unlike the prayers we said in school, which were in English, the prayers we said at home were always in Spanish. All the talk of war made us concentrate our prayers on this subject, so much so that my five-year-old brother Enrique decided the line in the Lord's Prayer, "... *no nos dejes caer en la tentacíon*" (literally, ... don't let temptation fall upon us), should be changed to "... *no nos dejes caer una bomba*" (... don't let a bomb fall on us). This brought the prayer session to a halt because none of us, including my mother, who we thought was the most pious person in the whole entire world, could keep a straight face after that. All of us knew prayer was a serious endeavor. We knew that because of what we were taught at school, and what we did in church and at home.

With the war over, the joy at my father's return from Waco as our own personal war hero was short lived. Our talk and prayers quickly turned away from bombs and toward the task of finding my father a job. After much looking, the job had finally come but not in Brownsville, where we were still living. The work was in Edinburg, where my father had lived as a young man.

On my first day at St. Joseph in Edinburg, I was told to go to Sister Celine's room. I found a nun who looked and sounded different from any nun I had known before.

Young and slight, Sister Celine could have passed for one of the older girls in school. She had smooth red cheeks, and when she was upset, which in my two days in the fourth grade happened many times, the red in her cheeks turned into blotches. I became convinced when the blotches came in my direction that Sister Celine hated me. I felt it only fair to hate her back.

Sister Celine patrolled her class with short, quick moves, the same short, quick moves which her eyes made as she monitored each student in her fourth-grade class. Her voice raced through subjects as if she were flipping the pages of a book. Before you could see the whole of the first page, she was already on the second. Evidently, no one found this process troubling, or if anyone did, no one remarked on it and, most important, no one ever interrupted her.

When I first met Sister Celine, she said she was from Kansas. I had never known anyone from Kansas, didn't even know where Kansas was except it was up there somewhere in the North. I had never heard of anybody going to pick anything in Kansas and thought the poor people of Kansas didn't even have fruits or vegetables to eat.

Although I had studied geography and knew about places on maps, a place like Kansas was as unreal as what I later read in the book about Dorothy and her yellow brick road. Since Kansas was the one thing I found strange about Sister Celine, I focused on Kansas as the reason why my meeting her had turned out so unpleasantly.

In fact, our mutual short-lived animosity had nothing to do with the nun's home state and everything to do with the fact that Sister Celine was a culturally different person. That cultural difference seemed so great, it went beyond the surface of the red in her cheeks and her Kansas origins into a realm I could not understand. I didn't begin to comprehend any of this until many years later.

As an adult, I came to see the metaphorical complexity of those two Kansas influences. Sister Celine, the youthful woman, the first truly American nun I knew. And Dorothy, the girl whose adventures down the yellow brick road brought her joy, fear, and the eventual wisdom to see things from a different perspective. In a way, both of these feminine images had significant meanings in my life and added to the myriad influences of women who shaped my own attitudes about who and what I was.

Long after I no longer knew Sister Celine, I carried with me the lessons of the spirited young American woman, whose stubborn re-silience to what must have been an extremely trying teaching situation left an indelible model for me to follow. I also discovered as my experiences with American schooling broadened, bringing an array of different literary figures and imagery into my life, that I, too, would search for my own symbolic version of an Emerald City.

When I arrived in class that first morning, Sister Celine had my table and chair ready at the back of the room. Since all the desks in St. Joseph classrooms were occupied when we registered at mid-year, and without desks we couldn't attend school, my father had resolved the problem by buying two small tables and chairs for my sister Alma and me to use.

I had reluctantly accepted this solution, equating my loss of a real desk with my loss of a town, a house, and a school. When I saw where my table and chair were placed, I was convinced things were going from bad to worse. I always sat in the front of the room at Incarnate Word, and considered myself, if not a perfect student, at least one who formed part of the nun's inner circle. This was not true for the other interactions we had in any town we lived in, including Brownsville. The opposite was true. We were always on the periphery.

The dictates of my father's on-again, off-again jobs left us on a precarious edge from which I was convinced we would never escape. We had to fabricate a sense of solidity and a significant part of that for the children in our family consisted of what we did at school. The relationship I had with the nuns who were my teachers thus magnified in importance. Since we were coming to St. Joseph late in the school year, our chance of establishing significant relationships was jeopardized. The placement of the table and chair symbolized the upheavals we were facing as a family. The moves further aggravated the situation.

I spent the first day at St. Joseph doing what Sister Celine called "orientation." She told me to watch what everybody else did, and in this way I would be able to make the transition from one school setting to another. The pedagogical strategy in the convent schools I attended emphasized recitations, and the situation at St. Joseph was no different than at Incarnate Word. What was different at St. Joseph was the method of discipline. Penalties for classroom transgressions required the doing of times tables on the board, and whenever the board was full, the students were required to do these at their desks. From my cursory look around the room on that first day, I concluded the students were assessed more penalties than any other school task, because it seemed that everyone was constantly getting up to do times tables on the board. The day was quickly filled with recitations and times tables. Before I realized what had happened, the class day had ended and it was time to walk home.

The next day, Sister Celine called on me to do a recitation from the lesson for the day. I fumbled around, not knowing what to do. When she questioned me more closely, I told her I did not know what the lesson was. She informed me the assignments were written on the top right-hand corner of the board, and it was each student's responsibility to read and prepare them. If we didn't, then we had to endure the humiliation of doing the times tables. If this occurred often enough, the student would have to return to the third grade.

I couldn't believe what I was hearing. Not sitting at a regular desk was bad enough, but I regarded the embarrassment of going back to the third grade as the most fatal of humiliations. This seemed to me on the par of making an "F" on your report card and this had never happened to me. When I tried to tell Sister Celine I did not understand the words on the blackboard were my homework, Sister Celine cut me off at mid-sentence. She had no time for explanations, she said. If I could read the blackboard, I could do the homework like everybody else.

The only words I spoke for the rest of the day were the ones I said during prayers. Praying was the last thing I wanted to do, but since the prayers were stacked up in my memory like the pages in my notebook, I automatically knew which lines came first and which lines followed. I mumbled the words but my thoughts were elsewhere. I knew God was already preparing some giant punishment for me because I had not done my homework. We were always told nuns and priests had a special relationship with God, and since Sister Celine was a nun, she could probably talk directly to God in a way I never could. Surely God was at this moment coming down and telling Sister Celine to send me back, not to the third grade, but to the second grade with the little kids. My days at St. Joseph or at any other school were at an end.

"I'm not going back to school," I told my mother as I entered the house, slamming the door so hard that even Tío Daniel, who was usually the calmest person in our family, looked startled.

My hope was to keep one step ahead of Sister Celine, so the plan I concocted on the way home from school was to quit before the nun sent me back to the second grade. I launched into an explanation, bunching up the sentences so fast, Tío Daniel said the words were like the twists of the dominoes he taught us to play. One little misstep and the logic of the argument would come tumbling down. My mother, whose patience and insights astounded us, eventually fit all the pieces together.

"I'm not going back to that school," I said in between sobs. "I'm not going back to that school."

The solution was straightforward and without reason, first from my mother and then from my father when he came home from work.

"You have to go back to school," they said.

I could not understand how they could be so unbending. Nothing I said altered their position.

The next day, my father missed work in the morning and went to talk to Father Mozos. Father Mozos concluded that this was a personality conflict and rather than prolong the issue further, he resolved the situation, much to the nuns' displeasure.

I received an automatic promotion, along with my table and chair, to the fifth grade with Sister Helena. I was to stay in the fifth grade until the end of the semester, at which time I would probably not be ready to be promoted to the sixth grade, so I would remain in the fifth grade another year and still be with my regular class.

Sister Celine did not think much of the solution, but since Father Mozos, as pastor of the Hispanic congregation, had official jurisdiction over the school, there was nothing she could do about it. As a younger nun, she had even less of a say. I had heard snatches of the discussions my parents had with Father Mozos. Sister Celine had made it clear it was not a matter of my not having done my homework. She thought my previous work at Incarnate Word was in some way inferior and had not prepared me adequately to handle the more accelerated work being done at St. Joseph.

Although I emerged from this academic fiasco with my pride intact, I had no confidence about doing fifth-grade work. And nothing I said changed my parents' minds about letting me quit school. Though my father called Sister Celine "*esa monja desgraciada*" (that vile nun), the leeway I had in this decision was limited. In the end, my father said, "You either go back to the fourth grade with Sister Celine, or you try your best to work with Sister Helena."

Skipping grades was not uncommon at the time, a privilege reserved for the brightest of students. My sister Alma, who was especially gifted in math and science, had skipped three grades. My situation was different. I was a "B" student, which in our family was okay, but not good enough to warrant taking an accelerated path through the grades.

To the surprise of everyone, including myself, I was promoted to the sixth grade at the end of May. I could not contain my joy throughout the hot summer. The prospect of joining the ranks of the best students had done a great deal to restore my self-confidence, but the anticipation was short lived.

In the fall, I received another shock. Sister Celine took over the upper grades for Sister Helena, and she became my sixth-grade teacher. I knew Sister Celine had spent the entire summer on her knees conspiring with God to teach me a lesson, but I didn't know the kind of a lesson it would be.

By now, I knew that quitting school was not an option. And neither was getting skipped another grade. Since coming to St. Joseph, I had ridden a roller coaster of high and low feelings about myself and my abilities. Sister Celine was linked to whatever insecurities I had about my capacity to do well in school, but the unexpected promotion to the sixth grade had done a great deal to restore the sense of what I could accomplish.

Faced with the unexpected challenge of Sister Celine, I made up my mind to prove to her I was not the dummy she thought I was. My grades took a leap in the sixth grade, as did my relationship with the young woman from Kansas. But before that happened, I spent some memorable days in the fifth grade with Sister Helena, a time whose significance would not be clear to me for many years to come.

Sister Helena moved toward me with tentative steps. "E-e-y-dah," she began slowly, giving my name one of the several pronunciations she had been trying out during the week. "Please read the last paragraph, and please stand and speak loudly, so the rest of the class can hear you."

I was still upset about the events of the week before, but after getting repeated lectures from my mother, I knew I could not risk having anything go wrong again. Sister Helena had gone out of her way to be friendly and had not called on me to do anything in class before this. I wanted to please her by doing the reading well, so I could show her that even though this was the fifth-grade reader, I could handle the material. I tried my best to hide my hands under the book so no one could see they were shaking. I started to speak, but the words stuck in my throat trying to decide whether they were going to stay there or come rolling out the way they usually did. I could feel the time rushing by, faster than it had done before I stood up. Everyone in the class was looking at me, and as the silence stretched out, the students from the other grades were beginning to turn in my direction. Finally, I heard the beginnings of my voice, but instead of the sounds I expected, there was a crackling noise and then a whisper.

"A little louder, E-e-y-dah," Sister Helena urged me, "so the rest of the class can hear you."

I waited a few moments, then swallowed and started again. I read slowly and carefully, but as I became more confident, I started going faster. I was now at the end of the reading and felt good about my performance. I saw the last word and it was spelled "s-p-i-d-e-r-s." Without stopping to catch my breath, I said "speeders."

The class burst into laughter.

Sister Helena tried to gloss over my mistake, motioning to the class to stop laughing. "That was very good," she said in her kindest voice. "And that last word was just an oversight. The word is 'spiders,'" she said, giving the word the correct pronunciation.

"Spiders," I mumbled in a barely audible whisper. I sat down quickly and pretended to read my books for the rest of the school day.

I never forgot the "speeders" story, but it was years before I realized there was a connection between the embarrassment of that day and the perception that such pronunciation gaffes defined my knowledge of English.

I knew I learned English when I first went to school, but I had no recollection of going through any language-learning difficulties, nor was I aware of having been laughed at because I couldn't speak the language. The nuns at Incarnate Word had never made an issue of the language I spoke.

At the time, I thought of the spider story as an embarrassing incident, like many I went through in the process of growing up. But the story, like others in my childhood, came to define the concept I had of myself as a Mexican American. It was also important in the work I chose to do for Hispanic children, whose difficulties with the English language produced analogous stories for them.

Years later, as I analyzed the best approaches to take in creating a multicultural, bilingual program like *Carrascolendas*, I came to see the significance of what had actually happened that day at St. Joseph.

I had grown up hearing stories about spiders, scorpions, and snakes, subjects common to growing up in South Texas. As children, we were convinced the only reason these creatures were around was simply so that we could tell stories about them. I heard and told my share of them. I remember hearing the story of the time my Tío Daniel Craig was bitten by a black widow spider and how he was near death for days. And I vividly recall, as a four-year-old living in Roma, seeing my mother take a broom to dozens of tarantulas that had taken up residence on our front porch.

The difficulty I had that day in the fifth-grade classroom was not with knowing what spiders were. Nor was it with the process of reading. I could read the word easily enough. What I did not know was the English for the word "*arañas*," so I automatically gave the "i" in the word a Spanish sound.

CHAPTER TWO

▪ Angels

THE TWO CATHOLIC schools I knew as a child were as different as the towns in which they were located. Incarnate Word was a convent school in Brownsville, a border town with Mexico on its doorstep. The school had a lineage almost as old as Texas, campuses in three different locations with multi-story buildings, and a substantial population of students, nuns, and caretakers. St. Joseph was a small, struggling parochial school in Edinburg in the upper Valley, far enough away from the border to give it another cultural ambience. Classes were held in a modest frame structure, more on the scale of a house than an institution of learning.

Although these distinctions were important, another difference would be critical to my own personal and professional formation. Incarnate Word was an all-girls school, with a hierarchy dominated by the nuns themselves. St. Joseph permitted both boys and girls to attend, but the ultimate control of its governance was in the hands of the parish priest.

The history of the nuns of the Incarnate Word and Blessed Sacrament was closely tied to the history of Texas Mexicans, and especially to Texas Mexican women. The nuns were proud of their history and told us stories about the four young sisters who in 1852 left the mother house in Lyons, France, to start a school in Brownsville. The Texas they encountered had few women, little opportunity for education, and none of the niceties of living common to European cities in the mid-nineteenth century.

If the roughness of the Texas terrain was daunting, coming to terms with the cultural complexities of the region was even more so. The nuns of the Incarnate Word established their school in the aftermath of the Mexican War, at a time of strong resentments between Americans and Mexicans. The Treaty of Guadalupe Hidalgo ending the war in 1848 had granted people living in the newly acquired area American citizenship, but no government document could easily change the Spanish–Mexican cultural makeup of the region. Texans struggled with their cultural identity, especially Texas Mexicans, who were torn between adapting to the process of becoming Texans and defending their cultural and linguistic connection to Mexico.

The nuns added their lifestyles and languages to this mix, rising to the challenge as they carved out a place for themselves and their school. They overcame linguistic hurdles by translating and printing their textbooks and conducting classes in French, English, and Spanish. The resulting multicultural and multilingual atmosphere contributed to the identity of the Incarnate Word Academy itself as well as to the identity which the students themselves developed.

Since their pupils were drawn from families from both sides of the border, the sisters developed their own version of intercultural diplomacy. Integration was a matter of religious intent as well as practical expediency.

As the years passed, the nuns and their students witnessed additional racial tensions as more Americans came to the area. The cultural ethos that evolved at Incarnate Word was shaped by those tensions, and the highly politicized situations affected the way one culture felt about another. The partisan attitudes and other questionable tactics of the Texas Rangers, called the *rinches* (derived from the English "rangers") by the Texas Mexicans, added to the turmoil.

Although there were notable exceptions, unscrupulous "Anglos" (the colloquial word used in Texas for a non-Hispanic Caucasian, regardless of actual ethnic background) looked upon the Mexicans with disdain, regarding them as culturally and racially inferior. The dispossession of many Mexicans as a result of shady land deals further exacerbated the antagonistic feelings the groups had about each other.

In 1859, when the Incarnate Word had been in Brownsville seven years, the nuns witnessed their first full-scale border battle. Their reputation for neutrality, however, preserved their position in the community and assured their survival.

The Cortina War exemplified the strained relationships between Texas Mexicans and Anglo law enforcement officials and arose as a result of a conflict between Juan "Cheno" Cortina, a rancher, and the Brownsville city marshall. The altercation was described as a bandit assault by the Anglos and a heroic defense by the Mexicans. Cortina lay siege to Brownsville with his cry of "*Mueran los gringos*" (Death to the gringos), but he carefully posted his men around the convent in order to protect the nuns. Classes were put on hold for the duration and the Texas Rangers and federal troops were brought in to settle the dispute.

Outside the convent walls, the lyrics of the earliest border *corrido* proclaiming the deeds of Cortina contrasted with the "*Ave Marias*" the nuns sang within the safety of their cloistered quarters:

> *Ese general Cortina*
> *es muy libre y soberano,*
> *han subido sus honores*
> *porque salvó a un mexicano.*

> That general Cortina
> Is very free and lofty,
> His honors have risen
> Because he saved a Mexican.

Order was restored and the sisters resumed their teaching, ameliorating the racial tensions because of what they symbolized as well as their daily comportment. They did as much to alter the cultural complexion of the region as the Rangers and Cortina and his men.

Rosa Solis was twelve years old in 1853 when word spread through the tiny community of Port Isabel that four French nuns, who could barely speak English and Spanish, were coming by boat to establish a monastery in Brownsville. The sixth of seven children of Francisco Solis and Anastasia Rivas, Rosa was born in Matamoros but as a young child moved to Port Isabel, part of the territory that was ceded to the United States after the Mexican War.

If one part of Rosa's upbringing taught her the survival skills necessary to living in a region constantly subjected to borderland skirmishes, the other part gave her the requisite talents to circumvent the limitations of growing up in a frontier area with few opportunities for personal and intellectual development, especially for young girls. As soon as the nuns had their school ready, Rosa became one of the boarders at Incarnate Word Academy, mastering in quick succession English, mathematics, French, and religion.

The same year Cheno Cortina's secular heroism was immortalized into border-ballad history, the religious heroism of Rosa Solis was celebrated in a more solemn ceremony. With music that lacked the popular cadences of the well-known Cortina *corrido* but that nonetheless was equally familiar to the community of Catholics in the area, the eighteen-year-old Rosa became the first Texas Mexican postulant to join the community of the Incarnate Word. Initiating a legacy that was to have an impact on Texas Mexican girls over six decades, the young woman took the name of Sister María Teresa. She became known by the more familiar Teresita or Thérèse, depending on whether she was dealing with Spanish or with French speakers. Sister María Teresa soon displayed an exemplary ability to interact with others as well as the intelligence to undertake substantial roles within the community of nuns.

Working her way through the hierarchy of the convent community, Sister María Teresa became a teacher, school accountant, director of novices, convent treasurer, and assistant superior, finally ascending to the top leadership position as mother superior. Mother María Teresa spent thirty-eight years as a nun in Brownsville and at fifty-seven, she followed in the missionary footsteps of the four French nuns who had originally inspired her. Returning to a Mexico which was on the verge of revolution, she spent the rest of her life developing and assisting with Incarnate Word missions in Tabasco, Chilapa, and Puebla. She died at the age of eighty on January 16, 1920, on the sixty-first anniversary of the day she first entered the monastery of the Incarnate Word at Brownsville.

Other young Mexican women followed Rosa Solis into the Incarnate Word convent, not only from the Texas side, but also from Mexico. They joined nuns from France and Ireland, continuing multicultural and multilingual traditions and passing these on to the girls who studied under them. By joining a community of women whose cultural and linguistic makeup was different from hers, Rosa Solis demonstrated an independence of spirit that went beyond the norm of her Texas Mexican contemporaries. The image she created affected those who knew her during her lifetime as well those future generations of young Texas Mexican women who would come under the influence of the nuns of the Incarnate Word.

In Brownsville, we lived in two houses, but the one we lived in the longest was the shotgun white frame house on Third Street, between St. Francis and St. Charles. The house sat in the middle of a row of five identical structures owned by a man named Valentín. The houses sat on pier-and-beam frames, resembling by their very anonymity the properties on a Monopoly board. Like the Monopoly houses, whose worth to a player can be substantial, the houses on Third Street were worth the rent money Valentín received from his tenants. The worth to us, however, had nothing to do with the ownership of property. Rather, the value came from the more elusive sustenance we received from having a place to live.

Each house had a kitchen, two rooms, and a front porch with steps leading to a tiny strip of dirt yard before hitting the sidewalk. A back porch was sectioned off to accommodate a shower for the adults and a toilet. The children in the family bathed in the kitchen in a number two aluminum tub purchased and set aside for this special purpose.

On really hot days, my mother did not let us go outside and play but instead instructed us to stay indoors during the hottest part of the day. To counteract the heat, I developed my own version of climate control. I laid down by the screen door in the front room and covered my body with a wet towel. The water in the towel made me feel cool at first, but as the drops of moisture began to dry, I felt tiny pin pricks running all over my body. The pin pricks made me shiver and fooled me into thinking the temperature was much cooler than it was.

The number of people who lived in our house went up and down depending on the money situation of our different relatives. The immediate family was made up of my mother and father, four kids, and Tío Daniel, my mother's great-uncle. My mother's brother, Tío Raúl, his wife Amparo, and their son Raúl, whom we called Raúl Chiquito or Sonny, came for extended visits. They stayed weeks or months, depending on Tío Raúl's working situation. Although our living conditions were overcrowded for the adults, the children had no difficulty in accommodating to the numbers. For us, it meant more tellers of stories, more participants in games and playacting, and more variety in the songs we sang.

The elder in the group was Tío Daniel, who acted as our surrogate grandfather since all our grandparents had died before we were born. Even though Tío Daniel was half Irish, his name, Daniel Craig, was given the Spanish pronunciation "Dah-knee-elle Crehg." He spoke no English.

Tío Daniel was a slight man, with thinning hair and a voice as gentle as his disposition. He was our companion, playmate, caretaker, and father confessor. He taught us to play dominoes, Chinese checkers, and card games. Although I enjoyed playing the games, my favorite Tío Daniel activity was combing his hair. He sat patiently while I came up with one outlandish creation after another. His response, after a look in the mirror, was mock anger, leading to other experiments in search of a satisfactory hairstyle.

As a young man, Tío Daniel had been beaten in a mugging which caused a cerebral hemorrhage and he had lost his capacity to walk and talk. After a painstaking recovery, he regained most of his faculties but he was never able to function at full capacity again. When we lived in Rio Grande, Tío Daniel made a modest living by selling *pan de dulce* (sweet bread) on the street. But once we moved away from Rio Grande, he was not able to integrate himself into a job, so he lived either with us or with my Tía Tencha.

On school days, Tío Daniel walked us around the corner past Doña

Albina's grocery store, called the Corpus Christi, and up St. Francis five blocks to Incarnate Word. We knew Corpus Christi was the name of a town in Texas and we also knew it was part of the Latin we heard in Church. The Corpus Christi on the corner of Third Street and St. Francis was not important to us for those reasons. It was important because sometimes we stopped there after school and Tío Daniel bought us a *golosina* (treat). My favorite was a bag of *pinole*.

Pinole was a fine powder the color of the golden ground toasted corn, honey, and spices that had been used to make it. The trick in *pinole* was in the eating and it was only after many hours of practice that you could do it well. You had to pour the powdery dust into the palm of one hand, then scoop it up quickly with your tongue. If you weren't careful, you'd end up with *pinole* all over your clothes; and if you got too much of the *pinole* in your mouth, you could choke because the dust was so dry you could hardly swallow it. Eaten correctly, *pinole* was as tasty a treat as you ever hoped to have.

At Incarnate Word, I first went to the Little Convent, a one-story structure large enough to accommodate the teaching for the first and second grades. In the third grade, I went one street over to a much larger building called the Big Convent. The Big Convent was a large, two-story brick building taking up an entire block on Eighth Street, between St. Charles and St. Francis Streets. It had a playground with swings all along one side and a patio with a grape arbor on another side toward the kitchen and the laundry room where the sisters went to do their daily constitutionals and prayers.

The nuns at Incarnate Word wore habits the color of the thick cream you saw on the top of milk bottles. Down the front of their robes, they wore a long crimson scapular with an intricately embroidered blue monogram. On cold days, when we played outside on the swings, the nuns folded their hands behind the scapular, creating the illusion they had no hands and no feet. All of us knew the sisters did not have hair like normal women, and a favorite pastime at recess was trying to catch glimpses of the nuns' heads as the gusts of wind caught at their veils.

The nuns were not like ordinary people. When I was at Incarnate

Word, I thought nuns and priests never got sick and never died, and indeed, all the time I was growing up, I never heard of a priest or nun missing a day of work because he or she was ill.

Incarnate Word was a convent school, which meant responsibility for the day-to-day operations resided with the hierarchy of nuns who lived in Brownsville. Nuns may have come from other countries or originated with the mother house in France, but the community was essentially responsible for its own maintenance. The mother superior's domain extended beyond the realm of the spiritual. She was the chief executive officer of convent affairs and was as competent in running the operation of the convent as any chief executive officer of a mid-sized corporation. As students, we soon learned there was more to life than saying our prayers.

Convent life was a business, and we were the nuns' mini-corporate staff. Everyone was enlisted in the effort, from the girls in high school at Villa Maria across town to those of us in the beginning elementary grades. Our chief aim was to raise enough money so the nuns could make it through the summer without the tuition stipends which the students paid during the school year. We became the line workers as we canvassed our neighborhoods selling tickets for raffles and other convent functions. We put on large-scale operettas with casts numbering in the several hundreds. These amateur theatricals were designed, staged, scored, written, and directed by the nuns.

One year I was a white bird in one of these end-of-the-year extravaganzas, and my Tía Tencha, the family dressmaker and general costumer, spent hours cutting and sewing hundreds of paper feathers. Another year, Tía Tencha turned her sewing machine to the task of converting her Texas Mexican niece into a village belle, complete with long billowy dress of yellow organza, matching ruffled pantaloons, and a wide brim hat.

At times, what was in current fashion for girls our age conflicted with the nuns' concept of what was appropriate attire for growing young women. On one such occasion, my sister Alma, who had the role of a cloud in one of the theatricals, showed up for dress rehearsal wearing a net skirt over a petticoat that was cut too short to pass the nuns' careful scrutiny. The solution was quickly resolved and my sister appeared on stage with the petticoat hem let out three inches below the net skirt. The show proceeded with Alma's wobbly elementary-school knees modestly hidden from view. As devoted as my mother was to the nuns, she was not pleased with these interventions.

The nuns were as distinct in personality as they were in their manner of speaking. We quickly learned their nationalities and picked up their speech patterns and accents. Since the majority of the students were Texas Mexicans, most of us learned English at the time we went to school. But unlike many Spanish-speaking students who went to public schools where the teachers were largely Texans who spoke with regional accents, we did not have any Texas drawls to imitate. What we did have was a crossing of accents that made our speech colorful. In due time, our English became standardized, and if anything, our language was devoid of idiomatic regional expressions since the women who were doing the teaching had learned the language in formal settings.

In Spanish or English, I was among the most talkative of the students. This was a problem, or at least for the nun who was my teacher in the first grade. Sister Imelda was a spontaneous dark-skinned woman from Mexico, and she believed that a kind word backed by a stern glance did more for the unchanneled enthusiasm of her first graders than any other measure of discipline. On one of my more energetic days, Sister Imelda bid me to be silent several times without success. She changed her tack. She came to my desk and placed a quarter on top of the pile of construction paper strip link chain I was working on. She said, "You can keep this quarter, if you can stay quiet for one hour. *One hour*. But during that hour you cannot say one word—*not one word*." I could still hear the emphatic "*not one word*" as I went up to the front of the room some fifteen minutes later. Reluctantly, I placed the quarter on her desk, "Here, Sister, you better take the quarter back."

In an era characterized by the absence of any contentious debates on bilingual education, the nuns did what was expedient and logical with respect to language. Driven by common sense, the nuns placed the first graders at the Little Convent in the care of a Mexican nun. Although the curriculum did not follow any specific dictates, English textbooks were employed and Spanish was used on an "as-needed" basis. The result was a school day that stressed academic achievement but took into consideration the language capability of the students.

Evident in the approach was the nuns' strength in humanistically oriented skills, and oral repetitions were fundamental to the pedagogy. Everything in the school day contributed to building and reinforcing this approach: the recitation of prayers at designated intervals during the day, the recitation of readings of secular and biblical stories, the recitation of dialogues for the theatrical performances.

Although we did not realize it, those recitations were oral exercises in learning the cadences of the English language. We sang, we chanted, we memorized. We did this as part of the school day, and all the students were involved in doing exactly the same thing. I don't ever remember any of the nuns ever telling me I didn't know how to speak English or saying I had a drawback because I couldn't speak the language. Nor do I remember anyone ever saying I should stop speaking Spanish so I could get ahead in school. Language seemed secondary to what you were doing and learning.

We soon identified which nuns were softies and which ones were not. We had our favorites, as the nuns themselves had their pets among us. Sister Ignatius and Sister Gertrude, two Irish nuns, were direct opposites. Sister Ignatius had stooped, round shoulders, and her face looked like it may have, many years before, resembled a nice oval balloon. But by the time I knew Sister Ignatius, the air had long since been let out, and the only thing left was the crumpled balloon. Sister Ignatius taught second grade, the last grade at the Little Convent, so whether you liked it or not, if you had any hopes of going to the Big Convent, you had to go through Sister Ignatius.

Once you passed that hurdle, you could go on and have Sister Gertrude, who taught third grade. Sister Gertrude was a tall, motherly woman who spoke so softly, it was almost a whisper. If you listened carefully, you could hear the sound of one word begin before the last sound disappeared. I loved to hear Sister Gertrude talk and went around trying to make my words sound like hers, until everybody said they could not understand a thing I was saying. I thought the reason for this was that I had been born in Texas and not Ireland, and so I would never be able to talk like Sister Gertrude no matter how hard I tried.

Tiny Sor Javier was popular with all the girls. At home, we always said Sor Javier's name in Spanish instead of Sister Xavier in English. This was because Sor Javier was Eva Ramirez from Rio Grande City and was distantly related to my family. If Sor Javier had not been a nun, we would have called her "Tía."

Sor Javier taught at Villa Maria, the high school located in a distant building on the other side of the city, so we generally did not see her during school days; but on Saturdays, my mother would make flour tortillas and we would take them to her at the Big Convent where she lived. At Christmas we would take her tamales made from the deer and javelina my father had killed on his hunting trips. She loved these treats and shared them with the other Texas Mexican Valley nuns like Enriqueta Vela, who had become Sister Berchmans.

We knew we could always go to Sor Javier whenever we had any problems. A big problem occurred when I was in the second grade and Sister Ignatius was my teacher. Sister Ignatius was cranky and on some days, she was crankier than others. I must have done something awful although I never knew what it was I did. Sister Ignatius became so angry, she hit me on the back with a ruler. The ruler left a big red welt that lasted for days.

My mother and father believed in "regañadas" (scoldings) as disciplinary tactics rather than any form of corporal punishment. They were angry, and my mother wrote a note to Sor Javier telling her about the incident. I was sent after school hours to deliver the note, and on the way, I ran into Sister Ignatius.

"Ah-í-dah," she said, accenting the "i" in my name, which was different from the way my name was pronounced at home.

Years later, I would finally concede there were going to be people, especially those aficionados of the opera *Aida*, who preferred this pronunciation of my name, but, at the time, all I could think was that this lady had never even bothered to learn how to say my name correctly.

"Ah-í-dah, where are you going?"

I could tell Sister Ignatius was not pleased I was in the school grounds after hours, as she had not been pleased when she hit me with the ruler.

I tried not to look at her and spoke as fast as I could so I would not have to talk to her very long.

"My mother sent a note to Sister Xavier, Sister, and I'm taking it to her," was my rapid-fire, monotone answer.

"O-o-h?" her mouth gathered the sound, finally letting it go in a slow, up-sweeping motion.

Sister Ignatius had really small eyes, and if you were standing in the back of the class, you could not tell in which direction her eyes were looking. But on the day she intercepted me in the playground, her eyes were as large as any I had ever seen. They kept going from the note in my hand, up to my face, and then back down again to the note.

"Let me see," she said, and before I could do anything, she took the ruled paper from my hand.

I knew she would not be able to read the note because it was in Spanish, but I was still afraid that somehow she might be able to understand what my mother had written. I had no choice but to show her the note.

Sister Ignatius was no dummy. She carefully analyzed each line, looking for clues as to what was in the note. She may not have understood the language, but she was smart enough to know what "Sor Ignacia" meant, and these words appeared several times on the sheet of paper.

"This is my name," she pointed accusingly. "I can tell this is my name."

"I-I-I . . . ," I could not think of anything to say.

Abruptly, she handed the note back to me and turned and walked away with a flat, "I know that's my name. I know that's my name."

I do not know what happened between Sor Javier and Sister Ignatius, or what kind of clout Sor Javier had over the Irish nun. All I know is that Sister Ignatius never hit me again.

At St. Joseph in Edinburg there was no Sor Javier to call on when there were problems, making it especially scary when I first went there. Although I was too young at the time to really perceive the complexity of the distinctions between the two places, I was old enough to recognize the schools in Edinburg and Brownsville were worlds apart. Before we moved to Edinburg, my father had gone to St. Joseph to see about matriculation for my sister and me. Because his father died when my father was still a child, the reversals in his family's finances had changed the opportunities he had to get a good education. He nevertheless grew up with family traditions upholding the value of learning and knowledge. In South Texas and northern Mexico, this meant schools that were private and Catholic.

During the nineteenth century, my father's family, like many others in the region, lived and traveled freely along the American and Mexican sides of the border; but they went for advanced schooling to Monterrey and Saltillo, some three hours away in the northern Mexican states of Nuevo León and Coahuila. Unlike the rougher Texas, Monterrey offered an array of intellectually sophisticated academic institutions. Saltillo was the site of the famous liberal school Fuente Atheneum, where Venustiano Carranza had studied, a figure whose later political role would affect the ranchers of northern Mexico and South Texas, including my father's family.

The area of northern Mexico was also critical in providing a cultural and ideological haven for those Mexican families who were rapidly losing the battle in Texas for political and territorial dominance. If the Mexican War gave the edge to the American side in settling geographical boundaries between the two countries, it did not make allowances for the cultural, intellectual, and linguistic allegiances which the people carried within them.

As education in Texas improved during the twentieth century, the shift was made to schools on the American side, but the emphasis, especially in the early years, remained on private schooling and the foundation which this could provide in Spanish/Mexican language and culture. Often Texas Mexicans formed their own schools and recruited teachers from Monterrey or other places in Mexico to do the instruction, thus giving subsequent generations linguistic and cultural continuity. My grandfather's brother, Francisco Barrera Guerra, was one of the founders in 1897 of El Colegio Altamirano in Hebbronville. Altamirano's reputation was well known among the people who lived in the ranches of Jim Hogg and Starr counties, and this is where Texas Mexicans of the area sent their children. My grandfather's youngest brother, Rosendo, became Altamirano's first teacher, a position he held until his death.

The ties to northern Mexico went beyond education. South Texas Mexicans had a common philosophical foundation with their Mexican brethren which extended into other realms. My father was exemplary of these complicated interconnections. A man of strong opinions, my father was liberal and somewhat anticlerical. Like others of his generation, he grew up amidst the Mexican political ideologies of the early decades of this century and reacted to the things he heard about the Catholic Church's excesses in Mexico. But unlike the anticlericalism of some of his contemporaries, my father's was tempered by a strong family attitude of accommodation toward the Church.

During the Mexican Revolution, a resurgence of anticlericalism occurred involving some of Venustiano Carranza's armies. Although Carranza's stance toward the Church was moderate, the atmosphere of anticlericalism affected the thinking of those northern Mexican and southern Texas ranchers who participated in the rebel leader's forces. My father's formative years were spent in this political and philosophical milieu. My father inherited a family tradition of fighting for political ideals, and in the case of the generations that preceded him, these attitudes favored peaceful postures toward the Church.

My father's family had come to the lands bordering the Rio Grande River in the 1750s at the time of the earliest settlements in the region known as Nuevo Santander. The Barreras, Guerras, and Hinojosas made up a huge clan that settled in places like Mier and Reynosa, in, among others, the land grant called San Salvador del Tule. Their movement across the river north or south to what was then the Jurisdicción del Nuevo Reyno de León, or to any other part of what was later called Mexico, was a matter of practical expediency. They had no consciousness of going from one legal nation to another.

During the civil unrest in Mexico from 1905 to 1924, the family had ranches and businesses and, for the most part, conducted their life in Texas in towns like Rio Grande City, Sam Fordyce, and Hebbronville. But allegiances to causes south of the border were so strong that when rebel forces gathered against Porfirio Díaz, my father's father, Enrique, returned to Mexico to become a lieutenant colonel with the Constitutionalist forces led by Carranza. Carranza, whose roots were in the north, was a conservative. He was an advocate of education and backed the concept of church schools.

My father, who was born in 1900, had grown up amidst these upheavals. He had been too young to take part in the fighting, but he had been old enough to have some of the Carrancista ideology become part of his philosophical formation. The political situation had an even greater impact because his father had been killed in one of the rebel battles, which severely altered the finances within his immediate family and changed the circumstances of his youth. As a result, his schooling was limited and at a young age, he started working to support his mother and younger sisters.

My father was not a Carrancista in the same sense that his father might have been, but his ideas about education and church schools were in keeping with the Constitutionalist leader's philosophy. Although my father's work brought a low and uncertain salary and paying private school tuition was a distinct hardship, he always insisted we attend Catholic schools. When he inquired at St. Joseph, he was told the school had filled all available desks and there were no more spaces available. The nuns were polite but firm. They could not accommodate us. We would have to be enrolled in the public school.

No amount of entreaty would change the principal's position. In desperation my parents went to the pastor of Sacred Heart and asked for his intercession.

The pastor was Father Sebastián Mozos, a young, handsome Spaniard whose gift of oratory filled the Sacred Heart Church on Sundays and all holy days of obligation. Father Mozos' favorite target were the "*protestontos*," his coined expression mixing "*protestantes*" (Protestants) with "*tontos*" (fools).

What Father Mozos lacked in ecumenical spirit, he made up in a personality that was engaging and friendly when he was not sermonizing from the pulpit. Everyone seemed to attribute his bombastic outbursts from the pulpit, which they thoroughly enjoyed, to the fact that people from Spain had an exaggerated fear of Protestants.

My father and Father Mozos became immediate friends. My father's own heritage of rebellion meshed with the priest's outspoken bent, and whatever natural chemistry did not handle was taken care of by Father Mozos' appreciation and understanding of my father's name.

My father's name was Fadrique, a name that perplexed everyone who heard it. No one, Mexican or Anglo, could pronounce it, and everyone wondered how his parents had chosen such a name. He was alternately called Fabrique, Federico, Fabricio, and a host of other less worthy variations. The most Anglos could manage was Fred.

Father Mozos pronounced the name easily and correctly on the first try. My father was understandably intrigued and questioned his ease of pronunciation. Father Mozos said anyone who knew Spanish history would have no difficulty with the name.

My father, who was a history aficionado, was delighted to hear there was a whole line of Fadriques who had been kings of various regions of the Spanish empire from the thirteenth through the fifteenth centuries. The question of our matriculation at St. Joseph was quickly resolved, and my father bought two small tables and chairs so Alma and I could be squeezed into our respective classrooms.

Since St. Joseph was a parochial school, it was attached to a particular parish and legally under the jurisdiction of the priests connected with that parish. St. Joseph was staffed by the Sisters of Mercy and controlled by the oblate priests of the Sacred Heart Parish. The school and the church were housed in modest white frame structures on opposite corners from each other. I remember hurrying to church every morning, a sheet of notebook paper attached to my hair with a bobby pin, then back out again after mass, across East Kuhn Street, through the dirt playground with the one lone crossbar that was the bottom half of a seesaw, and up the porch steps to the T-shaped building where classes were held.

It was at Sacred Heart Church that I said endless nine-day prayers called "novenas" to grow long nails and received holy communion on nine First Fridays, guaranteeing I would not die with a mortal sin on my soul and run the risk of going straight to hell. I prayed endless penances of Hail Marys and Our Fathers for essentially the same type of sins. In my case, the sins were disobeying my mother and on occasion doing such things as telling my youngest brother he was going to turn into a girl on his sixth birthday.

St. Joseph had a total of five rooms, with the fifth, sixth, seventh, and eighth grades sharing one room, and primer through fourth grades each having one of the others. A hallway in the middle of the school housed a closet converted into a library the year I was in the seventh grade. I became one of the librarians, helping to catalogue and check out the used books donated by a parishioner.

The school was staffed by four nuns who stayed in Edinburg from one to two years. It was unusual for the mother house of the Sisters of Mercy to leave a nun at St. Joseph for a long period of time. A Texas Mexican secular teacher alternated primer and first-grade teaching duties with Sister Imelda, the American nun who was the principal. The year I first went to St. Joseph, these two beginning classes had as many as seventy children each. Total student enrollment was around 250 students, mostly Texas Mexican children from generally poor homes. Some children from middle class old-line Texas Mexican families also attended, as did a few Anglos, one or two of whom were children of wealthy Catholic families whose interest in a religious education for their children took precedence over whatever material advantages may have been available in Edinburg's public schools.

Public schools, neighborhoods, churches, and businesses in Texas were generally segregated, and Edinburg was no different from other cities. The elementary schools in Edinburg followed an east–west pattern cut along ethnic, racial, and socioeconomic lines. Five blocks away from St. Joseph, across the railroad tracks to the east, was Austin, the Mexican public school. Carver, the black school, was three or four blocks further toward the same end of town. Sam Houston, the Anglo school, was on the west side of the city.

The nuns at St. Joseph belonged to the Irish-originated Sisters of Mercy of the Union of the United States, whose American mother house was in St. Louis. The Sisters of Mercy had come to this country in 1843, among the first large wave of Irish immigrants. The Irish accounted for 45 percent of all new arrivals during the 1840s, and among other things, provided the country with much of the leadership of the Catholic Church. The nuns established themselves throughout the Northeast in cities like Pittsburgh and New York, where there were large numbers of Irish immigrants. From there they went throughout the Midwest, eventually to St. Louis and New Orleans, and finally, in 1875, to Indianola and Refugio in Texas.

The sisters came to the state initially to set up schools where groups of Irish immigrants were founding settlements, but as the community of the Sisters of Mercy spread geographically, its schools were established wherever the need occurred. The nuns eventually went to Laredo on the Texas–Mexican border, and then, in 1907, to the Rio Grande Valley.

The Sisters of Mercy went to Edinburg in 1916 during a period characterized by ethnic tensions and war. Shortly after their arrival, events such as the Zimmerman telegram incident polarized the country against Germany and Mexico, and within a few months led the United States into World War I. President Woodrow Wilson's ideas of Anglo American superiority heightened an overzealous surge of patriotism, intensifying notions of cultural conformity and appropriate cultural values. Texas lawmakers echoed these sentiments, declaring in 1918 that public schools had to teach patriotism and conduct classes in English.

In Edinburg, the Sisters of Mercy originally were public school teachers employed by the State of Texas, but eventually, public school reforms, plus Ku Klux Klan sentiments against Catholics and especially against having religious orders connected with public school teaching, brought this to an end. In 1921, the Sacred Heart parish opened St. Joseph and asked the Sisters of Mercy to take over the teaching tasks.

The ethnic tensions facing the Sisters of Mercy were different from those facing the sisters of the Incarnate Word when they first came to Brownsville after the Mexican War. Edinburg was some sixteen miles from the Mexican border, which meant the relationships between Texas Mexicans and Mexico Mexicans that existed in the Brownsville school were not analogous to those occurring in Edinburg.

The history of the Sisters of Mercy was not connected with the history of Texas Mexicans to the same degree that occurred with Incarnate Word. Perhaps more important was the fact that by the time the Sisters of Mercy came to Edinburg, the balance of cultural power in areas further from the border had shifted toward the Anglos, a factor which affected whatever was happening in individual parishes, as well as any corresponding parochial schools.

For Texas Mexicans, the new mandates instituted by the state legislature did nothing more than add another page on what were recurring chapters in their history. If indeed there was renewed vigor on the part of the state's political leaders to change the cultural and linguistic landscape of the schools, Texas Mexicans continued to instill in their children their own brand of cultural and linguistic survival. This did not mean, however, that Texas Mexicans were closed off from other cultural and linguistic connections. In what generally has been and continues to be the cultural paradox of many American communities, while ethnic tensions prevail at a political level, a secondary ethnic dynamic can and does exist at a personal level.

As more ethnic groups came to South Texas, the cultural makeup of communities such as Rio Grande City and others in the Rio Grande Valley developed and flourished, albeit not totally without ethnic tensions. In some instances, the resulting hybridization, with an overarching dominance of Spanish–Mexican heritage, created a peaceful cross-cultural coexistence among the families populating the area.

Marriages in my own family during the nineteenth and early part of the twentieth centuries combined names like Cox, Oosterveen, Landin, Dougherty, Campione (later Champion), Saunders, Danelli, Dreumont, Kramer, and Craig with Barrera, Guerra, Hinojosa, Vasquez, and Hernández. The cultural and linguistic mixes imbued the families with a diversity which was acceptable and seen as normal. But the prevailing sense, at least within families, gave precedence to Spanish and Mexican values and language without necessarily denigrating any of the others.

When I was growing up, we knew some cities in Texas were Mexican and others were not. Laredo, Brownsville, and Rio Grande City were Mexican towns. We knew that many people in these cities spoke Spanish, whether they were Mexican or not. This was especially true of places like Rio Grande City. Everyone there, including the Anglos, had names that were mexicanized.

I grew up hearing about "*el doctor* Hoeness," for example. It was not until I was an undergraduate student at the University of Texas taking a Spanish literature class and beginning to question the roots of Texas–Mexican Spanish that I thought about asking my parents how you spelled "Hoeness." "J-o-n-e-s," was the ready reply I was given, and it was only then that I realized the doctor was not Mexican.

My mother's family heritage was half Irish, yet no one in the family, with the exception of her Irish grandfather, spoke much English. The children of that grandfather had names which were all pronounced in Spanish: Rosa (Rose), Mereh (Mary), Daniel (Daniel), and Rineh (Irene).

One of my father's sisters, Isabel, married a man named Henry Danelli, and we knew he was Italian because Tía Chabela went to New York to live and learned Italian. My father's youngest sister, Rosenda, married a man named Abel Dreumont. All of us thought Tío Abel was Mexican because they stayed in Rio Grande City and the only thing anybody ever heard Tío Abel speak was Spanish. It wasn't until I was an adult that I found out Tío Abel was French.

Edinburg was not a Mexican town. Part of this was due to the dominance of Anglos in the political structure, and part was the result of the absence of a Mexican history connected with the city. But as kids, we were not necessarily aware of these things. What we knew was that Edinburg was not Mexican because more people there spoke English than Spanish, or when they spoke English, they seemed to speak it better. And if they spoke Spanish, they did not really understand the jokes or the words with the double meanings.

But even in Edinburg, there were strong currents of Mexican culture and language which filtered in through the electronic media. There was a distinct following for XEW, the Mexico City radio station my family listened to in the evenings. Every other commercial on XEW (pronounced "*equis, eh, doh-bleh oo*") seemed to have the refrains advertising the soap and the orange soft drink—"*Por fin, Camay*," and "*Ya es hora para tomar un* Spur."

We never tired of hearing the announcers giving the English words Spanish pronunciations, and in our own repetitions of the commercials, we would also say "Cah-my" and "Es-p-oo-oo-r-r," with that special intonation we knew was unique to anyone living in Mexico.

We were also fans of the program featuring the rapid-fire questions of "*El doctor* I.Q.," whose questions about everything, including Mexican history, were as drawn out as the "E-e-e—C-oo-oo" announcing the quizmaster's name.

When we weren't parroting the commercials and challenging each other with miscellaneous historical facts, we were duplicating what we thought were exact replicas of the songs we heard on the radio. *Rancheras*, *corridos*, *danzones*, *boleros*, *pasos dobles*, *valses*, *norteñas*, *tangos*, *mambos*, and other forms filled our childhood musical repertoire, educating us through oral mimicry in the sounds and nuances of the language.

We also had Valley Spanish-language radio programs, although these programs when they first began broadcasting suffered discriminatory scheduling practices and were placed either extremely early in the morning or very late at night, the two times considered the most undesirable in radio. Eventually as the station owners became convinced of the commercial potential of these programs, the schedules improved, but into the 1950s and 1960s the programs still populated the periphery of the broadcast day.

At least in its initial years, KURV in Edinburg, owned by Judge J. C. Looney, chairman of the Hidalgo County Democratic Party, and Texas Senator Rogers Kelly, placed the two Spanish-language programs they produced in the early morning and afternoon but eventually shifted the afternoon program to late night. Regardless of the disadvantages of the hours, the two disc jockeys in Edinburg became local heroes. These two programs competed for audiences which sometimes were interpreted as divided by class distinctions, one appealing to the working class and the other attracting a more middle class base. In actuality, the class differences were largely superficial since the majority of listeners were poor and the majority worked at ordinary and not professional jobs. Rather than class, the audience split favored preferences for musical and language styles, which some could interpret as having a semblance of language snobbery, since one group closely identified with the homegrown *norteño* accordion and guitar sounds of Texas Mexican artists and the other group wanted to retain the original flavor of the *mariachi*, *ranchera*, and *bolero* styles of artists who came from Mexico.

The Edinburg announcers, both in language capacity and countries of origin, turned the tables on any linguistic stereotyping which may have been superimposed on them. The Mexican-born Pedro Suarez filled his early-morning program with the conjunto Texas Mexican regional music of Narciso Martinez, known as *El huracán del Valle* (The Valley Hurricane) and Santiago Jimenez, whose son Flaco later became a well-known artist. Texas native Ramiro de la Garza, whose program came later in the day, filled his time slot with the *mariachi* and *bolero* styles of Mexican singers such as Miguel Aceves Mejía, Lola Beltrán, and Amalia Mendoza. Both announcers had melodic and appealing voices, but the preferred program at our house was Ramiro de la Garza's, for reasons that had little to do with class distinctions. Since my mother largely controlled the radio dial, she gravitated to lyrics that she could readily memorize, and Ramiro's singers succeeded in doing this for her. More important, however, was the fact that Ramiro's program had women singers, and their songs had themes which appealed to women. In contrast, *conjunto* artists of the time were largely male. An added aspect was the fact that Ramiro was from an old Valley family, known to my parents and their extended circle of friends and relatives, and these familial connections provided important points of identification.

All of us looked up to Ramiro, whose slim frame and gracious demeanor seemed to be eternally youthful. Like others of the time, Ramiro had had no media preparation. His training had started in the late 1930s when at fifteen he would ride around with Jimmy Longoria in a car rigged with a homemade sound system. The two would wander through the corrugated cardboard *tejabanes* (shanties) hidden in the citrus orchards owned by the Bentsen family, known for their extensive land holdings as well as political prominence. In those out-of-the-way, dust-filled treks, Ramiro would announce the Saturday night Mexican movies that were shown at the Aztec theater, the only venue having any Spanish-language cinema. The people who lived in the shanties were the Mexican nationals who crossed the border illegally to pick the citrus and other produce belonging to landowners like the Bentsens, and the ambulatory advertisements were meant to attract them to the movies scheduled for 11 to 11:30 P.M., after the English-speaking audiences had seen the earlier American shows. The Aztec was owned by Dr. L. J. Montague, my father's family doctor, who early on had recognized the potential of appealing to Mexican audiences.

The Mexican-movie gimmick proved so popular that Dr. Montague had been able to increase his theatrical holdings, leaving the Aztec for American movies and Saturday serials and opening up El Teatro Juárez, devoted exclusively to Mexican fare. Eventually, he also opened the Citrus, which became the main English-language theater. El Teatro Juárez, where I had my first job, brought Mexican movies and live variety shows to Edinburg.

Jorge Negrete and Pedro Infante, the great singing Mexican *charros*, were larger than life as heroes of the downtrodden. María Felix and Sara García, with their respective depictions of the glamourous movie queen and the older woman of wisdom, were the protagonists in dramas that were as filled with as many emotional complexities as the ones they elicited from the audience. The comics Cantínflas and Tin Tan, as well as a host of others, brought laughter as well as a welcome respite from the tears that inevitably occurred during a good Mexican movie.

The larger crowds, including increasing numbers of Texas Mexican kids, went to the Citrus, where they saw John Wayne and other American heroes whose movies were more polished; but nothing compared to the unspoken cultural messages received from the Mexican productions. Although we did not recognize it at the time, nor could we have articulated it in words, there were pluses for those of us who frequented the old-style, sometimes ill-conceived, and largely homespun melodramas of the Mexican films.

While the kids who only saw the John Wayne movies had the advantages of technology, those of us who were spared much of this viewing were also spared the deplorable depictions of Mexicans shuffling around in some *cantina* (bar) invariably playing second banana to the dashing American stars.

There were ethnic divisions at St. Joseph that went beyond the easy familiarity of tortillas and tamales that existed with some of the nuns at Incarnate Word. The sisters at St. Joseph were Americans and the prevailing ethos at St. Joseph was Anglo. There was Sister Celine, the nun from Kansas who was to receive such prominence in my life in those early years. Sister Stephen was from Rhode Island, Sister Judith from Oklahoma, and Sister Regis from Texas. Sister Imelda, the principal and first-grade teacher and the nun with the longest tenure while I was at St. Joseph, was actually Canadian, of Irish ancestry; but to the students, Sister Imelda was identified as an American.

We thought of the nuns as Anglos, and those of us who were Texas Mexicans did not identify with them, either because they didn't speak Spanish or because their Angloness predominated in some other way. The secular teacher in the school was a Texas Mexican but because of her lay status was not part of the religious hierarchy, and so we, as children, knew she was not very important.

There was no overarching sense of multiculturalism or multilingualism in Edinburg, as there had been at the convent school in Brownsville. The nuns did not speak of their cultural heritage, nor we of ours, at least not in the context of the school setting. These nuns did not overtly discriminate against the Texas Mexican students, nor do I ever remember anyone ever saying that we could not speak Spanish. Rather, these nuns presented themselves as Anglos, and as such, belonged to the larger Anglo world and whatever was happening there. The atmosphere that prevailed at the school and at the parish that had jurisdiction over it was one of ethnic and racial separation.

The hierarchical structure was also different at St. Joseph. Whereas the management at Incarnate Word placed the ultimate responsibility on the women, who ran the complex business of the convent, the gender roles at St. Joseph were more traditional. The nuns at St. Joseph taught at the school, but it was the parish priests who actually controlled the school operation.

By the time we moved to Edinburg, the parish of Sacred Heart and what eventually became the parish of St. Joseph had been split. The historical intention was to segregate the American and Mexican congregations. Father Alfonso Jalbert, the first oblate pastor of the Sacred Heart Church, told his superiors in 1927 when he first arrived in Edinburg that although both groups worked in harmony, a church for the English-speaking Catholic people would eventually have to be built in some other part of the city. Father Phil J. Kennedy became the pastor of Sacred Heart in 1929, at a time when priests and other church officials considered it a "handicap" to have to minister to two races in two languages.

Perhaps because of limitations on the number of priests, the church continued as one group until 1942, when the congregations were officially split. Since there was only one church at this time, both groups continued to use the same building for services. Father Kennedy became the pastor for the Americans and Father Mozos was appointed pastor for the Mexicans. Eventually, two new churches were built and the congregations went their separate ways; and also in due time, an American Catholic school was also built and the Anglos transferred to the new school. Father Kennedy took the name St. Joseph with him and the Mexican school changed its name to Sacred Heart.

I knew Father Kennedy as a distant, enigmatic figure. I knew he was part of the Anglo congregation, and I knew he had seniority in some way, but I was not clear on how he had come by that stature. I guessed it had something to do with his age, but I had a suspicion that perhaps it had more to do with his being an Anglo. Father Mozos was clearly the junior priest, even though he was called the pastor of Sacred Heart.

The day Sister Stephen told us that Father Kennedy was going to have a silver jubilee, we were all excited, not because we really knew what a jubilee was, but because we figured this would give us a welcome break from the routine of studying. The highlight of the festivities would be a schoolwide ceremony at which an angel would present Father Kennedy with a gift of silver coins. The angel would not only represent the whole school but would deliver a speech especially written for the occasion.

I was as shocked as everybody else when I was chosen to be the angel. My father joked about the fact that he had never seen any dark-skinned angels and I would resemble "*una mosca en leche*," (a fly in milk) if I wore a white costume; but my mother knew this was just my father's outspoken manner, and she had no such qualms about her daughter's abilities to execute the starring role. My mother immediately mobilized the family and neighborhood, and soon practically everyone we knew was involved in the design of the angel costume, the finding of appropriate seamstresses, and the selection of suitable fabrics. My sister Alma coached me as I memorized my speech and my five-year-old brother Tadeo became an audience of one as I practiced my delivery and went around for days imitating "From all these people" and making the grand-arm gesture Sister Stephen had instructed me to do.

The costume far exceeded everyone's expectations. It had a long glittery white gown with huge feathery wings, and a headdress that was certainly angelic, if not queenly. We had consulted with the nuns throughout these preparations, and they were delighted to hear of each new development, so much so that a couple of weeks before the event, one of the nuns asked if Dorothy Rogers, a girl from the Anglo congregation, could borrow the costume so she could be the angel in a separate ceremony the Anglo community was planning for Father Kennedy. I was not happy at the prospect of having to share what I considered the symbol of my theatrical achievement. My family discussed the issue for days. We talked at length about the delicacy of the costume and about my selfishness and lack of charity. I felt guilty but remained unmoved.

In one of our more heated exchanges, I told my mother, "I will not let anyone else wear my costume, and if Dorothy Rogers wants to be an angel, she can make her own costume." My mother would hear no more. Dorothy Rogers borrowed the costume.

Years later when we were both recently out of high school, Dorothy and I worked at the local newspaper. We came to know each other, although we never discussed Father Kennedy's jubilee. Years later Dorothy would tell me she was oblivious to anything that had occurred with respect to the angel costume. At the newspaper, I had found her to be a pleasant and friendly woman, but we didn't become close friends because at that time in Edinburg little socializing occurred between Anglos and Mexicans. I remember thinking about that silver jubilee and all the acrimony it had caused. Even though I realized there was a lot more to my childish rebellion, I nonetheless felt remorseful at having been so petty and mean spirited.

As the years passed, it became clear that the angel incident meant more to me than someone wanting to borrow an article of clothing. In fact, borrowed and hand-me-down clothing was a way of life when I was growing up. Borrowing was done in the immediate family and among cousins and others in our extended circle of friends. The children did it and so did the adults. It was our way of stretching the few clothes we had and having whatever was needed for special occasions such as baptisms, holy communions, weddings, and funerals.

Borrowing and a childish reaction to it may have been the surface issues with the angel costume, but the more fundamental problem was the other, more elusive, subject of angels with light and dark skins my father had talked about.

As I was growing up, I developed a special rapport with the song "*Angelitos negros*" (Little Black Angels), first made famous by the African-Mexican singer Toña la Negra (Antonia del Carmen Peregrino), a favorite singer of my mother's. Eventually Pedro Infante, one of the heart throbs of Mexican cinema during the 1940s and 1950s, made a move called *Angelitos negros*, and later on Eartha Kitt recorded the song in Spanish for American as well as international audiences.

The lyrics were written by the Venezuelan poet Andrés Eloy Blanco (1898–1955), taken from his earlier poem about angels of all colors. In the poem, Blanco speaks lyrically about the painter who forsakes his town by forgetting to paint a black angel. Blanco's poem makes it clear the painter of religious tableaux has forgotten the people of the *pueblo*, the common folk with dark or black skins. The poem is a plea to the painter to rectify his error, with the implied cautionary note to the painter that if he ignores the people of his town, he is ignoring himself. The lyrics in the song focus on the same theme but soften the admonition to the painter. The singer reminds the painter that God loves all of us, regardless of our color.

The message of the Blanco imagery resonated in my own memory, telling me more about that angel incident with Dorothy than any explanations I could have received from anyone else. But it was years before I would realize their true meaning for me.

If I felt remorse about the angel costume, I also felt resentment and a sense of disillusionment at the meaning of Christian ideals, and how these had come to be applied to a situation that affected the lives of young schoolchildren. Nothing in what I was learning in the saying of those daily prayers in school or the Bible stories which we read in class told me it was necessary to separate the American and Mexican congregations in order to have religious worship. The conflicting currents of these feelings made the episode a problematic one for me.

While it may have been that some of the Texas Mexican students who attended St. Joseph did not think about racial separation, this was not entirely the case for me. I may not have been able to articulate it fully, but at least subliminally the feelings of segregation were there, and during the angel episode, those sentiments focused on Dorothy and her request.

A distance existed in Edinburg between Anglos and Mexicans which went beyond the ruler incident occurring in Brownsville with Sister Ignatius and my mother's note, but I never really thought about what it meant. During the angel incident, I was forced to think about it.

Both schools had the same racial mix of students, yet no one thought of Incarnate Word as the Mexican school. But St. Joseph *was* the Mexican school, at least for the religious orders and the Anglo Catholic families who were associated with it, and it was the second-class status and the racism the term implied that I was unwilling to accept.

If Anglos went to St. Joseph, they thought of it as a temporary situation, to be tolerated because no other solution was currently available. My father may have joked about the skin color of angels, but the reality was that skin color was an issue of paramount importance. It certainly was not language, because everything at St. Joseph, including the ceremony for the silver jubilee, was conducted in English.

The Anglo students participated in the school ceremony but did so as part of their school requirement and not because they felt it was their celebration. Their ceremony was the other event, the one where Dorothy and not I was the angel.

The requisite change in racial and ethnic content of the participants was the fundamental issue.

The "speeders" story and the incident of the two angels served as the
beginning and end of a transitional period for me and were critical in
the initial conceptualization I had for the *Carrascolendas* children's
television series and the goals it was intended to have.

The day I read the "speeders" passage aloud was the first time I
became conscious that something was not right in the conclusions I
was drawing about words and their meanings. At least it was not
right as far as the school setting was concerned. Up to that point, I
was aware people spoke in different ways, but the sounds they made
were invitations to mimicry rather than reasons for ridicule. My
"speeders" reading changed that.

The significance of the "speeders" story is that I remember it so
vividly, in contrast to having no memory of experiencing similar epi-
sodes prior to that time. Certainly, this was not an isolated case of
mispronunciation, given the fact that I spoke no English before going to school. If I had other similar situations, I have no recollection
of them.

As I have thought in later years about how young children learn
language, and especially about how children who grow up in bilingual
settings learn to manipulate several ways of expressing themselves, I
know part of the process has a requisite amount of stumbling with the
attendant mistakes, eventually leading to mastery of the second language. Part of growing up is to laugh at the mistakes your peers are
making, so the laughter of the fifth graders at St. Joseph cannot be the
whole reason why I remember the "speeders" episode so well. The
difference in the St. Joseph incident was inherent in St. Joseph itself,
and not only in how I perceived myself in that context.

I first became aware of Anglos at St. Joseph. Before that, people
came from different places, they spoke in different ways, and they
had different looks. It was a challenge to find your place among all
those different slots, and that seemed to be how people functioned in
the world. The differences in people evidently propelled them through

a process of identifying themselves that was different for each person. That process eventually told them where they belonged.

At Incarnate Word, I perceived I had things in common with Sor Javier because she was from the Valley and perhaps more distantly, with Sister Imelda, the Mexican first-grade teacher. I could not have said the same for the Irish nuns, Sister Ignatius and Sister Gertrude, yet those distinctions did not take precedence over the personalities these nuns had and my reactions to their individual styles.

If I thought of ethnic differences at all in later years, I thought of them as analogous to a jigsaw puzzle in which each unit of the puzzle has a unique configuration. Each piece contributes and fits into the whole. On their own, the pieces have no meaning, but without them, the puzzle cannot be.

At St. Joseph, Angloness and the language defining Angloness was important. In that setting, mistakes, especially mistakes about language, were critical. That Angloness made me resistant to lending Dorothy Rogers my angel costume. The racial composition of the students at Incarnate Word and St. Joseph was the same, with the larger group being the one I belonged to, yet the first was a source of strength, while the second placed me in the weaker role of the outsider.

At St. Joseph, I was the person who made mistakes in speaking. I was the person who did not have the right credentials to merit a position with the congregation that counted.

Although I am sure we begin to form a concept of who and what we are from the moment we are born, a conscious memory of how identity develops comes at a later stage. The "speeders" and the angel incidents crystalized this process for me and made me aware of the cultural duality I would have throughout my life.

I saw myself as a Texas Mexican, a person who was a polar opposite to the Anglo. That polarity placed the entire definition out of balance. "Texas Mexican" was a term with little meaning in an outside world dominated by Anglos, yet was complete in itself in the world I knew at home.

The school changed the meaning of the words, and school and the values within it were critical for the children who eventually viewed the *Carrascolendas* television programs.

CHAPTER THREE

The Other Side

DISCUSSIONS OF LANGUAGE were important in our family, but if any stigma was attached to language, it was not about being able to speak Spanish. Time and again, we heard about Tía Chabela, who although fluent in Italian and English, had forgotten her Spanish. On one of her rare visits to South Texas, she tried to rationalize her behavior by saying there was no one in Rochester, where she lived with her Italian husband, with whom she could speak Spanish.

The excuse had no merit with the family, and my father, as the oldest of the four siblings, was adamant in his position: "You should have stood in front of the mirror and talked to yourself."

Feeling guilty at having slighted her mother tongue, yet unable to recoup all the years of lost time, Tía Chabela was quick, if not quite grammatically correct, in answering, "*Mañana enseña*" (Tomorrow learn).

As children, we took frequent trips to Monterrey in northern Mexico, where my paternal grandmother's only surviving brother lived. The visits to Tío Abrahán were accompanied by strict admonitions that (1) my sister and I were not to wear slacks or shorts because this was offensive to Mexican customs, and (2) we were to speak only Spanish while in Tío Abrahán's household, since no one on the Hinojosa side of the family spoke English. It was impolite, my parents reminded us, to speak in a language other family members could not understand.

Our visits to Monterrey always started with a mixture of excitement because we were going to make the trip and apprehension because of the hurdles we had to overcome in order to get there. A major obstacle was the suspension bridge joining Roma on the Texas side to San Pedro in Mexico.

Crossing the swaying bridge rated in my mind on a level with the hurricane of 1933, one of the worst disasters in the Rio Grande Valley. I had not witnessed the hurricane but my parents and other relatives mentioned it so often and with such terror in their voices I was convinced that if the bridge fell, we would all go floating down the river like the hurricane victims had done.

The opening of the bridge in 1928 signaled the beginning of the modern era for the people of Roma and Rio Grande City. They welcomed the faster means of transportation and were happy to see the closing of the ferry, which had been used previously to cross the river. But for me the bridge was a symbol not of modernity but of a physical challenge that had the potential for disaster. The only way I could meet the challenge was to maneuver the seven hundred feet of creaky wooden slats by staring straight ahead, being careful to avoid glancing down at the rushing water or up at what seemed to me to be the flimsiest of cables.

Once we crossed the bridge, we joined the rest of the small crowd boarding an old Ford bus for the ten-mile ride to Comales, where La Linea del Norte came from Matamoros to pick up passengers before winding its way past Aldamas and Herreras, and finally some four or five hours later arriving at Monterrey.

The train ride through Mexico was an adventure. We sat in straight-backed wooden seats and looked out the window at what seemed like land that went on forever. The flat expanse of mesquite and brush gave way to the semi-arid Tamaulipan desert, filled with hundreds of *palmitos* standing like toy soldiers wearing white plumed caps. As the train rolled forward, the track seemed to push the land into small hills, throwing the palmettos into all sorts of skewed positions.

To pass the time, my mother and father told us stories or taught us songs. A memorable one was a humorous *corrido* called "La Bola de la Maquinita," about a derailment. My mother loved to sing and she learned songs by hearing them or by buying songbooks called *cancioneros*. Sometimes the publishers of the songs printed the lyrics in loose sheets of *papel de china* (tissue paper) or found other, more innovative, ways to distribute the words to the public. Lydia Mendoza, a singer of the 1930s and one of my mother's favorites, had learned the words to the song that made her famous, "Mal Hombre," from a chewing gum wrapper.

For us, *corridos* like "La Bola de la Maquinita" were lessons in community history since these ballads related actual happenings. In the case of ballads like "La Maquinita," they were also important lessons in Mexican humor and, specifically, showed the particularly Mexican attitude of defiance, with an implied acceptance of the in-evitability of death. Although the *corrido* was a lengthy one, a few stanzas capture its central theme.

El tren que corría sobre la ancha vía,
de pronto se fue a estrellar,
contra un aeroplano que estaba en el llano
volando sin descansar.

Quedó el maquinista con las tripas fuera
y mirando al aviador,
que ya sin cabeza buscaba el sombrero
para librarse del sol.

Los zopilotes estaban
sobre los muertos volando
y la máquina seguía
chu-chu-chu-chu y caminando.

The train that ran over the wide rail,
suddenly crashed,
against an airplane that was in the plain
flying without rest.

The engineer was left with his guts hanging out
and looking at the aviator,

now without a head looking for his hat
to free himself from the sun.

The buzzards were
flying over the dead
and the engine continued
Choo-choo-choo-choo, and running.

Just when we were no longer able to sing another verse of the
corrido that seemed as interminably long as the train ride and had
eaten all the lunch my mother had packed, the faint strip of moun-
tains that Tío Abrahán called the Sierra Madre Oriental could be seen
in the distance. But it was not until we saw El Cerro de la Silla (Saddle
Mountain) going way up into the sky that we knew we were in
Monterrey.

Monterrey offered an array of sights having no comparison to the small
towns of South Texas. There were taxis at the train station, a park called
La Alameda where people rented bicycles, a carnival, and horse-drawn
buggies. We didn't have bicycles at home because my father said these
fit into the "People want ice water . . ." category, so when we went to
Monterrey he always let us rent bicycles. At night, the entire city lit up
like a Christmas tree. My favorite neon light was the one with a can of
paint that seemed to be forever spilling down but never did.

In Monterrey, we usually stayed at a *casa de huéspedes* (house of
guests) where we ate our meals like we did at home and not like in a
restaurant. Sometimes we stayed at a small hotel named El Fronterizo.
I especially liked El Fronterizo because it had a pinball machine in
the lobby and we could keep pulling the handle even after we had
run out of Mexican coins to put in it. Although the desk clerk was
generally friendly, his forehead went into a frown whenever we kept
this up for too long.

All the houses in Monterrey had bars on the windows, including
the places where we stayed and the house where Tío Abrahán and his
family lived. Tío Abrahán's house looked small from the front but it
seemed to have an endless supply of rooms leading to other rooms

that went on and on. I used to think that the rooms probably kept on going until the house reached the other side of the block, but we never found out for sure because my mother said it was impolite to go exploring in other people's houses. Besides, El Sultán, Tío Abrahán's dog, kept a close watch on us when we went to visit.

El Sultán was a mastiff and the largest dog I had ever seen. He protected the house from burglars and, I believed, from people like us who went to visit. Although Tío Abrahán always told us we didn't have to worry because El Sultán would never harm us, I never quite believed him. I knew El Sultán could not be trusted. I knew this because El Sultán did not like laughter, so how could you trust a dog that didn't like laughter.

My father was renowned among his family and friends for his sense of humor. Everyone who came to our house talked about his colorful vocabulary and his ability to tell jokes. They said he was *muy célebre*, which meant he could twist the story in such a way that he would make you laugh in the end. Whenever we went to Tío Abrahán's, my father would immediately start on one of his stories.

Tío Abrahán's reserve quickly dissolved in my father's presence and before long he and my father would be matching each other joke for joke or singing songs from the old days. Some of the songs were family originals, like the one my father, in the spirit of the flapper era, had made up when his father's sister, Rafaelita, and her two daughters, Flavia and Encarnacíon, had bobbed their hair:

> *Estaban las tres pelonas,*
> *Sentadas en su balcón,*
> *Flavia, Rafaela,*
> *Y Encarnación.*

> The three baldheaded ones,
> Were seated in their balcony,
> Flavia, Rafaela,
> And Encarnación.

Even though we had heard the song many times before, we always laughed at the end. At the laughter, El Sultán would bound up and start barking. He seemed to know who had laughed the loudest, which usually happened to be me, so he'd look directly at me and bark in my direction. In many ways, El Sultán was the most memorable member of the Hinojosa family.

Tío Abrahán was tall and slender and was easily the handsomest Mexican Mexican man I had ever seen. He always wore dress clothes, the kind you only wore to church and for special occasions. The creases in his white shirts matched the smooth, straight lines of his neatly combed gray hair. He always chose his words carefully, measuring each sentence with the same attention for detail that Tía Inés, his wife, used in preparing the meals we ate at their house.

Tía Inés was a small thin woman with blondish hair. She had a birdlike quality and moved about with dainty little steps, quietly checking on the cooking in the kitchen and straightening the lace doilies in the living room while letting Tío Abrahán take center stage in the conversation. She was famous for her thick bean soup, which she strained in a colander before serving it in bowls that all looked alike. My mother, who was famous for her cooking, always complimented Tía Inés on her soup. I have to admit that as hard as I tried, I could never find a single visible bean in that soup.

Tío Abrahán had three children, and I was in awe of all of them. A son, Gustavo, was tall like his father and had a mustache. Gustavo was so handsome he looked like a movie star, but there was a debate as to whether he looked like Jorge Negrete, the famous Mexican movie *charro*, or Clark Gable, known to everyone including the anti-American Tío Abrahán. I thought he looked like somewhere in between. If Gustavo was not a movie star, he dressed like one; and he always had money.

During our visits, we saw Gustavo only briefly because he was always going to do something or was coming from having done something. We never knew what kind of work Gustavo did but we all thought he might be doing some smuggling, although we couldn't be sure what he was smuggling. It was possible the smuggling rumor was made up by Gustavo himself, who was not above adding to his own mystique.

Tío Abrahán's daughter was named after her mother and everyone called her Inesita. Inesita was tall like her father and as slender as the strips of palm leaves that were given out in church on Palm Sunday.

She was dark like the Hinojosas but had the simplicity of style of her mother.

Everyone worried because Inesita didn't have a boyfriend and might never marry, but the impression that Inesita gave was that she was not concerned about this. If anything, she fit the *dicho* that said "*Mejor me quedo para vestir santos que para desvestir borrachos* (Better that I dress saints than undress drunkards), which is what women who didn't marry said about themselves.

Well into her thirties, Inesita surprised the entire family when she married what all the relatives called "a very nice man," or maybe they just said that because they were relieved she wasn't going to have to dress the saints in church.

Tío Abrahán's second son was more of a mystery than Gustavo. His name was Ernesto and everyone whispered about him because they said he was adopted. The whispering was really not about his being adopted; the relatives were convinced he was Tío Abrahán's child with a woman who was not his wife. No one could be sure about this story, because the relatives also said Tío Abrahán was a proper and faithful husband, which was not said about too many Mexican men. Regardless of the truth, everyone was sure Ernesto did not look like anyone in the family.

Family stories and family lands were always a topic of conversation in those visits to Tío Abrahán's. The important thing about the family lands, those land grants that were deeded by the King of Spain to families like the Barreras, Guerras, and Hinojosas, was that they had been there in the past but weren't there in the present, or at least they weren't there for the poor branch of the family. The story of how the poor branch came to be poor was much repeated. The narration of the uncle who in the early years of the twentieth century appropriated his brothers' lands and went on to become a millionaire led the stories on the family lands. The uncle's children became doctors, lawyers, and judges and had great affluence. The other side of the family struggled with no land, no money, and little or no education.

The years crystallized the divisions between these haves and have-nots, with the haves doing little socializing with the have-nots. One of the have-not aunts, who was a great beauty, married well and was subsequently restored into the have side of the family.

Family names were as important as the family lands, and the retention of one was as critical as retention of the other. The Barreras intermarried with the Guerras so often that reading their birth and marriage records created a blur between the two names. Following Spanish custom, people had two last names, the first one for the father and the second one for the mother. Because of the crisscrossing of marital partnerships, there were people whose names were Barrera Barrera, Guerra Guerra, and in the case of my own grandmother, Hinojosa Hinojosa.

The Barrera Guerra combination had a cachet that some other names didn't, so descendants whose actual name was only Barrera and not Guerra hoped to capture the prominence, if not the legality, by using the two names. There were so many Barrera Guerras, it was not easy to tell who was legitimate and who wasn't. One thing was sure, saying you were a Barrera Guerra gave you immediate prestige and saying you were a descendent of land grant holders gave you even more.

As children, we thought you couldn't get much higher than being a Barrera Guerra, but in those visits to Tío Abrahán, we soon discovered that the name Hinojosa had an equal claim to distinction. Gustavo, whose irreverent style equaled my father's, told us there were two branches of the Hinojosa family, one known for insanity and the other for its connection to the island. He assured us they were related to each other because after family members went crazy, they were all sent to the island. I thought there was a special island for the Hinojosas who were insane.

Years later, I learned that indeed an island, Padre Island off the coast of South Texas, had initially been part of the Hinojosa family land holdings, but the connection had nothing to do with insanity. Rather, it came through Padre Ballí, one of the three sons of Rosa María Hinojosa, a colorful and enterprising woman who was married to a Ballí and who after being widowed became one of the largest land grant owners in South Texas. Padre Ballí had been the owner and founder of Padre Island.

As pleasant as the visits to Tío Abrahán's were, they were filled with some tension. The main reason for this was my parents' Spanish-only rule. Since we could speak only Spanish at Tío Abrahán's, my sister Alma and I remained largely silent during these visits. Because we were not permitted to speak English, we struggled with the Spanish home vocabulary we knew but could not use the vocabulary we were developing in school.

When I was growing up, I thought I had an English brain and a Spanish brain. The English brain went to school, did homework, and received grades on a report card. The Spanish brain visited relatives, told stories, and laughed at Spanish jokes that other kids in school didn't understand. When the brains got together, everything was fine. But when they didn't, there was trouble. Sometimes on those visits to Tío Abrahán the two brains would not connect. The words would not come or they would form combinations that caused someone like Tío Abrahán to laugh.

A famous family story about one of our trips was the time when I broke my own self-imposed silence and ended up doing something worse. Walking along one of Monterrey's commercial districts, I was impressed by a tall, antique slant-front desk in a store window, and not having seen anything like it before, I called everyone's attention to "*el* desk *alto*," (the high desk). Although Tío Abrahán and his family were usually quick to correct any mistake we made in the use of Spanish, this particular combination of words brought laughter from the Hinojosa family, even the dignified Tío Abrahán. But it was the kind of laughter that said, "A-ha! You didn't say that correctly."

I did not know it at the time, but the gaffe I made at Tío Abrahán's was a *pochismo*, an inappropriate mixing of Spanish and English. Making such mistakes was what made Texas Mexicans *pochos*, or "*los mexicanos de este lado*," Mexicans from this (the American) side, as opposed to "*los mexicanos del otro lado*," Mexicans from the other (Mexican) side. The Mexicans from the Mexican side were the more authentic Mexicans. We were "*los vendidos de* Santa Anna" (the people "sold" by Santa Anna to the United States as a result of the Treaty of Guadalupe Hidalgo of 1848). Being a *pocho* was somehow being at fault. A *pocho* didn't have a home. A *pocho* didn't belong anywhere.

This sense of displacement became critical in the creation of the *Carrascolendas* television programs. As a child, I knew that my sense of place and the language connected with it were somehow being brought into question in those visits to Tío Abrahán's, but it was not clear how this was affecting who and what I was. It was not until I was an adult and studying Spanish literature formally at the University of Texas at Austin that I questioned the fine line which designated certain words as *pochismos* and others as acceptable Spanish.

I remember asking Ramón Martínez López and Ricardo Gullón, both Spanish literary scholars who were my professors, why Spaniards who used "*jersé*" (pronounced "herr-seh") for "jersey" and Mexicans from Mexico who used "*suéter*" for "sweater" were not called *pochos*. On the other hand, if Texas Mexicans used "*troque*" for "truck," they were *pochos* and spoke incorrect Spanish.

University Spanish literature departments of the 1960s and 1970s made concessions to literature from Latin America, but anything produced by U.S. Hispanics was not accorded first-class literary status and consequently was not included in course readings. Furthermore, the linguistic canon in these departments made it clear there was a correct way of speaking and an incorrect one. Using *pochismos*, Tex-Mex, or Spanglish was incorrect, and literate people who wished to be thought of as educated were discouraged from using any of these forms.

The more conservative Martínez López did not concede the point of my question on the word *troque*, but the iconoclast Gullón laughed off the distinction as arbitrary. "You people were unfortunate enough to be born on this side of the Rio Grande River instead of the other side," he said, "and that's why your language is criticized."

Talking about "*el* desk *alto*" was a natural solution in my struggle to accommodate the two languages I knew with the one language that Tío Abrahán knew. But the linguistic dictates on those Monterrey trips were no less stringent than the requirements demanded of my scholarship as a university student. In each instance the message was clear: the origin of the words and what you did with them was not as important as the origin of the speakers.

Our trips to Mier were not as frequent as our visits to Monterrey, but they underscored our grounding in our Mexican heritage. If Monterrey was the periphery, with its bright lights and big-city attractions, Mier was the unadorned center, the Spanish/Mexican origin, where it had all begun.

The antecedents of my bicultural makeup had originated during the mid-eighteenth century as the Spanish frontier moved north into the present-day continental United States. My ancestral home, both culturally and genealogically, was in that part of northern Mexico and South Texas that at a certain point in history represented the absence of a border rather than the presence of one.

My forebears had come with the first Spanish and *mestizo* families into those *porciones* south and north of the Rio Grande River in the Spanish land grant area which José de Escandon had called Nuevo Santander and which eventually formed the geographical division between the two countries. Mier was on the south side of that division and Rio Grande City was on the north.

Located in the northern state of Tamaulipas, a few miles southwest of what used to be San Pedro and is now Ciudad Miguel Alemán, Mier is a sepia-dusted little town that has lost in historical importance what it has gained in mythical significance.

The Mier of today looks like it might have been created by a Hollywood production designer for an old western. Cracking mud facades that look more like stage pieces abut teeter-tottering sidewalks bordering streets that have lost countless battles with several centuries of repairs. But unlike the westerns of another era, there is no Gary Cooper or John Wayne coming triumphantly to save the day. There are no blonde heroines and no dark-haired, spit-fire señoritas.

Instead, just off the main square with one of the streets named after my grandfather, Enrique Barrera Guerra, and around the corner past the dilapidated structure my great grandparents once called home, live some of the descendants of the families who originally settled there in 1752.

The name Barrera Guerra is immediately recognizable to those residents, now in their eighties and nineties, who knew Enrique as the revolutionary hero with the debonair mustache, and Baudilia Hinojosa Hinojosa, the tall woman with the large deep-set eyes and formal demeanor who had been his wife.

I never knew my grandparents, but as children when we went to Mier to visit Tía Mila, a cousin of my father's, we were told of the house that had belonged to my great grandparents. The house had my great grandmother's name, Encarnación Barrera Guerra, carved on one of the *vigas* in the ceiling, the beams traditionally used in buildings of the time. Encarnación Guerra was the wife of José Miguel Barrera Guerra, a descendant of Juan Ignacio Barrera, whose marriage in 1768 to María Manuela Flores Hinojosa was the eighth recorded marriage in Mier and whose family of eleven children and their progeny for generations afterward contributed to the energetic town that Mier became during the subsequent centuries.

Although my father was proud of the family heritage and its connection to the larger events in Mexican and Texas history, his tongue-in-cheek admonitions always left us with a bit of humor which essentially said, "Take these stories and listen to them with a sense of pride, but never forget that you do with your life what you want to, irrespective of who or what came before you."

When we were children, my father reminded us of the unofficial motto for Mier, "Mier *da para todos*," he told us, "is the most important thing you can remember about Mier."

The motto played with the word "*mierda*," meaning "shit," and the verb "*dar*," which means "to give." The dual interpretation could be "Mier gives to all" or "Shit to all." But if the saying had the edge typical of much of Mexican popular humor, the motto ingrained in us the attitude that life, like Mier, could be a two-sided coin, and it was up to us to choose which side we wanted to emphasize.

In those trips to Mier, the family stories we had been told before suddenly had relevance and meaning that went beyond the words we had heard. If Mier had given sustenance to the previous generations of Barreras, it also nurtured us in ways we could only begin to fathom. One of our most memorable trips to Mier happened during a time of family sadness, shortly after the death of my six-year-old brother Enrique. The death was sudden and sent all of us into a state of shock.

Enrique was in the first grade at St. Joseph, the all-boys Catholic school in Brownsville. He came home from school one day in November and, still in his uniform, started coughing. The cough did not seem serious and was not enough to deter his taking my younger brother

Tadeo and our cousin Sonny to play in the papaya trees in our backyard. My mother cautioned him against overexerting himself, but the sounds of running and laughing that came from the backyard assured her that the cough was only the symptom of a mild cold.

I always thought of the papaya trees as giant, graceful umbrellas which sent spotted, lacy patterns to the ground below. The patterns reminded me of the delicate lines of my mother's *velo*, the black, lacy *mantilla* which she draped around her head whenever she went to church. The trees were a favorite gathering spot both because they were a rallying point for the games we played with the other kids in the neighborhood and because they produced the large, oval-shaped orange papayas with the black, BB-like jelly seeds which we ate for breakfast.

The day of Enrique's cough, nobody thought about the papayas. The only thing we could think of was the wheezing, choking sound my mother called "*una tos de perro*" (a dog's cough). After that day, I thought of the lacy patterns the papaya leaves made on the ground, but I could only see them against the white of my mother's face. She wore her black *velo* for a long time, even though she wasn't going to church. Weeks and weeks passed before we saw the papaya trees again, and when we finally did, they reminded us of the last time Enrique had been able to run and play.

Dr. Vidal Longoria came to the house and said Enrique had the croup. He told my mother the boy would be up and about in a few days. But instead, the few days turned our tiny household into a nightmare. Enrique stopped his choking sounds with my sister Alma holding him. My Aunt Amparo, Tío Raúl's wife, said he had become asphyxiated.

The correct diagnosis of diphtheria after Enrique died stunned my family as well as everyone in the neighborhood. The black sign on the door and the little red flag hanging on the post of our front porch served as the signal that everyone should stay away from our house. We could not understand the reasons, nor could we understand why my sister Alma and I could not return to school. All we knew was that my mother couldn't stop crying, so we cried with her and missed Enrique and all the curls on top of his head that all our aunts called "*caracoles*."

Our family went into mourning, with my mother observing full *luto*, which meant she dressed all in black for over a year. Because we were children, Alma and I dressed in navy blue. We didn't listen to the radio or go to the movies. My mother's singing stopped and for days there was no laughter.

Being in Mier made us forget about our sadness as we concentrated instead on those things that were different in Mier from the life we knew in Texas. Mier was much smaller than any of the Valley towns we knew, yet it had the most active social life we had ever seen. The town's electricity was turned off at ten every night. This meant relatives and friends, who were treated like relatives because we were taught to call all grown-ups *tío* and *tía* regardless of whether they were real aunts or uncles, came to Tía Mila's to visit until that hour. Since our sleeping quarters were in the living room, we couldn't go to sleep until everybody left. Although at first my brother, sister, and I thought this was an exciting departure from our nightly routine in Texas, after a while, we found the schedule exhausting.

The cooking at Tía Mila's was done on a hearth and not on a stove, and it was on the hearth that Tía Mila's daughter, Nena, cooked her famous *panochas*. *Panochas* were a thick, unleavened flat bread that was made in a deep, cast iron skillet covered with a lid. We all thought these *panochas* were delicious and my four-year-old brother, Tadeo, or "Telo" as we called him, was especially fond of them. One day, when Nena's *novio oficial* (formal boyfriend) came to call and had overstayed his visit way beyond our mealtime, Telo, whose entreaties about being hungry had been ignored, blurted out, "*Yo quiero panocha de Nena*" (I want Nena's *panocha*).

A flustered Nena quickly ushered the red-faced *novio* out the door. We didn't learn until years later that the word *panocha* was the off-color label given in popular Mexican culture for a certain part of a woman's anatomy.

More than anything, those trips to Mier, like the ones to Monterrey, were lessons in the divisions between Mexicans and Americans and in the hurtful behavior that continued to maintain those divisions. There were two José's in Tía Mila's life, Tío José, her husband, and

Tío Pepe, her brother, who was also a José. Tío Pepe was a colonel in the Mexican army and in his military uniform, he was an imposing and authoritative figure.

As children, we were in awe of everything Tío Pepe said and did. We knew that whatever he told us had to be true, and one of his often repeated questions to us was, *"¿Qué le dijo la bandera mexicana a la bandera americana?"* (What did the Mexican flag tell the American flag?) His quick answer was, *"Por taruga te estrellaron. Ponte águila como yo."* (Because you're such a dolt, you were smashed. Become astute like I am.)

The meaning of the words went beyond the plays on the words. *"Estrellaron,"* from the verb *"estrellar,"* means both "to spangle and cover with stars" as well as "to smash." The word *"águila"* also has a double meaning. It can mean "eagle," the symbol on the Mexican flag, or it can have the figurative meaning of "astute."

Obviously, the joke captured more than the twist in the words, but it was a long time before we discovered the complex irony behind Tío Pepe's joke, which, along with the humor, demonstrated the disdain one flag, along with the people who had allegiance to that flag, showed for the other. But these nuances escaped us, and when Tío Pepe asked us about the two flags, we almost heard them talking to each other. We laughed along with everybody else each time the joke was repeated.

More obvious in its meaning was Tío Pepe's story about his encounter with some American tourists, another event that became part of our family stories. On a tour of duty in one of the Mexican border towns, Tío Pepe had come upon a group of Americans taking photographs of some poor Indians who were begging in the street. While they were ignoring other more pictorial attractions, the tourists were enticing the Indians to pose for them by giving them money. Tío Pepe became so enraged at the group, he took their camera, ripped out the film, and muttered to them in his best, broken English, "Go tahk yur pitures somwhar els."

The story was intended to highlight the insensitivity of the American tourists, but the altercation also brought home questions which were difficult to resolve. Tío Pepe's anger made us sympathize with the Mexicans because obviously the picture taking insulted them, but it also placed us in the ambivalent situation of not wanting to condemn the Americans because we thought of ourselves as Americans, and castigating the Americans was like castigating part of ourselves.

I did learn one thing from Tío Pepe. I still react negatively whenever I see tourists of any nationality focusing their cameras on "picturesque" indigenous people.

In my family, it was as important that we retain our sense of Mexicanness as it was that we continue to speak Spanish. My mother was critical of people who became *agringados* (anglicized), especially those who translated their names from "José" to "Joe," or worse, from "Flores" to "Flowers," or who pronounced their Spanish names with an English accent. Plays on language of this sort were relegated to jokes or satirical literal translations which lost meaning for anyone other than someone who knew both languages, such as the one about "Juan B. Caro" (an actual person) who was called "John B. Highprice," or "*Fulano de tal salió por debajo de la mesa*," which was literally translated as "So-and-so came out under the table," instead of the idiomatic "So-and-so made a mistake."

Retention of the Spanish language and a sense of Mexicanness had nothing to do with lack of loyalty to the United States. At one point in my family's history, as in the case of my father's father, allegiances had been to Mexico and the political struggles that were occurring there. Theirs was an understandable position given the fact that during the nineteenth century my grandfather's parents had been nurtured on the bitterly fought battles over what constituted Mexican and American territory, not the least of which was their individual title to property rights over that territory. But by my father's generation, these old war wounds had begun to recede. In fact, the emphasis was the opposite.

My father had readily volunteered for military service during World War II, as did many other Mexican Americans throughout the country. It was a point of honor to come to the defense of his country. Once honorably discharged, my father kept his military relationships active through membership in the American Legion.

At the time of his death in 1984, he was given a military funeral, a point he had stipulated to his die-hard veteran buddies, who would get together and tell war stories in the best American good-old-boy military tradition. The only thing different from the stereotypical image which gatherings of this sort generate was that they included Anglos as well as Mexicans. The connections between these American Legion buddies of my father's transcended racial and ethnic barriers in much the same way that Mexican American troops who distinguished themselves in battle during the war were accepted as equals with their other American counterparts. Not lost in these gatherings was the fact that events following the war marked a distinct turning point for Mexican Americans, as returning veterans like my father became more vocal in resisting overt practices of racial discrimination in their hometowns.

Nor did our retention of our Mexicanness have anything to do with thoughts of national separatism or aspirations to Mexican citizenship. Rather, the contradictory pulls within the Mexican American psyche came to be expressed in the popular vernacular people used to describe their ethnicity, which incorporated both strands of the duality: we may be "*los vendidos de* Santa Anna" (the sold outs of Santa Anna), but "*lo mejor que hizo* Santa Anna *fue que nos vendió*" (the best thing that Santa Anna did was to sell us). No one wanted to become "*mexicanos del otro lado*" (Mexicans from the other side) and no one wanted to trade what they had for what they saw their Mexicans-from-Mexico brethren had. The continual flow of Mexican immigrants into the United States told them more than any government document ever could.

Retention of the Spanish language and my mother's insistence on not becoming *agringados* (anglicized) fed the Mexican American psyche in other, more elusive, ways. It had more to do with fulfilling and being part of a myth than it did with acknowledgment of a reality. The reality was that everything around you was in English. English was the union card to schools, jobs, and everything that went along with an American version of a middle class lifestyle. No one advocated a resistance to learning English. The opposite was true. There was an insistence on learning Spanish, which did not necessarily exclude English.

In many ways, this insistence was a form of collective wish, a way of yearning for something that was no longer there, a way of returning to a cultural heritage that was supposed to define us and tell us who and what we were. But if the goal was to verify ourselves as part of a collective mythology, we had failed to accomplish it. While it was true that our heritage had been Spanish/Mexican, we were no longer Spanish/Mexicans like Tío Abrahán and Tía Mila and their respective families. We were something else, and it was that vague something else that continually fed our dual cultural and linguistic dilemma.

As we progressed through the school system, my mother insisted we relate the events of the school day to her in Spanish and not in what she, half in jest, called "*ese inglés falso*" (that fake English). This became more difficult to do as we gained fluency in English and did not build a corresponding vocabulary in Spanish, so my sister and I took turns translating, a process that inevitably produced a mixture of the two languages.

The process had its effect, however. The point was driven home in these after-school sessions. Whatever that something was that we were a part of was important enough to spend time trying to retain it. Our connection, our rootedness, must be retained at all cost. We knew that Tía Chabela had gone off to New York and lost that connection, not by marrying an Italian, but by not practicing her Spanish. My father's other sister, Tía Chenda, who had married a Frenchman, had not lost it. Nor had my mother's grandmother when she married an Irishman. For us, the lesson was to not follow Tía Chabela's example.

I soon learned that language was something that did more than communicate the specific meanings of words. Language designated membership in a group, and it was also used to grant or take away status. What had been implied in those visits to Tío Abrahán's house was that the language we spoke was inappropriate. I could understand the notion of not speaking in a language that someone else did not understand and doing so out of courtesy. I could also understand striving to use language correctly, according to designated rules. We did that in school, and whether there or at home, we were constantly trying to better the way we spoke and the way we wrote. Furthermore, I could also understand trying to retain a cultural commonality, a way of knowing about your family and your family's history.

What I could not understand was that language could be used for one-upmanship, or as a means of transmitting messages that communicated attitudes and emotions that were not in the words themselves. I could not understand why Tío Abrahán's children could correct our Spanish, but we could not correct their English whenever they made attempts to speak it. I began to see that if Tio Abrahán and his family were displaying cultural pride in their knowledge of Spanish, they were also betraying a sense of envy because we, as Americans, even poor Americans, enjoyed a lifestyle that many Mexican families from Mexico did not have.

Their corrections were a way of saying, "You may be Americans, but because of that, you have lost your authenticity, your Mexicanness, and whether you like it or not, that loss has taken away from your wholeness, that which you once were, that which we still are."

But they were doing much more.

At a certain point in time, the Hinojosas and Barreras were both Mexican families and lived within the same national jurisdiction. An accident of history changed the geographical boundaries, causing one side of the family to become Americans and the other to remain as Mexicans. The racial composition of the family remained the same, but their ethnicity had changed. No longer could the dictionary definition of ethnicity (a group of people "classed according to common traits and customs") be entirely true if it was applied to them. The ethnic destinies of the two sides of the family would now go their separate ways.

That separation implied a loss, and their descendants were trying inadequately to explain that loss. They were seeking to redefine themselves, and that redefinition was proving troublesome. It was problematic because the members of the groups were not quite sure where they had been, and they were even less sure of where they were going. The only certainty was that human nature, rather than ethnic peculiarities, was the reason why our Mexican Hinojosa relatives felt they had to put us down linguistically.

My own immediate family tried to do the same thing that Tío Abrahán and his family did. I saw that my father's criticism of Tía Chabela was a way of telling her that she had gone on to another life and had left her brother and sisters behind. There was a mixture of regret and envy in his comments. She had gone on to other places and other languages, and the intervening years had done more than separate them geographically. It had changed them completely as people.

My father's unyielding posture was another way of saying, "We are hurt because we are no longer the same. We are no longer the family we once were, and we don't like it. We want things to be as they were, and they will be, if you would act as you once did." Tía Chabela's desperate "*Mañana enseña*" was a way of saying that she would make an attempt to go back. But she did not. She could not.

My mother's "*inglés falso*" was a replay of the same impulse. She saw us growing up and growing away from her, and like any parent, she wanted us to stay close to her. She wanted to stop the changes which were inevitable, the changes that would place alien layers over her children which she wouldn't be able wholly to understand. Speaking the language of her childhood was a means of making us share in what she had shared, knowing what she had known. It was a way of sharing with her what we were learning on the outside and telling her of those things we were coming to know. It was also a way of keeping us intimately connected, both to her and to our personal history.

If the events of my childhood propelled me in the process that eventually became *Carrascolendas*, then the years I spent as an adolescent in Edinburg and the readings I did later as a student at the University of Texas at Austin gave me the working tools to come to terms with who I was as a Mexican American and what that meant in the context of being an American. This mix of influences helped me in assembling the building blocks I needed to create a children's multicultural television program.

When I was growing up, no one in my family talked about our Americanness. That was taken for granted. It was taken for granted that we would grow up, become educated, turn into productive individuals, participate in the political process, vote, or, if the desire was there, run for office, ascend to political power as our Barrera Guerra relatives had done in Starr and other South Texas counties, pay our taxes, serve our country, and do whatever else was necessary to maintain our status as good citizens. In other words, we would do everything that everybody else in the country was doing or that they were supposed to be doing.

What had our parents worried was our Mexicanness. It was our Mexicanness that we were in danger of losing. Our Mexicanness was that something extra that we had. It was the thing that made us special. It was like being a Texan, except better. If being an American was the skeletal structure, being Mexican and being a Texan were the meat or the substance that gave contour to the skeleton. The contour of each skeleton was different, but it was what made people what they were.

No one had told my parents they were acting out an American tradition by speaking Spanish to us and retaining a sense of our Mexican cultural identity, for contrary to what many people believe, part of our tradition as Americans has been to incorporate a panoply of colors, nationalities, and languages within our borders. Indeed, this tradition has been with us from the beginning.

My parents, like legions before them, were following the part of our heritage that says we are and will continue to be a multicultural and a multilingual society. But if my parents were exemplary of one part of the American cultural situation, they were also confronting the other side of the conundrum, the one saying we are and should be a melting pot, a pot which makes cultural and linguistic conformity the requisite for being an American.

Rather than contradictory traditions, these are cultural currents reflecting dual aspects of a more fundamental and complex phenomenon, analogous to archetypal representations. Expressed as mythological traditions, these two metaphors function as symbolic archetypal representations of the American psyche. They are the forces which give us a necessary meaning, in terms of the mythology that each cultural group has about itself.

That mythology explains the minority ethnic dilemma and projects the fundamental ideals that give us a group definition. Both traditions act in syzygial relationship to each other, functioning as paired opposites which serve as symbols of the cultural phenomena that reveal the split nature of the American ethos.

As ethnological polar opposites, multiculturalism and monoculturalism are symbolic terms which are important to us at times when we especially feel we are the victims of political schisms. Both of these symbols have been the necessary creations of the ethnic imagination and have little to do with the actual reality which surrounds us.

We are a country of many cultures, yet we willingly and enthusiastically participate and contribute to one American culture. We are one American culture and yet there has never been a time in our history when we have not had people within our borders who were outside of what was considered the mainstream culture and language.

On a more culturally specific level, multiculturalism and monoculturalism make it possible for us to preserve our mythological heritage irrespective of our position within either of these traditions. And this heritage is the component which gives our life its meaning.

From the beginning of our history as a nation, multiculturalism has been a vital ingredient of our makeup as Americans, and in keeping with its configuration as an archetypal symbol, it has changed from generation to generation as well as from individual to individual within one generation. My parents, like those who came before and after them, clung in varying degrees to some measure of identification with the mythological metaphors projected by that cultural symbol. They saw themselves as apart and different and they wanted to come up with a definition of themselves that told them who and what they were.

Whether people came as immigrants or whether they were already here, Americans have sought to retain an ethnic and cultural base which they could identify as their own. People have set up Cuban Little Havanas in Miami, Jewish Squirrel Hills in Pittsburgh, Mexican Pilsen Barrios in Chicago, and other comparable neighborhoods throughout the country, wherever they found the foods, languages, customs, places of worship, and faces that reminded them of themselves, the symbols that gave them validity as a group and defined their place in the world.

The situation continues to be essentially the same today as it was over three hundred years ago. The impulse for cultural identification has continued to make multiculturalism even more pertinent an issue now than it has been throughout the history of the country. Those of us who belong to identifiable cultural groups within the United States continually seek a connection with our historical past as a way of explaining who we are in the present and who we might become in the future.

We want to go from the cultural alienation in which we find ourselves to a mythical alignment with what is culturally known and acceptable, restoring within us a sense of unity and wholeness. This impulse is the energy behind ethnic revivals and movements; festivals with art, music, dance, and native dress; restaurants and food markets; and nostalgia media productions that celebrate Irish, Jewish, Hispanic, Italian, African, and other traditions.

At a policy level, this impulse was the philosophical thrust behind programs like bilingual education and revisions of school curricula to accommodate non-Western cultures within the established canon.

Along with the impetus for multiculturalism has been the other tradition, the one that says we should assimilate and make the melting pot a reality. This tradition seeks to strengthen the commonality with those who make up what is perceived as the mainstream culture of the country. It yearns for a symbol of national identification, a stamp that would make all of us look, speak, think, eat, and live like one people, because this would then give us a clear and easy definition of who we are, which in turn would give us a cultural, historical, and mythological identification as a group, as a nation.

This is the philosophy which drives phenomena like the English-only movement and the initiatives to eradicate bilingual education programs. This is the impulse that says that multiculturalism is a temporary lapse in our cultural landscape and that if we apply ourselves diligently, we will erase all traces of it and become assimilated into what we truly should be: one country, one flag, one people.

If there is a definition of an American, it is not within one tradition to the exclusion of the other. Rather, the defining element of an American comes from the tension which exists between these two traditions. Nowhere is this more evident than in the question of public policies affecting language and culture.

From the beginning of us as a nation, these subjects have been played out on numerous battlefields, with the numbers at any point in time determining who the victors and the victims were going to be. Exemplary individuals have been on both sides of the arena, and so has a lot of misinformation or misapplication of what has come to pass for our philosophical aspirations as a nation.

Part of the reality of the coming-to-be of this country has been the unification of diverse peoples under one national emblem, but that unification was more the result of our coming together as a nation-state under one constitutional system than what this could mean in terms of cultural and linguistic conformity. Our diversity, as well as the lack of it, did more than define the realistic facts of our existence. It provided the terms for the definition of "American."

Multiculturalism and monoculturalism are reflected throughout our history, both in the people who make up the country and in the ambivalent relationship which continues to exist between the two traditions. If the victories have been there, on one side or the other, so has the tension, which seems destined to last as long as neither tradition succeeds in eliminating the other. And if that ever happens, we will cease to be Americans. We will become something else.

Initially, we had the Americans who were here, and perhaps it was only then, before we had a consciousness of being a nation-state, that a true separation of cultures could have existed. As new people have continued to cross our geographical borders, they have brought with them their languages, customs, lifestyles, and particular views of the world, but brought these not into isolation but into coexistence, albeit a distant and strident one in some instances, with other groups who had their own languages, customs, lifestyles, and particular views of the world.

This continual migration yielded a multiculturalism which carries with it an implicit coexistence, rather than just being a compilation of distinct and separate cultures, independent and making it on their own. That brand of multiculturalism still predominates in the country, but what is not evident is the exact meaning of that multiculturalism. Nor do we know the extent of the linguistic and cultural diversity or unity which any particular ethnic community has.

If there is a test for citizenship, there is no test for the more fundamental ideal of Americanness. Language proficiency exams, if they are actually given, and other polls to define the demographics or the marketplace do not reflect the complexity of the unconscious cultural and linguistics feelings and abilities of any one person at any specific point in time and place. The results are approximations, vague attempts at characterizing what we perceive as American reality. With that reality comes tension, and this can happen either between the people that riot in our streets and litigate in our courtrooms, or it can occur within the same person.

If our history has shown us anything, it is that we have been unable to come to any specific determination with respect to public policies affecting language and culture. Furthermore, these issues continually have been the subject of ambiguous debate and emotion. Oftentimes, the cultural and linguistic clashes appear to be taking us over the edge, as contentious discourse focuses on such issues as bilingual education in the elementary schools. Whether the threat is to eliminate years of using Spanish and other languages to assist immigrant children in making the transition to all-English classes or whether the decision favors the continuing of bilingual education, the debate seems to be almost historically preordained.

If the debate has a familiar ring to it, so does the confusion and ambivalence that follows these upheavals. As we have seen throughout our history, passing policy dictums is one thing, and implementation into the classroom is another. Legislative mandates have generally caused confusion and have thrown school districts into chaos, because of unclear legal interpretations, unavailability of teaching materials, or complaints that previous methods of bilingual teaching were effective.

It is no easy matter to determine fair policy on culture and language. We do not know what the future of an issue such as bilingual education will be in this country, but if the past has taught us anything on this, it is that these questions will always be a constant in our local, state, and national agendas. They are constants for us in the present as they have been for us in the past.

Some of the most articulate views on the multicultural myth have come from people who were not born in the United States, but even here the driving impulse was toward cultural unity. Perhaps it is the experience of being outsiders that produces a greater consciousness of the implications of diversity, with its requisite corresponding conformity. Being on the outside may also have caused a predisposition for searching for defining metaphors for the American predicament.

Historically, we have only to review one of the earliest American historical documents to see the importance of multiculturalism. Tom Paine offers some early examples of this situation in *Common Sense*. Published in 1776, Paine's document ushers in an era of independence and republicanism, as well as establishing a defining standard that tells Americans about their identity as a distinct people and about their destiny as a nation.

Paine's appeal is to the public, the *publicus*, and not just to one individual or one group of individuals. In rejecting England as the parent country of America, Paine does more than just deny England exclusivity as our country of origin. He establishes an inclusive multicultural basis for those who would call themselves Americans, an inclusivity which although restricted to Europeans nonetheless speaks to an acceptance of outsiders.

Paine's vision of America is global. He sees America as an asylum, the antithesis of an elite grouping. The choice of the word "asylum" is important because of the nuances which the term brings to the definition of America. The definition of "asylum" has to do with the shelter given to criminals, debtors, political refugees, the destitute, and the afflicted. America was to be a refuge and a sanctuary for the unwanted, the outsiders.

Michel Guillaume Jean de Crèvecoeur solidified the concept of the American cultural myth by giving us a term which could easily be popularized. If Crèvecoeur had published his *Letters from an American Farmer* today instead of the 1780s, media pundits would have said he had written the perfect sound bite. Crèvecoeur takes Paine's idea of American brotherhood and gives it physical contour. He talks about individuals of all nations being melted into a new race of men.

Crèvecoeur gives us the birth of the new American, the melted man. He provides us with the myth of our origins, but what is forged as metaphor passes into the popular imagination as stereotype and not prototype. The simplified image could not function alone. It needed a corresponding symbol of diversity in order to respond to the more fundamental needs of the American collective ethos. A closer look at Crèvecoeur shows that both the man and his vision encompassed more than the stereotype.

Crèvecoeur, who came to America from France when he was twenty-four years old and became a naturalized citizen at the age of thirty, was not a melted American. He was a man of broad interests whose writings included sentimental stories of Indian legends, slavery, and the disappearance of Indians. We do not know what Crèvecoeur's intentions were when he wrote about the new melted race of men, but we do know that his metaphorical reference gave the country a symbolic reference for the yearning which it had for unity, as well as a way to define itself in terms of that conformity. Crèvecoeur recognized the multiple aspects of the definition and included these in his document.

Like Paine, Crèvecoeur talks of America as an asylum, a place where people were a mixed breed. This new America was hardly a place filled with people of one look, one language, and one culture. Crèvecoeur's America was not blended. Rather the country was variegated, with an assortment of individual flavors. Crèvecoeur, who lived off and on in England, France, and Germany, saw America as reflecting the same multiculturalism he had lived and the multilingualism that he himself had.

If Crèvecoeur gave the American cultural myth physical attributes, Israel Zangwill provided the container and the requisite divine element necessary to complete the symbol and make it the subject of legend. The interesting point about Zangwill is that so many people adopted the melting pot ideology without ever taking the time to really see what Zangwill had written. Zangwill wrote a play in the early 1900s, populating it with unmelted immigrants and foreigners who spoke half-English, accented English, or no English at all, and giving the starring role to a protagonist whose alter ego can be found in the pages of *Don Quixote*.

Zangwill's David Quixano falls somewhat short of his namesake, Alonso Quixano, the name Miguel de Cervantes tells us Don Quixote acknowledges as his real name, when, shortly before his death, he regains his sanity and gives up his life of chivalry. Cervantes and

Zangwill may not have had equal talents as writers, but what they did have in common was their ability to give the world two mythical symbols which corresponded to their respective national psyches.

David Quixano voiced the words which were destined to be forever engraved in America's memory. He calls America "God's crucible" and a "great melting pot," echoing Zangwill's vision of a place where the races of Europe are melting, a place where the fusion of the races will surely produce a "superman."

David Quixano's name never made it into our heroic annals, but the play *The Melting Pot* became a Broadway hit. Zangwill, the son of East European Jewish immigrants who grew up in London's East End, took the term "melting pot" from its common usage in England and used it as a metaphor to tell the story of David Quixano, a young American Jewish immigrant who feels that ethnic diversity should give way to ethnic unity. *The Melting Pot* focused attention on the subject of culture as this related to American identity. It popularized the concept of one culture and one nation and catalyzed the multicultural debate that continued off and on throughout the twentieth century.

The important thing about the melting pot is not that it did not happen, but that it was and is a part of our mythology. That fact is still as relevant today as it was in the 1780s. It does not matter that the myth has little to do with actual reality. What does matter is that we want the melting pot myth to be real. We betray our wishful thinking in everything we do, including the ongoing debate about multiculturalism, which generally expresses an aspiration toward as well as an antagonism to the melting pot ideal. In fact, without the melting pot, we would have no debate.

If our aspiration was to bring unity out of diversity, the motto is as true today as it was at the beginning of our consciousness as a country. The myth continues to plague the image we have of ourselves as Americans. The metaphor of the melting pot may have misrepresented the actual reality, but it embodied what we as a country wanted to become. We yearned for a mythical unity in which we would have little conflict because we would all be similar. We wanted that similarity precisely because we were dissimilar.

The irony of the melting pot symbol is that, like the mythology that it embodied, once it became a part of the American psyche, the container simply could not be contained. The symbol passed into the popular imagination and from there it was misinterpreted, quoted out of context, or used to serve the purposes of whatever was being promoted at the moment.

A bit of Zangwill migrated to Texas and became transformed into what may be yet another version of the Texas political tall tale. Although we can never be sure of the origin of what becomes folklore legend, there are enough similarities to the Zangwill work to justify at least some relationship. In *The Melting Pot*, Zangwill shows that bigotry exists among recent immigrants toward each other as well as outside these circles. Kathleen O'Reilly, the Quixano's anti-Semitic Irish maid and an immigrant herself who speaks English with a heavy accent, is quick to show her impatience with Frau Quixano, David's great-aunt, who speaks only Yiddish.

A number of exchanges in the play pit Kathleen, with her propensity for frustration at being in a Jewish household and not understanding the family's customs, against the language Frau Quixano uses. The conflicts are symbolic of the generational ethnic transitions the Quixanos are making since the older woman's behavior goes beyond not knowing English. In one of these moments, Kathleen explodes with the line, "Why doesn't she talk English like a Christian?"

I have never seen *The Melting Pot* performed, but I grew up with the Texas version of Kathleen O'Reilly's line. Unlike the O'Reilly expression, however, the version of the line I knew applied to the circumstances of Texas Mexicans.

Stories about racial discrimination in Texas are as common as the number of signs that people have reported seeing outside of business establishments saying, "No Mexicans or Dogs Allowed." Also common is the humor that sometimes laces these stories together, perhaps because people want to take the edge off the transgressions and make them and, by extension, their lives, more palatable. Texas Mexicans sometimes add a comedic twist to their stories, not as a way of condoning the nature of the offenses but as a way of lifting themselves from the role of the victim. Laughing at one's victimizer may also be an attempt to provide a bridge out of the inevitability of living with the reality of a cultural and linguistic divide.

Language debates and the tensions these have produced have come in for their share of stories, told and retold until they have become a part of Texas popular culture. Along with this tradition has been the propensity in the state to capitalize on the colorful characteristics of some of its politicians, sometimes as a tool for simple satire and political commentary or sometimes as a publicity gambit the politicians themselves have utilized as a means of being remembered at the polls.

In the era of the sound bite no less than in the documentation we have throughout the history of the state, we have seen elected officials whose political personae projected the very essence of caricature. Whether in the style of dress, the cultivation of a Texas drawl, or the campaign speeches peppered with outlandish one-liners, Texas politicians have alternately been the object of admiration or ridicule, depending on the political circumstances.

I grew up with the tradition that told me about the inequities regarding language and culture prevalent in Texas, and I also grew up with the tradition that told me that sometimes Texas politicians were less than just with respect to the policies they promulgated regarding these issues.

Our way of capturing the impact of the first with the moral implications inherent in the second produced the line that was attributed to an early governor who was in office about the time it was made illegal in Texas for schoolchildren to be taught in any language other than English. The legislative prohibition was first enacted as part of the Texas Penal Code in 1918, which would have trailed behind *The Melting Pot* by a number of years, but which would have captured the anti-immigrant sentiments prevalent at the time.

In paraphrasing *The Melting Pot*, our version of the Zangwill line reflected what we thought were the attitudes of our political leaders rather than what may or may not have been said.

Our one-liner cultural sound bite for the early Texas governor who was responsible for our linguistic predicament was, "If English was good enough for Jesus Christ, it ought to be good enough for the schoolchildren of Texas."

The echo of those words did not prevent us from coming up with our version of what we imagined Americanism to be. If ethnic divisions hindered the progress of our parents, we made up our minds that the situation would be different for us. The impact of the reality of the gulf symbolized by those words served as an impetus to hone our own youthful determination to become full participants in the American story. Like American young people throughout the history of the country, our resiliency overcame whatever exclusionary attitudes we perceived in our surroundings.

That resiliency was nurtured and guided by mentors who encouraged our study and thinking in ways that went beyond the acceptable norms in the school curriculum. Long before it became popular to do revisionist history, there were those teachers who supported what eventually became our own revised vision of Americanism.

Frank Dugan was a short man whose upper torso provided the willpower for the rest of his body, or so it seemed to those of us who sat in his high school history classes. It was obvious that Mr. Dugan's chest was the general barking the orders and his pants were the rebel forces bent on striking out on their own. Every class period with Mr. Dugan was filled with suspense, not only because he made every battle and upheaval in history come alive, but because we thought that at any moment his trousers were going to fall. But in the middle of whatever historical altercation he happened to be describing, the chest issued the command and Mr. Dugan's arms dutifully followed the order and hitched his pants up. The moment this happened, and it did a number of times during each class period, all the students heaved a collective sigh of relief that once again the chest had won the day.

Students at Edinburg High School in the 1950s took the required American and Texas history classes with Mr. Dugan, and those who succumbed to Mr. Dugan's enticements into the glorious adventure of history, as did my sister, myself, and a number of my closest friends, added Junior Historians to their list of extracurricular activities.

Mr. Dugan's history lectures were filled with information about the immigrants that came to America in unprecedented numbers in the decade after 1900. The Progressive Era and events leading to World

War I caused the development of Americanization programs from social settlements like Hull House and from patriot societies such as the Daughters of the American Revolution.

I did not learn until later that the Americanization efforts of the settlement movement of activists like Jane Addams included nuances of bias such as the ones that Addams herself had, which favored immigrants like the Irish and Germans as opposed to those who fell lower down the scale like the Russian Jews, Greeks, and Southern Italians. But if I didn't know about historical figures like Jane Addams with the depth that more advanced study would provide for me in the future, what I did have at the time was an instinctive reaction against the patriot societies which Mr. Dugan told us about in class.

At Junior Historian meetings, in which our debate was more free wheeling and informal, I questioned societies like the Daughters of the American Revolution, whose dedication to the social integration and Americanization of immigrants included restrictions of membership, which by their very nature excluded immigrants from participation. If groups such as the Daughters of the American Revolution were attempting to revitalize the notion of Americanism by doing lectures on loyalty and American history, I reasoned, why were they also teaching that there were those in the society who could never be true Americans in the sense that they could qualify for membership in the DAR itself?

Mr. Dugan encouraged the debate, as he encouraged our pursuit of the study of history as an integral part of our own cultural and ethnic background. My sister Alma won first prize in a statewide Junior Historian contest because of an ethnographic folklore essay she wrote on the entertainment of early South Texas Mexican settlers. I, too, published my first teenage scholarly effort in the *Junior Historian Magazine* on José María Carbajal, a nineteenth-century revolutionary and legislator active in some of the borderlands disputes between what eventually became Texas and areas of northern Mexico.

While our discussions at those Junior Historian meetings did not delve into in-depth study of ethnic history and culture, as would present-day ethnic organizations, they did serve to encourage our own individual thinking about concepts of Americanism. In a way, the talk on the Daughters of the American Revolution and its Americanization ideals provided an opportunity for me to present Mr. Dugan with a solution to the dilemma.

The closest that I could come to the DAR was the DOG. Since I had grown up hearing about the initial settlement of South Texas and the land grants that had been given during the eighteenth century by the King of Spain to the original families, my father's among them, who had come to the area, I concluded that if authentic family lineage was what was required for status, being a Daughter of the Original Grantees certainly merited inclusion in membership in the DOG.

Of course, the notion that the King of Spain had a legitimate right to give land away to anyone was as flawed as the snobbery attached to the necessity for having an ancestral pedigree as a requisite for judging whether or not you were an American. To my Texas Mexican girlfriends, and those of us in the Junior Historians, these nuances were irrelevant. What was relevant was that we had come up with our own idea of being an American, one that had as much validity as anybody else's.

This vision of Americanism served as the philosophical underpinning for what would become one of the first American multicultural television series for children, a series whose principal goal would be to present definitions of Americanism that were as varied as the young children who would be viewing the programs.

CHAPTER FOUR

▪ The Black Blobs

UNLIKE THE CHILDREN who became my first television students, I did not grow up with television or know much about the medium when I was hired by the educational television station in the Austin–San Antonio area in 1962. KLRN was an emerging station in what was then the newly formed Public Broadcasting System (PBS). KLRN's emphasis was on instructional programming broadcast to schools in Austin and San Antonio, the dual geographic base of its Federal Communications Commission license. The central studio for the station was in Austin, in one of the older buildings on the campus of the University of Texas, with which it had a management agreement.

One of the goals of the station was to do a core program schedule on subjects such as art and science, which could be used to supplement what was already taught in the schools. But in addition to the established subjects, KLRN wanted to include an experimental sideline and proposed Spanish as direct instruction, since none of the elementary schools in the area were offering second-language classes. Spanish was a natural choice, not only because of the Hispanic heritage of the state but also because doing a Spanish program for children gave the station a promotional slant for publicizing its television instruction.

The schools responded with enthusiasm, but the problem was finding a suitable teacher to do the televised instruction. Since no Spanish classes were taught in the schools, no teachers were available with the appropriate credentials to do the teaching. The station management turned its recruiting efforts to the teaching assistants and other students in the Spanish literature program at the University of Texas. Women who spoke Spanish as their first language were asked to audition for the role of the television teacher. I was in the pool of invited applicants.

My experience with television was nonexistent, as were my credentials for teaching young children, but the prospect of a job which paid more than the part-time employment I had as a student was enticing, so the decision to audition was easy. The station management adopted the attitude that no guidance was the best guidance; the only thing we were told was to stand in front of the camera and pretend we were teaching a class to little kids.

The method of choice at the time for the teaching of a second language was the audio-lingual approach, based on the instructor voicing a series of dialogues, with the students reciting a repetitive drill that varied one or two words on each subsequent repetition. The goal was to get the students to speak the language rather than have them only attain reading proficiency, as previous methods had tended to do. Since we were simulating a television class, rather than actually holding one, I decided to conjure up a class using the television crew in the studio as the "students" and a small desk bell to signal them to repeat the phrases in Spanish. Presumably, the student viewers in their different classrooms would follow my on-camera cues and do the same thing the crew was doing.

I giggled my way through the attack of nerves as I focused on the little red light perched on top of the six-foot-high gangly RCA extra-terrestrial-looking camera in front of me and pretended I was looking at a classroom full of children. I made a vague attempt at covering up my jitters by slamming the pencil-eraser-sized knob on the bell with as much energy as I could muster.

The station managers offered me the job, concluding that my ability to speak English and Spanish without an accent in either language was an advantage. Harvey Herbst, the station manager, later said if I had succeeded in rallying the less-than-enthusiastic television crew to repeat the phrases in Spanish, I would have no problems with an energetic bunch of kids. Even though I knew nothing about what I was going to do, and even as I was beginning to think that the bruise on my bell-ringing palm might become a permanent element in my life, I said yes to the offer.

I thought the job was going to be like the audition. Someone would do the logistics of getting the program together and I would be given a script which I would use as a textbook. My role would be to stand in front of the camera and pound on the bell.

The cold reality was that it was a we-learn-as-we-go, we-have-virtually-no-money operation. Overnight, I became researcher, textbook author, scriptwriter, teacher of young children, producer, and on-camera host. There were no textbooks and no models to follow. The sort of Spanish programming I was going to do was either not being done elsewhere, or if it was, nobody knew anything about it.

Mr. Rogers' Neighborhood, among the earliest public broadcasting children's programs, was being broadcast at WQED-TV in Pittsburgh, but it would be five more years before National Educational Television, the precursor to PBS, would broadcast it. *Sesame Street*, with its hard-hitting concept targeting inner city youngsters, would not go on the air for another seven years. Children's programs were being broadcast on the commercial networks, but these programs had scant relevance to the programs I was going to do.

The term "diversity" had not entered the public vocabulary. Neither had "multiculturalism." Although there were the beginnings of what would eventually become bilingual education school programs, this approach to teaching was largely confined to particular school situations and had not yet attained the prominence it would achieve toward the end of the 1960s and during the 1970s.

Even if other similar programs had been available on television, access was impractical since the videocassette, with its easy transportability, was still a technology of the future. In any event, I didn't have time to watch anything, much less study comparable teaching methods. The other television teachers chosen at the same time had their own experiences in the classroom to guide them, but those subjects had little applicability to a program dealing with Hispanic culture and language.

I became an on-the-spot-on-the-job trainee, but the catch was that I had to come up with my own training program. I spent three weeks observing the best teachers in Austin in the first, second, and third grades. I talked to kids and I asked them what they did when they were not in school, what games they liked, what songs and toys were their favorites. I tried out mini-lessons and saw how they responded. I checked to see if I was going too fast or too slow, or whether I needed to vary the subject content in order to keep the pace interesting for the children.

I found out how critical voice could be. One teacher I observed controlled her class simply by lowering the pitch of her voice, and the children, who strained to hear what she was saying, not only listened with rapt attention but were models of comportment. Another teacher had no control of her class because her voice had no modulation and her pitch was always at a high and strained level.

I recalled my father's admonitions to Tía Chabela and decided to follow what he thought was an obvious technique for language learning. I practiced in front of the mirror until my family thought I was losing my grip on reality. Although they continued to support my efforts, they were highly skeptical of what they thought were questionable exercises which had little bearing on my doing a television program.

On the surface, I had been hired by KLRN to do Spanish language programs, utilizing the techniques used in second-language instruction. But this assumed the programs would be seen by an audience of non-Spanish speakers who would all be hearing Spanish for the first time.

Unlike college students, who went through some process of testing or classification, with opportunities for placement into more advanced classes for those who knew some Spanish, the elementary school children who would be receiving the televised instruction had no such advantage.

The programs were going to be seen by all children, regardless of their linguistic, cultural, ethnic, or racial backgrounds, and although the Texas of the time still had elementary schools that for all practical purposes were ethnically and racially segregated, the viewing audience was not going to have such divisions. And, indeed, some classrooms had children from varied backgrounds, so the audience, whether anyone anticipated it or not, was going to be mixed. Depending on the technical capability of each school, some campuses had television monitors in every classroom, while others would take several classes, sometimes of varying grades, into the school cafeteria for group viewing.

The nature of the television we were going to do was another important factor. Schools were not technologically savvy the way they became several decades later. Educational broadcasting was new and innovative. Some people were skeptical and some teachers were apprehensive that television was going to render their function in the classroom obsolete. But by and large the reaction in this early period was positive.

Schools were equipped with television sets and teachers were receptive to the idea that the television programs were going to enhance their curriculum. Educators and teachers were even more excited at the thought of having direct, interactive instruction via television, an idea that was more advanced than having programs that would only supplement what was already being taught.

Even more critical was my own participation in these telecasts and the reaction to them in the Hispanic population of the area. Hispanics were not visible participants in the television of the time, even at the local level, and the fact that a Mexican American woman was going to do television programs in Spanish and English was striking.

Mexican Americans in the entire broadcast area of San Antonio and Austin and surrounding towns responded overwhelmingly to the idea. Their reaction was not solely because programs to teach Spanish were going to be produced by the station. Rather, the reception I received was because the programs were going to be about them, their language, and their culture.

The strong response from the Mexican American community was also because I was Mexican American. And as a Mexican American, I was going to present images on television that talked about Mexican

Americans. Regardless of the initial intention of KLRN, these early productions became experiments in bilingual, multicultural education.

I made the decision at the onset that the diversity of the audience would predetermine the core of the programs as one going beyond mere second-language instruction. The programs had to begin from a cultural center and not a purely linguistic one. I had to do more than teach the Spanish words for "table" and "chair" or the standard greetings of "Good morning" and "How are you?"

The cultural core of the programs had to be Spanish/Mexican, but within the context of an audience of children who came from a variety of cultures and had differing degrees of knowledge about the Spanish language and culture. I was interested in teaching both Hispanic and non-Hispanic children, and I wanted the learning experience to be conducive to expanding all children's awareness about cultural and linguistic backgrounds that were different from their own.

I wanted to appeal to all children. And because I was Mexican American, I wanted the programs to be inclusive of Mexican American children, their language and their culture. It was only by having a program that would be appealing to all children that the programs could be successful.

Not having any models to follow and in the absence of textbooks, I turned to the one model I knew. I consulted my mother, who was my first teacher and who, as we were growing up, mastered the art of keeping us entertained with an array of games and songs that were a part of a child's world in Spanish.

My mother carried within her generations of Hispanic memory and had a gift for sound and poetic devices that was unrivaled. She only had three years of formal schooling, but what she missed in the classroom, she read and learned from the world around her. Although my mother's family was in South Texas for generations and one grandfather had come from Ireland, the things she transmitted to us came from Spanish and Mexican culture.

As a young girl, my mother had become the protégée and confidante of María S. Guerra, a gifted painter and as close to an artistic doyenne as Rio Grande had. Mamá María, as we were taught to call her, gave my mother books and exposed her to the fine arts and the intellectual world of ideas and literary expression. More importantly, Mamá María opened the possibility for my mother of an identification with a global Spanish-speaking intellectual family, one that went well beyond the borders of her South Texas upbringing.

Crucial to this exposure was the poet and Mexican nun, Sor Juana Inés de la Cruz. Sor Juana, who wrote the first known manifesto in the New World on the intellectual rights of women, inspired her contemporaries as well as the generations which followed with her wit, intellectual depth, and daring as she debated church authorities of the time, who were intent on silencing her. Also important to my mother's intellectual development was the Nicaraguan poet Rubén Darío, as well as other historical and literary figures prominent in the Spanish-speaking world.

My mother absorbed the stories of these heroes and heroines, whether literary or historical, and subsequently transmitted them to us in her teachings, through repeated recitations of poetry, through historical accounts she would relate, or through songs she would sing.

We learned and internalized what we heard just as she had learned and internalized it. This process of internalization was different from subjects we learned in school because what we learned at home became an integral part of our ordinary, everyday life. My mother's admiration for the poet Rubén Darío, for example, was not relegated to the confines of something you only learned about in a book, took a test on, and forgot about. Rather, Rubén Darío became part of the things that were talked about at home and shared with friends who had similar interests. In one such case, one of my mother's close friends, Hilda González, named her first born Rubén Darío in honor of the famous poet. Rubén Darío was a distant figure whose poetry we heard and memorized and at the same time a playmate who played tricks on us when we played *a las escondidas* (hide and seek).

While the poetry of a seventeenth-century Mexican nun or a Nicaraguan modernist of the nineteenth and early twentieth centuries did not transfer easily to 1960s Central Texas public television, what it did do was to provide formal structures for the endless uses of language.

Rubén Darío's "Canción de Otoño en Primavera" is one example:

Juventud, divino tesoro,
¡ya te vas para no volver!
Cuando quiero llorar, no lloro . . .
y a veces lloro sin querer.

Youth, divine treasure,
you are leaving never to return!
When I want to cry, I don't cry .   .   .
and sometimes I cry without wanting to.

Although Rubén Darío was not appropriate for children, the skill which went into the versification and the grounding this gave me in the sounds of the language were valuable as I went about the task of composing the content of each program.

Rubén Darío's lush "Sonatina" tells the story of a sad princess who, imprisoned in a golden palace garden filled with flowers, butterflies, peacocks, swans, and a fairy godmother, contemplates thoughts of a prince from India or from China. While the poem is far too complex for a simplified television presentation, it nevertheless provided me with some fundamental lessons in using language to appeal to a child's imagination:

La princesa está triste . . . ¿Qué tendrá la princesa?
Los suspiros se escapan de su boca de fresa
que ha perdido la risa, que ha perdido el color.
La princesa está pálida en su silla de oro,
está mudo el teclado de su clave sonoro,
y en un vaso olvidada se desmaya una flor.

The princess is sad . . . What is wrong with the princess?
Sighs escape from her strawberry mouth
which has lost its laughter, which has lost its color.
The princess is pale in her chair of gold,
the keyboard of her sonorous clavichord is silent,
and in a vase, forgotten, a flower faints.

My mother drew from a vast storehouse of Spanish/Mexican popular culture. She filled us with endless accounts that relied on humorous puns, rhyming couplets, and plays on words which she had memorized as a child and which we, in turn, also memorized. This had the effect of guiding us, soothing our fears, or simply breaking up the tedium when the Texas heat and humidity became intolerable.

Even our prayers to the saints, and we seemed to have one for every occasion, made use of poetic devices. The temperamental Texas weather was somehow more bearable after a quick,

> Santa Bárbara, doncella,
> que del cielo fuiste estrella,
> líbranos de rayo y centella.

> Saint Barbara, maiden,
> you who were star of the heavens,
> save us from a bolt of lightning.

And those notorious Texas spiders could always be controlled with,

> San Jorge, bendito,
> amarra tus animalitos,
> con tu cordón bendito.

> Blessed Saint George,
> tie up your little animals,
> with your blessed cord.

The rhyming folk game "Doña Blanca," which like Rubén Darío's verse featured a central female figure imprisoned by nature, was more adaptable to television. In the game, Doña Blanca is surrounded by pillars made out of silver, gold, and other substances like stone, wood, glass, and paper, protecting her from a wasp which buzzes around the circle. The children assume the different roles as they sing and enact the game.

> Doña Blanca está cubierta
> de pilares de oro y plata.
> Romperemos un pilar
> para ver a Doña Blanca.

¿Quién es ese jicotillo
que anda en pos de Doña Blanca?
Yo soy ese jicotillo
que anda en pos de Doña Blanca.

Doña Blanca is covered
with gold and silver pillars.
We shall break a pillar
to see Doña Blanca.

Who is that wasp
who is trying to get Doña Blanca?
I am that wasp
who is trying to get Doña Blanca.

Other singing and chanting games were easily adaptable to television, although always lost something in the translation. Unlike adults,
who thought the words didn't make much sense, the children readily
accepted these and incorporated them into the play experiences related to the programs.

Transcending the nonsense syllables of some of the songs and
rhymes were the cultural elements that were being transmitted, and
thus the value for television programming catering to children from
a variety of cultures. In contrast to Dr. Seuss' "Green Eggs and Ham,"
whose nonsense is in English, the absurdity here was in Spanish,
leaving the children free to fill in the gaps with their own imaginative
logic in whatever language they chose.

Naranja dulce
Naranja dulce,
Limón partido,
Dame un abrazo,
Que yo te pido.

Sweet orange,
Cut lemon,
Give me a hug,
I ask of you.

La víbora de la mar
A la víbora, víbora de la mar, de la mar,
Por aquí pueden pasar,
Los de adelante corren mucho,
Los de atrás se quedarán.

Like a winding sea snake, sea snake, sea snake,
You can pass through here,
The ones in front run a lot,
The ones in back stay behind.

Mata-rile-rile-ron
Amo a usted, mata-rile-rile-ron,
Qué quiere, usted, mata-rile-rile-ron,
Yo quiero un page, mata-rile-rile-ron,
Escoja, usted, mata-rile-rile-ron.

I love you, mata-rile-rile-ron,
What do you want, mata-rile-rile-ron,
I want a page, mata-rile-rile-ron,
You choose the page, mata-rile-rile-ron.

Both my mother and her only brother, my Tío Raúl, were gifted singers. Tío Raúl was a musician, although he had other jobs too, as did many Mexican Americans who were part-time professional musicians in South Texas.

Tío Raúl played the drums and sang in the *bailes de regalo*, the dances held in the ranches surrounding Rio Grande City in which the men gave the young women a gift in exchange for a dance. The mothers, who accompanied their daughters to the dance, carried a sack for the purpose of collecting the gifts. The gifts were usually pieces of *pan de dulce* (Mexican pastries), so the friends and extended families in the *ranchos* where the popular girls lived were always glad when these dances were held because they were the recipients of the overabundance of sweet bread the young women were given.

Venues for local live entertainment were plentiful, with the usual assortment of birthdays, weddings, anniversaries, and baptisms calling for serenades and other musical performances. Touring tent shows, or *carpas*, were especially popular during the 1930s and towns like

Rio Grande City, although small and isolated, were the beneficiaries of these traveling troupes. During my mother's youth, she was a fan of Lydia Mendoza, the young Texas Mexican woman who started her recording singing career in 1934 at the age of sixteen and who was called *la cancionera de los pobres* (the singer of the poor).

Along with the tango, "Mal Hombre" (Evil Man), Lydia's theme song about a man who violates a young girl, Lydia sang plaintive melodies that talked about sadness and a world of betrayal. One such song, "Mundo Engañoso" (Treacherous World), recorded a few months after "Mal Hombre," speaks of the plight of a young girl who has to launch herself into the world.

Vengan jilgueros, pajarillos, a estos prados
entonaremos estos cantos con placer,
pues yo comprendo que el gusto se me ha acabado
que en este mundo todo ha sido un padecer.

De la edad de catorce años me salí
a navegar con mi triste situación,
ahoy les cuento lo que sufro y he sufrido
por no llevar en el mundo dirección.

En otros tiempos me encontraba en otra esfera
a cualesquiera le podía yo hacer un bien;
ahora me encuentro y me ven como a cualquiera
y no soy digno que los buenos días me den.

Y esto lo digo porque a mi mismo ha pasado
con dos amigos de mi grande estimación,
que llegó el grado de tratarnos como hermanos,
ahoy se burlan de mi triste situación.

¿Mundo tirano, por qué eres tan engañoso?
¿Por qué a la vista te presentas tan formal?
El desengaño yo lo llevo por mi vista,
que en este mundo nada es cierto ni es legal.

Vendrá la muerte y quedaremos igualitos
porque en el mundo todo tiene su hasta aquí,
les aseguro que más tarde al cabo hay tiempo
se han de encontrar como yo me encuentro aquí.

Yo me despido porque vengo de visita
yo me despido de todos en reunión,
les aseguro que en capilla o en capillita
a cada santo se le llega su función.

Come goldfinches, little birds, to these meadows,
we shall sing these songs with joy,
well I know that joy has gone out of my life,
in this world everything is suffering.

I set out at the age of fourteen
to navigate with my sad situation,
now I am telling you what I suffer and have suffered
for not having direction in the world.

In other times I found myself in another sphere,
I was able to do good to anyone,
now I find myself being treated like a nobody,
not deserving of even a good day greeting.

I say this because this has happened to me,
with two friends I held in high esteem,
who were so close, we were almost like brothers,
and now they make fun of my sad situation.

Cruel world, why are you so deceitful?
Because at first glance, you present yourself so correctly?
I now recognize betrayal,
and know that in this world, nothing is certain or legal.

Death will come and we will all be equal,
because in this world, everything has its limit,

I can assure you that later since there is time,
you will find yourselves as I find myself now.

I will say good-bye because I have just come for a visit,
I take my leave of everyone at this reunion,
I know that in every small church or little chapel,
every saint will have his celebration.

Rather than being downers, a folk song like "Mundo Engañoso" elevated the audience from the travails of difficult depression years. The importance of the song is that it is told from the perspective of a young adolescent, barely out of childhood, whose comprehension of the world goes far beyond her years. In speaking of the world's betrayal and death as an equalizer ("*vendrá la muerte y quedaremos igualitos*" / death will come and we will all be equal), Lydia's empathetic appeal was to all listeners who found themselves beset by problems.

Perhaps, more critically, the lyrics signal the ephemeral nature of life in the concluding stanza, which begins by saying that the narrator, and by extension all of us, are in this world only briefly. "*Yo me despido porque vengo de visita*" (I will say good-bye because I have just come for a visit) reminds the listeners that their problems, like their lives, are transitory. The final line, "*A cada santo se le llega su función*" (Each saint has his celebration) further admonishes, "Your current situation will someday end, and you, too, will have your day." In its call to the world of the spirit, the song lifts the audience away from the material and makes bearable the circumstances over which the listeners have little or no control.

If the songs were about sadness or treachery, the context of transmission was just the opposite. My mother sang these and other similar songs so often that we all sang them and internalized their messages, the style of narrative, and their melodies. Within the context of family singing, the songs filled our days without necessarily leaving us with a sense of despair. If, indeed, there was talk of sadness, all we had to do was wait a few moments for a bit of levity to return to the conversation. Lydia Mendoza's music and her songs were no exception.

As children, we often heard the family story about the time Lydia Mendoza came to Rio Grande in a *carpa* show and the resulting hub-bub that occurred. Filemon and Lupe Garza were two of my parents' closest friends. Filemon wanted very much to see the performance, which was the talk of the town, but Lupe, pregnant and concerned about the couple's finances, did not want to go. The night of the show, Filemon and Lupe had a heated discussion about Lydia, and Filemon finally agreed not to go to the performance. In the middle of the evening, Lupe had a craving for ice cream and sent Filemon in search of what at the time was still considered a delicacy. Not to be thwarted, Filemon took some of their grocery money and decided to sneak into the tent show to catch a glimpse of his favorite singer. His initial thinking was that he would work some extra hours, replace the money, and Lupe would never know about his innocent escapade. Capti-vated by Lydia's talent, Filemon lost track of time and stayed until he heard the last song. Filemon's explanations of the missing grocery money, the soupy container of ice cream he brought Lupe, and Lydia Mendoza's role in all of this were forever part of our family history.

Although my mother was not a professional entertainer like her brother, she had a professional's sense of timing and an instinctive artistic sense about what to do to capture an audience's attention. At times, my mother's entertainment for us turned raucous and was filled with popular folk humor, but here, too, poetic, rhythmic, and rhym-ing devices filled her recitations. These rustic and more antiheroic styles provided additional instances of language manipulation, show-ing me that words can be used in graphic ways to retain a child's attention.

One of these word-play songs dealt with a woman who is robbed of her jewels by a singing robber. The woman has a son-in-law named Tiempos (Times); a daughter called Lucía (Lucia, or Lucy, a name for a woman but also a form of the verb "*lucir*," to show); and a dog named Pellejos (Skins, or someone who is denuded and without cloth-ing). As the woman (W) is attacked, she yells for help, and when she pauses, the robber (R) sings his verses to complete the woman's words.

W: *¡Me roban! ¡Me roban!*

R: *La vida y el corazón . . .*
   La vida y el corazón . . .

W: *¡Tiempos! ¡Tiempos!*

R: *En que yo . . .*
   En que yo . . .

W: *¡Lucía! ¡Lucía!*

R: *Mis alajas . . .*
   Mis alajas . . .

R: *Y ahora me encuentro en estos tristes . . .*
   Y ahora me encuentro en estos tristes . . .

W: *¡Pellejos! ¡Pellejos!*

W: I'm being robbed! I'm being robbed!

R: Of my life and heart . . .
   Of my life and heart . . .

W: Times! Times!

R: In which I . . .
   In which I . . .

W: Showed! Showed!

R: My jewels . . .
   My jewels . . .

R: And now I find myself in these sad . . .
   And now I find myself in these sad . . .

W: Skins! Skins!

If the words in the songs or rhymes sometimes lost something in the translation, the cultural transfer of one value system to another was even more problematical. This was especially so with the subject of death and the violence that sometimes accompanied it. Dealing with death as an adult subject is difficult enough, but cross-cultural discussions at the level of a child can produce contradictory interpretations leading to hard-to-resolve misunderstandings. Without necessarily giving the edge to either Mexicans or Americans on this issue, we chose to look closely at each individual example and apply what appeared to be the most workable solution in each case.

Although border and other Mexican *corridos*, which have their fair share of death and violence, were not specifically intended for children, we learned and sang many of them at home. Américo Paredes' seminal work on the border ballads documents their pivotal role in depicting the cultural clashes between Anglos and Mexicans in Texas, especially following the Mexican War of 1848. The most famous of these is the classic epic ballad "El Corrido de Gregorio Cortez," in which the hero, a common and innocent man, defends his rights, "*con su pistola en la mano*" (with his pistol in his hand), which he uses to kill his Anglo enemies who have oppressed him.

If *corridos* such as "Gregorio Cortez," "El General Cortina," and others had themes of violent killings, they related these events in simple, straightforward terms. The ballads did not have the graphic depictions or the humorous twist shown in "La Bola de la Maquinita," the *corrido* we loved to sing on our train trips to Monterrey. Judged with an American yardstick, "La Bola de la Maquinita" might seem gory, with its graphic depictions of the crash. From the American perspective, the comic twist given to the violence might seem particularly macabre and insensitive to the plight of the people killed in the crash. Yet "La Bola de la Maquinita" did not seem gory to us. Rather, it served as a lesson in the tragicomic nature of life, and fit in with other traditional customs having to do with death, such as eating *pan de muerto* (a round loaf of sweet bread with a skull and crossbones baked on top) or giving sugared *calaveras* (skulls decorated with names across the forehead) on November 1, The Day of the Dead.

To me, "La Bola de la Maquinita" was no different from the traditional finger game "El Pollito" (The Baby Chicken) my mother had taught us as toddlers. "El Pollito" is played with the adult taking the child's hand and folding the fingers into the child's palm, as each one is characterized in turn in its role in the story, from the little finger, which is the baby chicken, to the thumb, which is the old dog. When all the fingers are bent over and the child has made a fist, the adult storyteller, acting like the old dog, does a finger crawl up the child's arm, hiding in the armpit, or the dog's little house, and tickling the child. In the process, the baby chicken is killed, peeled, cooked, and eaten, all to the accompanying giggles from the child, who endlessly asks for repetitions of the game, never tiring of the breathtaking buildup of suspense and the gobbling up of the baby chicken.

Este es un pollito,
Este lo mató,
Este lo peló,
Este lo guisó,
Y este perro viejo
Vino y se lo comió.
Y se fue,
Corriendo, corriendo,
A su casita.

This is the baby chicken,
This one killed it,
This one peeled it,
This one cooked it,
And this old dog
Came and ate it,
And he went,
Running, running,
Into his little house.

"Juana la Marrana" (Juana the Pig) was another humorous folk rhyme which dealt with the killing of an animal. While "El Pollito" proved too complicated for television, "Juana la Marrana" was adapted to the constraints of a generalized television audience. In the original story, Juana the pig is cut in half by a butcher. Although children in Spanish and Mexican culture took these stories in stride (I certainly had in my own childhood), I felt that this might not be the case in a situation where the cultural context could be misunderstood. For this particular rhyme, we adapted the visualization of the verse, and instead of an actual pig, we showed a piggy bank filled with coins which was broken at the moment the butcher was supposed to "kill" the animal.

I recognized that television representations are not accompanied with the extensive value structure that undergirds the transmission of culture in the family or community setting, so rather than risk an outcry from the educational establishment or from parents who might be perturbed at the thought that I was advocating the killing of a cute little pig named Juana (Jane), I opted for the simpler and more expedient solution. I felt it was important to include the rhyme for those Mexican American children viewers who would be able to relate to the verse within their social context.

Juana la marrana
Se cayó en el soquetal.
Vino el panadero y no la pudo levantar.
Vino el carnicero y la partió por la mitad.

Juana the pig
Fell in the mud.
The baker came and could not lift her.
The butcher came and cut her in half.

My mother had taken those same lessons in lyrical and melodic fantasies and had applied them creatively to the things that surrounded her. Her applications were geared toward the familial rather than the professional world of work. She had named her children Alma Nelda, Aida Nydia, Enrique Eduardo, and Aristedes Tadeo, exotic sound combinations which evoked other times and other places. She did the same thing with the rhymes and songs she taught us as children, making us conscious, both by example and by direct instruction, of the potential that words could have. As I encountered the challenge of creating a television program for which I had no preconceived patterns, I relearned those familiar rhythms, sayings, and riddles of my childhood and put them into different dramatic and visual settings. I filtered what I knew through what I did not know. At the time, I could think of no better way to use the television box as a transmitter of those cultural values I had received in my own childhood.

I quickly learned that television is essentially a dramatic medium, and unlike a presentation made to an audience that is physically present, television depends on dramatic and theatrical techniques to retain an unseen public. Television has a small screen, where large panoramic views get lost, and its essential intimacy requires close-up camera shots in order to capture the attention of the viewer, who establishes a one-to-one relationship with the limited scenes which are being presented.

The communication dynamic changes radically when the camera focuses on a person or an object. By isolating the object, the camera alters the peripheral vision, restricting the information that is being sent out about that object. The camera can manipulate the object, rendering the whole process extremely subjective. When the camera magnifies the object, it can call attention to it and highlight its importance. If the camera ignores the object or places it at a distance, it can take attention away from it and trivialize it.

Television is like art, as in *artificial*, and its reality is not a *reflection* of life, but a *recreation* of it. Television time is not real time, but instead television, like all art, takes the moments and concentrates them, sometimes to the point of unrealistic exaggeration.

In those first productions, I pretended children were inside the cameras and I walked among them and could almost touch them. I experimented with direct and interactive teaching techniques. I gave my television students instructions and asked them to repeat or to answer in chorus, or to sing or close their eyes, or to whisper or shout, or to speak slowly or fast—whatever succeeded in keeping their attention.

The persona I developed was "Señorita Barrera," who, given the bouffant helmet hairstyles of the period and my expertise with television makeup, looked like a combination between a Japanese Noh character and a Mexican revolutionary *soldadera*. All I needed would have been a bit more white powder and the crisscross ammunition holders.

Initially, the other television teachers and I attended special makeup sessions intended to prepare us for our appearances. Anxious to look my best, I followed the makeup consultant's instructions to the letter. The only problem was that the woman had given us makeup tips for blondes with very fair skins, and when I intensified the use of eyeliner and did what she recommended with the rest of my makeup, the results were more grotesque than flattering. After that first disastrous session, I started scrubbing away at the layers of makeup.

In those early days of television, I knew next to nothing about such technical matters, so I did some experimenting and went through the painful experience of watching and critiquing my own programs. I changed and adjusted and gradually arrived at a version of me that, if not Hollywood gorgeous, was adequate for the Central Texas video audience.

Austin–San Antonio audiences did not necessarily view those early Spanish–English programs because they were done so well, but because those viewers formed a personal connection with what they saw. Incident upon incident reminded me that people formed special relationships with television. They developed a close rapport with the fictional or real characters who appeared on their screens, and it was this link between the viewer and the screen that was critical in whatever changes television could bring into people's lives.

Viewers felt they could tell you intimate details about themselves, and they expected that you should do the same. Although the programs I did were on a regional level, I was continually surprised at people's reactions whenever I found anyone who had seen the shows.

Especially memorable were the women in the restaurant who kept sending me loving notes written on napkins when I was trying to make an impression on a first date, the young child who told me I looked just like their family maid, and the bank teller who held up a customer line for some thirty minutes while she asked me for details about my eye shadow, mascara, and makeup, meticulously writing down everything I told her.

If the question of color was of paramount importance in the context of a television production, it was even more so for Hispanics in terms of the color bias shown by the society that surrounded them. For some Hispanics, having a dark skin can be problematic, although I never knew anyone whose experiences with their coloring were like those of the Mexican American Richard Rodríguez, who wrote in *Hunger of Memory* about shaving his arms in the hopes of making them whiter, and whose aunts took large doses of castor oil during late pregnancy to prevent having dark children.

Although the subject of *prietos* (dark ones) and *güeros* (light ones) was not an uncommon one in our family, it was not something that was of overriding concern. My attitudes about skin color chiefly came from my mother, whose complexion reflected the light genetic heritage of her redheaded Irish grandfather, Daniel Craig. Her affinity for darker skin tones was well known in our household, and so were accounts of how she said novenas whenever she was pregnant in fervent hopes the child she was to have would have my father's brown eyes and darker *mestizo* coloring.

An incident reflecting the value that people place on color happened to my mother in later life, shortly after she left South Texas and moved to Austin. My mother, who was as chatty as the elderly Anglo lady who lived next door, struck up a quick friendship when they first met. But the casual repartee they enjoyed took a thoughtless, if unintentional, turn that caused my mother concern.

In one of their usual backyard-across-the-fence conversations, the lady had said, "Mrs. Bar-reh-row, Mrs. Bar-reh-row, I told the ladies at my church that I had a new neighbor lady, and she was Spanish. But I told them they would never know it because she was so white. I said, 'She's as white as I am.'" My mother, whose respect for the older woman took precedence over her chagrin in what she perceived as her ignorance, restrained herself in her answer, "Mrs. Pharr, I am *not* Spanish. I'm Mexican, and I'm proud of it."

Mrs. Pharr may or may not have known the geographical distinctions between Spanish and Mexican, but she knew enough to know that the word "Spanish," associated with "white," was a compliment, while the word "Mexican," connected with "dark," was not. After a few days, my mother, who felt the woman's age permitted her certain transgressions, let the matter drop and she and Mrs. Pharr continued to be good friends.

Skin color is an issue of considerable importance to Hispanics. Hispanics who are Spanish or Caucasian are able to "blend" into mainstream American society easily, but discriminatory practices are strong toward darker Hispanics who are *mestizos* or are mixed with African lineages, as in the case of some Hispanics from the Caribbean. In those first television programs I did, my discomfort came not from the fact that I was far from fair, but from the technicians whose lighting abilities failed to make me look like myself.

Darker skins, because they absorb light rather than reflect it, are harder to photograph. Furthermore, a dark-skinned person standing next to a very fair one presents even more complicated lighting problems. Trying to find a happy medium between the two extremes can often mean the edge on the tonal contours is given to the lighter person in order to give that person definition, while the darker person receives scant lighting. The lighter person ends up looking normal, while the darker one loses tonality and gets an overdose of shadows. The dark person appears far darker than he or she is in reality and because of the contrast, the facial features can almost disappear.

I developed an aversion to what I called the "black blobs" on the screen. In years to come, and especially in *Carrascolendas*, where I felt it was important to reflect the color variation of the Hispanic community in the actors who participated in the programs, production seasons would be preceded by my standard "black blob" lecture to the crew. If necessary, we brought in additional lighting personnel or compensated by choosing colors within the same tonal spectrum for the actors' costumes.

Although the problem of lighting continues to this day, it's not as bad because of improved cameras (which can now capture the finer shading variations in people's skins), increased knowledge about the medium itself, and greater minority participation in production crews.

The taping sessions were exercises in the art of on-the-spot performing. The programs were done as if they were "live"; that is, they were not edited. Although the programs were taped ahead of time, essentially the taping sessions began at the beginning and proceeded through to the end, with retapings permitted only in dire circumstances. These occasions happened all too frequently, but not because of any mistakes in content or delivery. The KLRN studios were on the flight pattern allocated to the nearby Bergstrom Strategic Air Command, and the planes from the base would cause sound wave disturbances every time their speed broke the sound barrier. The crew handling the cameras would react to these sonic booms with sudden jerks, giving the videotaped picture unexpected wavy ripples. On harried days, these minor mishaps would be overlooked and the program would bump along to its conclusion.

My first taping session was an event, well documented with banner headlines in the local media as the latest effort in television technology. Whereas our rehearsals had been simple affairs with only the minimal personnel needed to get the program done, the actual recording of the program was quite the opposite. What I most remember about it was that the studio suddenly filled with all sorts of people who had nothing to do with the production, the studio lights somehow multiplied overnight from the ones I thought I had seen when I was first shown the large cavern-like room, and my fanny was sore for forty-eight hours afterward from the stress of holding it so tight during the dry runs and final recording of the program.

Robert Squier, who later became a Washington-based political media consultant, was my first television director. Bob was considered a comer in the business. He was a man of medium height, with boyish good looks and boundless energy. He was filled with the confidence of knowing where he was going and how fast he needed to go to get there. Bob lost no time in setting the pace from his command post. He gave me what I could have sworn were dozens of instructions. I was to stand, walk, turn, hold, look, count, recap, time, and all while I was supposed to smile and keep my eyes fixed on whichever camera had the red light on.

Unlike the director, I felt underqualified—as well as ignorant of teaching methods and self-conscious about the correctness of my Spanish, which I knew everyone would conclude had a *pocho* ring to it. It also did not help that I thought I was ten pounds too heavy, had a mouth that was too big, teeth that were terribly uneven, and hands that were horribly bony with protruding veins that looked more like their sole purpose in life was to get intravenous injections rather than make graceful gestures for camera closeups.

My solution to my preoccupation with what I looked like was to speed through the delivery as quickly as I could. Those early shows were fifteen minutes long, and I generally wrote script outlines, rather than detailed dialogue sequences. Adrenaline pumping, I raced through these outlines under the false illusion that by speaking fast, I would somehow alter the passage of time.

In the first programs I taped, I frequently used up what I had to say with three or four minutes to spare, and, on camera, even a few seconds of silence can seem interminable. The crew soon became adept at following my extemporaneous conclusions, and, as I gained experience, I learned to control my nerves, and my pacing slowed down, at least to a point.

I never quite overcame the tendency to want to race through presentations, but, after a time, whatever extra minutes I had in a program were easily fixed with a retaping as new and more sophisticated video techniques made it possible to do postproduction editing quickly and efficiently.

I produced from sixty to ninety programs a year for six years, from 1962 to 1968. As more programs were produced, the shows for each year were retained and rerun throughout the KLRN daytime schedule.

The programs were intended for a viewing audience of children, but the actual viewers extended far beyond this expected group, and reflected, from the fan mail I received, a variety of ages, ethnic groups, and interests. The range included, among other anomalies, several gentlemen fans who offered proposals of marriage; home-bound housewives with restless preschool children; night shift workers who would wake up intermittently during the day and flip on the tube as a reprieve from interrupted sleep cycles; the widow who would later unknowingly become the equivalent of a Broadway angel for *Carrascolendas* and who avidly learned Spanish by watching reruns and repeats of reruns; retirees who thought that the programs beat the soaps for viewing fare any day of the week; and a host of Spanish speakers who wanted to renew their ties with their language and culture, or who wanted their children or grandchildren to do so.

The majority of these initial programs remained in reruns for some ten years. The impact they had and the testimonials I continue to receive are constant reminders of the void they helped to fill, although after the first few years of reruns, and given the changes in fashions and the improvements in my own abilities as a television producer, I was more self-conscious about watching these old shows than I had been about doing those first few on-camera sessions.

Little did I know that these initial programming attempts would serve as the precursors of *Carrascolendas* and the small wave of bilingual television that followed. What had been a part of my childhood would finally find a reality outside of the boundaries of my imagination.

CHAPTER FIVE

◼ The Bureaucratic Two-Step

MY FIRST CONNECTION with bilingual education came during the years I spent in the 1960s doing the regional Spanish and English language programs for KLRN, which, although they were not following any specific bilingual education methodology, were intended to help children who entered school with little or no knowledge of English. As a national program, bilingual education was meant for any child who had language difficulties, but because the majority of these children were Spanish speaking, the program essentially targeted their needs.

As chair of the Department of Romance Languages at the University of Texas at Austin in the 1960s, Theodore "Tug" Andersson was present during my first attempts at doing Spanish–English television programming. A tall man of Swedish stock, whose measured body movements and impassive speaking style could have come out of an Ingmar Bergman film, Tug would eventually be widely recognized nationally and internationally as a language scholar and one of the earliest proponents of bilingual education.

But when I knew Tug in 1962, I knew nothing about the academic discipline of bilingual education and had no concept of the stature that Tug had or would achieve later as a scholar. More than anything, I knew him as a self-effacing and insightful man who advocated hiring, whenever possible, "authentic" models as language teachers in order to imbue students with the direct and intimate experience of speaking a new language and learning about another culture.

For Tug, this was an ideal to aspire to and did not necessarily reflect the reality of the romance language department, where there were plenty of excellent teachers who were not native to the language and culture they taught. Tug's position did not denigrate these professors so much as acknowledge the importance of including native speakers in the language-learning experience.

In taking this stance and reaching out to populations that previously had largely been ignored, Tug positioned himself as a forward-thinking educator. Far ahead of his time, he was recognizing the legitimacy of having bilingual and multicultural capabilities. In fact, the Texas Penal Code prohibition against using languages other than English for instruction in public schools, initially passed in 1918, was still in effect during the 1960s. Tug's recognition of Mexican Americans and U.S. speakers of other languages as valuable resources in the educational endeavor made his advocacy of dual-language instruction for children a natural next step.

As Tug's activism grew, so did his recruiting efforts of public school teachers as part of his Teaching Associates Program within the department, a move he hoped would rectify the ethnic imbalance on the faculty of his department as well as link the efforts of his language department with the reality of what was going in public schools. His second and third recruits, in 1962 and 1963, went on to earn doctorates and distinguish themselves in the field. George Blanco, from El Paso, eventually became the director of the Office of Bilingual Education in the College of Education at the University of Texas at Austin, and Albar Peña, from Falfurrias in South Texas, whose role was so prominent at the end of the decade in the initial funding of the *Carrascolendas* programs, became the first director of the U.S. Office of Bilingual Education in Washington, D.C.

I met Tug in a roundabout fashion. I was doing a series of recordings and filmstrips called *Gloria and David* to teach young children Spanish and English. The series was being produced by Gib Divine, a man whose vision for entrepreneurial opportunities matched his interest in trying multimedia language approaches to enhance children's education. Tug was a consultant for Gib's company and it was through conversations with him and his advice which led to my becoming a student in his department. It was also through his efforts that I became one of the students who auditioned for the role of on-camera teacher for KLRN's proposed children's television programs.

Although Tug did not officially hire me for the University of Texas-based KLRN position, his general attitudes on language teachers who were native speakers were instrumental in shaping the process. So was his criticism of the scholarly community for hiring teachers solely on the basis of certification credentials and not on what he felt were actual qualifications, which included the valuable resource available through a person's home culture. This combination of factors probably influenced station management in my favor.

Tug's advocacy for the potential offered by native language instruction for those children whose first language was not English produced skepticism even from someone like George Blanco, who thought the idea sounded strange. George initially saw no virtue in teaching Spanish speakers to read first in Spanish and then in English, but after reconsidering, he concluded Tug's thinking was logical.

Along with subscribing to the method of teaching language by emphasizing hearing, understanding, speaking, and play—principles established by the National Defense Education Act of 1958—Tug also embraced the new audio-video uses of the language laboratory, television, and teaching machines. This, plus his emphasis on the educational breakthroughs that could occur by focusing attention on the bilingual child, made the climate propitious for the events taking place after that.

The bilingual child was the important issue in the federal legislation which followed and in my own thinking in the creation of the *Carrascolendas* series.

Responding to the ethnic unrest of the 1950s and the War on Poverty and civil rights legislation enacted during the 1960s, the U.S. Office of Education, as part of Title VII, the Elementary and Secondary Education Act (ESEA) and the Emergency School Assistance Act (ESAA), began programs in 1968 advocating the concept of bilingual education as an important part of the curriculum. Bilingual instruction was included in the compensatory education models designed to meet the special needs of children with limited English-speaking abilities.

Eventually, both of these pieces of legislation were critical to the funding of *Carrascolendas* and other programs similar to it. But at the time these initiatives started, there was little indication that the productions receiving funding under these acts would be the largest body of television ever to be done focusing on ethnic and racial minority populations. Nothing comparable has been done, either before or since that time.

The *Brown vs. Board of Education* Supreme Court case of 1954, which declared that separate educational facilities were inherently unequal and therefore unconstitutional, had stimulated interest in the needs of the poor and especially the education of poor minority children. The McAteer Act of 1963 initiated a series of congressional actions addressing programs for disadvantaged youngsters. Eventually a whole series of mandates came under the rubric of compensatory education for those students deemed "culturally deprived" who required more individualized attention.

The Bilingual Education Act followed in 1968 as part of these compensatory initiatives but left unclear whether the emphasis was the transition to English or bilingualism itself. From the outset, the program was characterized by politicization, a situation which has remained true throughout its history. Although initially President Lyndon B. Johnson opposed the legislation, the increasing activism of Hispanics, including dramatic school walkouts in places like Texas and California, as well as other highly publicized events which became known as the Chicano Movement, shifted the political situation. In 1968, President Johnson signed the act into law.

The surge of available federal money charged the atmosphere with fervor about educational reform, and as the announcements of new funds filled the halls of schools and other educational institutions, more attention was given to Mexican American children in the Southwest, where most of the children lived whose first language was Spanish.

Bilingual education had as many critics as proponents. Since its goals were linked to civil rights and low-income issues, the program came to be regarded almost exclusively within the province of the minority poor, rather than considered for its important linguistic and cultural merits. Rather than concentrating on what a program like this could do to capitalize on the cultural and linguistic diversity of the country, the program became part of other War on Poverty efforts. The concept of being bilingual was caught in the political maelstrom surrounding compensatory education and quickly became stigmatized as being a program for those disadvantaged children who were failing academically. In the special-interest shuffle which followed, the burden of proving the validity of the concept fell largely on schools with large Spanish-speaking populations, where most of the bilingual programs were being initiated.

Caught in these transitory educational and political concerns, bilingual education eventually came to be regarded as one of the most confusing and controversial educational reform movements, struggling since its inception to be accepted as a valid approach in the instruction of young children. By focusing participation on low-income students, the legislation diverted attention away from other youngsters within the school setting who could benefit from their exposure to another language and culture alongside students who already had some native connection to these subjects. This had the effect of leaving people with the perception that the program merely created academic ghettos and increased rather than decreased polarities.

Instead of promoting multicultural and multilingual environments—following the idealistic intentions of some of the original proponents of the program such as Tug Andersson, Albar Peña, and Severo Gomez, as well as the scores of teachers in Texas and throughout the country who were at the forefront during the initial stages of the program—the legislation sometimes was perceived as being used to keep children in isolated, poverty-linked programs. The results were and continue to be unfortunate, as the contentious educational reform movements in California in the 1990s and the attending English-only initiatives in a variety of states have demonstrated.

Ethnic and linguistic pride was to be cultivated only in people who were disadvantaged and supposedly culturally deprived. Although some programs existed which concentrated on a variety of other languages, the majority of programs instituted under bilingual education were Spanish–English programs and, consequently, linked to whatever ills were attendant on the immigration patterns of the Hispanic population. With each wave of new Spanish-speaking arrivals into the country came a renewed set of language problems to be visited on the schools affecting whatever studies were being done to evaluate these programs.

In the confusion of media and political attention these reports received, few people acknowledged that greater numbers of Hispanic youngsters were attaining fluency in the English language and were reaping the benefits of having teachers who supported their home culture and language because these teachers themselves came from the students' own communities. Some critics felt this fluency was not necessarily due to any special type of educational instruction and in particular did not want to credit bilingual education with any advances.

Others felt that the advances in fluency merely reflected the ongoing American immigrant story: progress in learning English, they reasoned, is a natural outcome of the assimilation and acculturation process. English fluency had come to all immigrants, the argument went, without special bilingual education programs. But this argument ignored the more fundamental benefits of a multilingual and multicultural education. Nor did it address the issue of regarding children whose home language is other than English as a valuable resource rather than as yet another problem to be fixed by the schools.

In the melange of positions, few stopped to consider that the widespread accessibility of the television programs which were coming to dominate children's lives might very well be an important linguistic factor. The video generation was beginning to come of age, giving children from all walks of life a common language and culture as well as further complicating whatever idealized concept people had of a multicultural and multilingual society.

I, like others in Texas, welcomed the role the state was playing on the national scene with respect to bilingual education. In spite of any shortcomings of the bilingual program, the bottom line was that Spanish-speaking children were going to be the recipients of federal attention. For those of us like me, who were already working in television and already teaching Hispanic culture and language to young children, opening up the possibilities of what could be done with the medium seemed like a natural next step. At least that's what I thought.

KLRN was not one of the principal players in the PBS system. It was not part of the elite northeastern educational broadcasting establishment, which emanated from New York and Boston, and it was too far from Los Angeles, with its proximity to Hollywood and the entertainment world. If KLRN was not a complete outcast, it was certainly not in the limelight, either.

One U.S. Department of Education official in Washington would later tell me he thought KLRN was in a "rustic" area. Another thought the station was too remote to really pull off any top-quality broadcasts. A person at the Boston station laughed at the suggestion that there might be confusion between the like-sounding "Austin" and "Boston"—Austin was beneath any such radar. And a corporate official out of Houston concluded that his company's major funding investment should go to the West Coast because Austin was too small to undertake a television production of any significance.

But if those were the comments I would eventually hear, my point of reference in those early years was strictly regional, with little or no exposure to the larger world of broadcasting. I had no doubts, however, about the potential for creativity at a station like KLRN, in contrast to commercial television operations, which produced what I considered rather perfunctory newscasts, with at times a talking-heads noon woman's show.

Even in a low-budget operation like KLRN, I was doing programs with countless changes of scenery, puppets and costumed fanciful characters, filmed inserts, live music, numerous props borrowed from local stores, and an assortment of five-dollar-an-afternoon student performers who had neither acted before nor done anything on television but whose energy and enthusiasm for the creative endeavor was unrivaled.

The plotlines were more slapstick than realistic, and the costumes, limited to one per performer for the entire year in order to save money, bordered on the silly. One of the actors in this early period was Nicolás

Kanellos, in the role of a fellow with knickers, who went on to become a well-known Spanish literature professor as well as the founder of Arte Público Press, a bilingual scholarly press at the University of Houston. Another was Graciela Rogerio, as a woman in a ruffled cap, who later became a medical producer for WABC, the flagship ABC station in New York.

The children loved the programs and I was overwhelmed with greeting cards when Ricardín, a Charlie McCarthy look-alike ventriloquist dummy purchased at a local store and rechristened for our purposes, celebrated his birthday. No one seemed to care that the programs were distinctively "homemade," lacking the polish and sophistication of television done out of the larger markets. What we were providing was not being done elsewhere, and this overrode whatever production deficiencies we had.

My office at KLRN was in a recessed attic vault, underneath the rafters, in one of the smaller, older buildings on the University of Texas campus. The building, which in time fell victim to construction demolition crews, was located adjacent to the main administration building of the University. After doing these initial productions, I was creatively restless and wanted to tackle a program which was more focused toward the needs of Mexican American children. I wanted to go to another level of production and had visions of doing something on a larger scale.

The *Gloria and David* Spanish and English recordings and filmstrips I did prior to my KLRN work were an outgrowth of some of the work being initiated by the League of United Latin American Citizens (LULAC) and the American G.I. Forum. These organizations, led by men like Alonso S. Perales, George I. Sánchez, Carlos E. Castañeda, J. T. Canales, Hector P. García, and Gus C. García, were instrumental in calling attention to the inequities suffered by Mexican Americans. LULAC's leadership in educational issues began as early as the 1930s when it challenged the segregation of Mexican American children in Del Rio schools.

In 1957, LULAC's Félix Tijerina organized the "Little Schools of the 400," a concept intended to teach four hundred basic words of

English to preschool children. The design centered on a series of radio instructional lessons known as *Escuelita del aire*. The idea did not gain widespread support, but there were those, among them Gib Divine, who felt the concept was worthwhile. Gib Divine had originally recruited me to work on the radio series, and when this did not materialize, he turned instead to the production of filmstrips and recordings. The concept for *Escuelita del aire* would also be instrumental in the thinking of educators who were involved in the Head Start initiative.

My parents thought of Alonso Perales as an exemplary leader and, as we were growing up, told us about his seminal work, *En defensa de mi raza* (In Defense of My Race). During the 1940s, Perales was a state and national activist on civil rights issues concerning discriminatory practices against those who had served in the military. As a veteran, my father was particularly sensitive to these problems. He, with others from Edinburg and South Texas, protested the comments of Anglos who complained because the city had become "completely Mexican." This narrower Anglo view called for the job restriction of Mexicans in order to give the returning American boys and their families a chance at jobs and housing.

Perales made a particular issue of the Edinburg situation in his testimony before the President's Committee on Civil Rights in 1947 and cited the incident as typical of what was happening in the country, including my father's name in his list of citations.

As a student at the University of Texas, I was familiar with George I. Sánchez' activism and worked for him as a research assistant when he was on the University faculty. George, a president of LULAC, had been instrumental in establishing the American Council of Spanish-Speaking People in 1951. The council's work on public school segregation and discrimination in housing, employment, restaurants, theaters, and other public places established its civil rights efforts on a national level, a cause eventually taken up by the Mexican American Legal Defense and Educational Fund.

George was a slight, wiry man with a line mustache that stretched out to near invisibility when he became irritated. He moved about the tiny office which we both shared with the speed and lightness of the former flyweight boxer he had been. He would get upset at the inequitable treatment of Mexican American children in schools and would decry the absence in the curriculum of any subjects that would inspire young Mexican Americans about their cultural and historical background.

One of George's interests was studying the highly developed mathematical symbols of the Mayans, and I remember sitting in his office doing painstaking drawings of the dots and dashes that made up the Mayan system, the illustrations for his scholarly research on the subject. He complimented me on my housekeeping and organizational abilities, saying that when two people had to coexist in such a limited work space, it was helpful if at least one of them had an exaggerated sense of order. When I went to him requesting a reduction in hours (and pay) because I was finishing the work he gave me too quickly, he was adamant in saying that since I was being paid ridiculously low wages, I should pretend the extra money was scholarship assistance, and I should use the free periods to study. It was the only time I volunteered to give up pay for work I completed too fast.

Although the stories that George told me would not translate directly to the plan I had of doing a bilingual television program for children, what was important was that George was the first Mexican American professor I knew. His ideology, along with those influences in my upbringing, formed a part of the background that eventually became the philosophical motivation for the work I was to do later. During the years I spent doing the Spanish–English language programs for KLRN, I heard the talk about bilingual education and thought the time might be right to try to get foundation or federal funding for a television program which would expand the nature of the productions I had been doing.

The hurdles proved to be far more daunting than I anticipated.

While it is true that concrete steps lead to specific actions in our lives, it would be erroneous to say I had a detailed outline of any plan the day in 1968 when I walked into the KLRN station manager's office and said that what I needed to do was to go to the East Coast and try to sell my idea of a bilingual television program. What I have found in my own life is that thoughts and ideas move around in that amorphous illusion which I call my mind, and then with what appears to be little explanation, partly based on logic and partly on intuitive consciousness, I find myself acting at a given moment in time almost without willing to do it. As clearly as I could ever define it, this was the sequence of events leading to my behavior that day.

I never knew Harvey Herbst to be unpleasant. He always seemed to have a composure about him and general smoothness of expression which kept everything he said at a uniform level. A man with a wide forehead and steady stride, his face was more sheen than shadow. I used to picture him as an old man, a handful of gray at the top, but no wrinkles. This same evenness of contour characterized his working style, and it set the tone for most of the others who were employed at the station. KLRN management preferred the unruffled pace that would eventually see tasks through to completion. They neither encouraged me in any particular endeavor nor discouraged me. Largely, they left me alone.

When I went to talk to Harvey about a bilingual television program, something must have triggered his thoughts to future possibilities, because the sequence of events that followed was unprecedented in our relationship. By that time, I had produced close to five hundred Spanish–English programs at KLRN. Although no other television teacher had a comparable production record, I had not been singled out for any special recognition.

Going to Washington and New York was an off-the-wall idea. I had never been to either city to do business of any kind. But I didn't really evaluate the merits of what on closer analysis would have seemed like a preposterous notion. I proposed to Harvey that KLRN pay my travel to the East Coast so I could investigate funding to expand the nature of the bilingual television programs I had been producing. The budget levels which were generally assigned to my productions were extremely modest, but in spite of this I concluded I had nothing to lose by asking.

When I walked into Harvey's office, I knew nothing about the letter.

If *Carrascolendas* had a fairy godmother, I would have to say it was Margaret Caldwell Scarbrough. Although Margaret's participation in the whole scenario was largely unintentional, her contribution still represented the first dollars generating the momentum for the eventual funding of the series.

Margaret was a woman of wealth and came as close to aristocracy as Austin had in the 1960s. She was married to Lemuel Scarbrough, a descendant of E. M. Scarbrough, who had been a cofounder in 1890 of Scarbrough and Hicks, a dry goods store in Austin. The Scarbrough family has been in the retail business since then and in the 1960s, Scarbrough's was one of the leading department stores in the city. Lemuel died in 1965 during the time when my bilingual programs dominated the daytime schedule of KLRN with new productions, reruns, and repeats of reruns. In the period following his death, Margaret sought solace by watching the programs I was doing on television. She found the assortment of puppets, songs, costumed scarecrows, and nonsense delightful. They distracted her and she launched herself into the learning of Spanish with all the enthusiasm of a young child.

As she increased her proficiency in Spanish, Margaret concluded that Señorita Barrera was one of the greatest things on Austin television. She wrote a letter full of praise to the station manager, enclosing a check for a thousand dollars as a contribution.

I walked into Harvey Herbst's office and told him about my idea of doing a series of children's programs which would officially be classified as bilingual and which would play off of the programs I had already been doing. The programs I envisioned needed a more extensive budget than the slim funding allowed under the present station production configuration. I told Harvey that what I needed was to go and sell the idea for the show and get someone to give me the money to produce the series. If the station would pay my travel, I assured him, I could do the rest. Although my pitch to Harvey was positive enough, I could barely believe the confident tone in my voice as I spoke the words.

Harvey told me about the Margaret Scarbrough letter and the check she had sent. He proposed that I get a portion of the amount. Harvey paid for my ticket and put the rest in the station general expenses fund.

The trip East was far easier when I imagined it than when I was faced with the actual reality of it. Going to a large city, especially a city like New York, was a daunting thought, and, in fact, when I made the reservation, I could not bring myself to travel alone. I talked my sister Alma into going with me and we accepted friends' invitations to house us during the trip.

Alma had always been the adventuresome one of the two of us and was fearless when tackling such things as snake-hunting expeditions with her biology teacher. I was considered the talker but generally the wimp in the family when it came to braving the unknowns of the physical environment. The prospect of strange streets and taxis maneuvering the crush of traffic was unnerving. Alma accompanied me on appointments—that is, she went with me but stopped short of actually going in to any office. She sat on street benches and waited on corners while I went in and made the pitch.

No one refused to see me, but no one helped me, either. In New York, I called on the Ford and Carnegie foundations. In Washington, I talked to people on Capitol Hill and in government agencies. Although I was not overly optimistic about my initial meeting at the U.S. Office of Education, it turned out that the South Texas-Mier-Hebbronville connection served me in good stead.

Albar Peña, who had studied under Tug Andersson at the University of Texas, had been hired by the U.S. Office of Education to serve as director of the Office of Bilingual Education. The congenial, naturalized Texan turned bureaucrat was charged with launching the bilingual programs being initiated through the newly established Title VII of the Elementary and Secondary Education Act.

Albar was born in Mier and his early schooling in the late 1930s and early 1940s was in Hebbronville, at the Spanish-language El Colegio Altamirano, the school that was started by my Tío Pancho and my Tío Rosendo, my grandfather's brothers. Albar was one of a growing group of Hispanics around the country in the 1960s and 1970s who had received doctorate degrees and were assuming positions of leadership as educators.

At the time I knew him, Albar, the first president of the National Association for Bilingual Education, was a man in his late thirties whose natty appearance complemented the brush mustache and the ready smile punctuating much of his conversation. He pointed out the difficulties of the programs I envisioned, although as a government employee he did not want to discourage me from any plans to do the series. His vision for bilingual education generally fell in line with the more traditional programs of instruction which were being planned for classrooms. He wasn't against the use of television per se, but he expressed reservations that the complexities of instructing Spanish-speaking children might be too difficult to undertake at a distance. We spent much of our visit talking about our South Texas–Mier connections. And, although the conversation ended on a congenial note, I had no reason to expect a positive outcome.

In the course of those first unproductive attempts to get funds, I made countless phone calls, received a complete dousing in the alphabet soup of government-speak, and met with enough people to find out that the bilingual monies which were available through Title VII could not be awarded to a television station like KLRN. But it was unclear whether or not I, as an individual, could make a request for funds to do a television program.

KLRN was a nonprofit institution but could not receive monies directly from the federal government under this legislation because it was not an LEA. An LEA, I found out, was a local education agency. Groups like public schools, regional educational service centers, and state education agencies like the Texas Education Agency were LEAs. The mother lode of monies, policy, and central guidance was USOE, the U.S. Office of Education, the education conglomerate I visited in Washington, which later changed its letters to DOE, the Department of Education. Periodically, different presidential administrations have threatened to dismantle the Department of Education, but this has never actually happened. USOE issued RFPs (requests for proposals), complex documents outlining detailed bidding procedures for grant solicitations. Panelists reviewed these proposal submissions and made recommendations to Office of Education personnel, who, in turn, decided who would receive the monies. In theory, this was the way it was supposed to work.

To an outsider like myself, the important information, once you mastered the jargon, was that the local education agency distinction kept funding limited within the traditional educational establishment, but no federal employee would come right out and tell me I could not write a proposal and submit it. What they did do was refer me from one person to another. I was left with the impression that the goal was to have enough people tell me to go to enough other people so I eventually would tire and go away. I soon learned that one of the key people in the process was the assistant commissioner at the Texas Education Agency. Severo Gomez was the assistant commissioner, and his office was in Austin.

Severo was another Texas educator who had attained prominence in the bilingual education movement. When I first saw him, I thought Severo almost fit the translation of his name, which in Spanish means "severe" or "stern." A man with an enigmatic countenance, Severo was given to deliberate and well thought out statements. He was the first Mexican American to be hired by the Texas Education Agency and had made his way through the agency's bureaucracy. From the point when I met him until he retired in the early 1980s, he was the highest ranking Mexican American educator in the state.

Like many multigenerational Texans, Severo had roots that went deep into the history of the state. His attitudes about educational reform had been shaped by a complex intertwining of feelings of allegiance to the state and of outrage at the inequities he had personally experienced and continued to see in the school systems. Severo readily recounted his Texas connections, saying he was a descendant of Plácido Benavides, a prominent Texas rancher who had been known as the Paul Revere of the Texas Revolution. Benavides rode from the battle at Agua Dulce Creek to Goliad to give notice of the arrival of José Urrea's army.

Severo's early experiences attending a racially segregated school in Woodsboro and the discrimination he saw there had a significant influence on his ideas about bilingual education. His vision for the programs was almost utopian. He wanted children to learn school subjects in both English and Spanish. In this manner, both languages would have equal status, and Mexican Americans and Anglos would be equal partners. Severo's vision for an educated American child was one in which the child could participate in several languages and cultures. For him, this was truly the American way of life.

Severo obviously wanted to do the best thing he could for Mexican American children, but it was difficult to see how this was possible, given the political battles besetting bilingual education and the difficulties of succeeding when the demands placed on the use of language made teaching so problematic for so many people. When *Carrascolendas* was finally launched, Severo became the chair of our national advisory board of educators, parents, and consultants, and his relationship with us endured throughout the six years we produced the series. I had the impression that in spite of his serious exterior, he genuinely identified with children; perhaps it was my own desire to break through his composure which led me to use his last name for one of our characters. Although I never told him the origin of the label, I named our bilingual lion, the lead character in the series, Agapito Gomez y Gomez y Gomez.

The afternoon I met with Severo in 1968 about the idea for a bilingual television program, we spent over two hours in conversation. He gave me every conceivable reason he could think of why the program was impossible. Although he did not come right out and say it, I concluded he thought the program did not meet federal requirements and, consequently, educators would not review the idea favorably. He was right.

The readers who evaluated the initial proposal I submitted gave it a zero rating on the grounds it was not what the legislation had in mind for a bilingual program funded under the federal guidelines for this initiative. But this was not information I would have until much later.

I went to my office that day after talking to Severo, took the Office of Education request for proposal, sat down in front of a manual typewriter in my attic-vault office, and started to write a document to send to Washington. I really do not know what propelled me to go forward with what certainly appeared to be a foolhardy plan. I had never written a proposal of any kind before and certainly had not received any encouragement from anyone. Furthermore, I had never struggled with the specific guidelines of submitting a federal solicitation for funding or dealt with the maze of curriculum requirements or behavioral objectives called for in the proposal.

Whatever the reason, I addressed all the items in the cumbersome set of instructions, and the station manager and I drew up what was an overly optimistic budget for $150,000 to do thirty black-and-white half-hour television programs.

I didn't realize it then, but the lesson I learned in how to respond to a request for proposal served me well in the other documents I would write during the next six years as the budgets for *Carrascolendas* grew into the millions. At the moment, my only concern was to send off the proposal by the required deadline.

Once the proposal had been sent off to Washington, I concluded that my work was probably in vain, and I forgot about it. No one was more surprised than I was when several months later I received a call from the Office of Education asking me to attend a meeting in Denver with some USOE staff members and other educators.

The call from Washington was typical of many I received in subsequent years. It was short and noncommittal, almost as if the caller was following a crib sheet outlining specifically what was and was not supposed to be said. The message of the distant voice was brief: "I am sorry, I cannot give you any definitive details about the status of your proposal."

Since the television station included San Antonio, an Anglo school official from one of that city's school districts was also invited to attend. He was to give his opinion regarding how the proposed television program would affect the Mexican American children in his area. I spoke with him on the telephone before going to Denver and agreed to meet him in the Denver hotel lobby before going to the meeting. At the time we spoke, he told me he had seen me on television and had met me on a previous occasion. I did not say anything to him during our telephone conversation, but in the course of the television programs I had done for KLRN, I had met hundreds of people, all of whom knew me but whom I did not really know. Not wanting to sound ungracious, I did not say anything and concluded that once we arrived at the hotel, he would recognize me and make the initial move to greet me.

Dressed in my most stylish mini-skirted suit, I went to the hotel lobby at the designated time, and as I was getting off the elevator, an overly friendly man greeted me with a big, "Hello, there!"

Thinking I couldn't place the man's face in my mind to determine exactly where I had met him, and smiling inwardly at the irreverent Mexican twist to the racist adage that all gringos look alike because they're all so pale you can't distinguish one from the other, I responded with an equally friendly gesture.

I started to walk with the man across the lobby, and although he continued to talk, he seemed to grow increasingly uncomfortable as we walked. After we had gone a few paces, he stopped to chat with a group of men whom he obviously knew. I also stopped and stood next to him as he spoke.

As the moments passed, the man became more ill at ease, and I was somewhat nonplused at the fact that he was not introducing me to the circle of men who had stopped him. The man grew increasingly flustered and his head made nervous little twitches as he glanced first at me, then at the group of men, and then back to me again.

Suddenly, I heard a voice behind me saying, "Miss Barrera, Miss Barrera. I've been looking all over for you. I thought I had missed you. The meeting is on the second floor."

As I moved away from the crowd of men, I could see the look of relief on the face of the man who had greeted me at the elevator. Embarrassed as I was, I managed to keep my composure as we made our way to the appointed room. The meeting was like none other I had ever attended before. The seven or eight people around the table seemed to think the idea for a bilingual television program had no merit, and I gathered that their questions were planned in order to prove this. At one point, I sincerely wondered why I had been asked to go to Denver at all, but then again I thought perhaps this was the way the government operated.

In Washington, people had not wanted to tell me directly that I couldn't receive any funding, and evidently those same people could not bring themselves to inform me by letter that the proposal was not going to be funded. I thought it made them feel better if they brought me to Denver, which must be happening to the losers in this competition, and then later they would tell me I wasn't going to get the money.

Richard Goulet was one of the Office of Education staffers officiating at the meeting. I didn't know it at the time, but he was intrigued with the idea of a bilingual program on television and had largely ignored the reviewers' comments about the suitability of funding such an endeavor.

Of French Canadian background, Richard had grown up with French and English and felt the ability to speak in two languages should be encouraged and nurtured. He thought television was a natural vehicle to get this job done and thought it was irrelevant that the legislation did not specifically address this issue. He had spearheaded the move within the Office of Education to get the proposal brought up for special discussion. But from the questions he and the others around the table were asking, I had no clue what had gone on behind the scenes.

After what seemed to be an interminable length of time, we paused for a break and Richard took me aside.

"How much did you ask for?" he asked. "One-fifty," I answered, trying to sound as breezy as possible, knowing full well at this point that all was lost.

"I think you're going to need two." he said.

"Of course," I answered, thinking I had misunderstood what he had said.

I hadn't. We got two hundred thousand dollars, and *Carrascolendas* was in business.

Those initial monies took me and the *Carrascolendas* I would come to know through funding and production upheavals lasting six years. In many ways, it proved to be an exhilarating, creative time. It formed me professionally and established my national reputation as a television producer capable of doing multimillion-dollar projects. But it was also a frustrating period, filled with the backstage intricacies of federal and educational bureaucracies, worlds I scarcely knew when I met with those Office of Education officials for the first time.

In the years that followed, I went well beyond the vision I had when I found myself in that Denver hotel lobby. In no small measure, I learned how to develop the skills needed to manipulate the systems I encountered, but most especially I learned about myself and the stamina required in order to make a difference to the audience of children I wanted to reach.

Those government initiatives of the late 1960s and early 1970s provided an impetus to invent and develop new ideas, yet because of many factors—how monies were allocated, competition for funds, political considerations, the nature of the public broadcasting establishment—these early experiments with multicultural programming were stopped before they could reach their full potential.

During fiscal year 1972, the source of funding for *Carrascolendas* changed from the monies it first received through the Elementary and Secondary Education Act to the competitive awards made through a special fund set aside for television broadcasts provided through the Emergency School Assistance Act. The act was designed to alleviate desegregation problems in the schools, and the television competitive awards were meant to promote an atmosphere conducive to greater ethnic and racial harmony. The television productions were intended to showcase a panoply of cultural diversity through broadcasting vehicles which had never had an opportunity to be produced before. The initiative was also a training ground for ethnic and racial minorities, who up to that point had had limited employment opportunities available to them.

The new competitions changed the nature of the funding game, making it possible for programs like *Carrascolendas* to expand their budgets beyond one million dollars and allowing television stations and other private nonprofit institutions to receive funds directly without seeking recourse through the schools.

The availability of the ESAA-TV funds opened a new avenue of funding, but because these contracts were available to anyone in the country who wanted to produce multicultural television programs, competition became fierce. Nonetheless the ESAA-TV program was not without its merits. In the mini ethnic and racial oriented television boom that followed, the ESAA-TV funds spawned two regional and three national bilingual television programs aimed at Hispanics, plus twenty-five other minority shows.

By the end of 1979, the federal government had invested nearly sixty-five million dollars in the production of these minority series through fifty competitive awards. The money seemed like a grandiose amount to those of us who had been used to smaller budgets in the past, but the funds needed to make these programs successful over the long run in a competitive marketplace far exceeded this amount. The nature of television programming generally calls for sustained financial and promotional backing over a long period of time in order to create and maintain an audience, and this element was not there for most ESAA-TV programs. Nor was there the impetus within public broadcasting, the educational community, or the private sector to take beginning programming efforts and extend their life with additional support.

Since the Emergency School Assistance Act had originated with civil rights, bilingual, and poverty issues, the programs produced under its television component carried a government taint which placed them in a quasi-ghetto within public broadcasting circles. The ESAA-TV programs were not segregated per se, but a number of factors placed these productions outside of the mainstream broadcasting community, virtually guaranteeing their demise.

The traditional funding source for public broadcasting, the Corporation for Public Broadcasting (CPB), had been left out of the loop of the funding decisions in the allocation of monies for these productions. And while a series like *Sesame Street* and other programs emanating from the Children's Television Workshop in New York were the recipients of government funds, those programs were in a league of their own, both in terms of the federal monies they received as well as the quality of production they achieved. The minority programs produced under ESAA-TV were not so lucky.

Reports from government officials connected with these productions indicated that the network for the system, PBS, as well as the Corporation for Public Broadcasting, did not value these programs, and, in effect, said that the programs lacked the popular appeal to warrant support.

Although nobody said so openly, these shows were generally regarded as second-rate minority productions, to be tolerated but not supported over what was considered the standard and better quality

PBS programming. Some PBS stations gave these minority productions poor scheduling time slots, broadcasting teen school-related series at 11 P.M. on week nights and bypassing them in the allocation of promotional dollars or other publicity efforts in favor of programs considered to have more general appeal.

In the case of *Carrascolendas*, one television critic charged that the productions were "unrelentingly lighthearted" and "maintained a strong Mexican flavor." The same critic cited a Hispanic Washington federal agency staffer as saying the program was "too parochial to survive" and "mainly geared to Hispanics in the Southwest." One top PBS executive told me the program should be less like Mexican television, indicating he thought the productions from that country were "abominable" and not on a par with American television.

Other barriers to entry plagued small, independent production groups when it came time to seeking funding through established public broadcasting channels. These smaller producers were considered outside of the PBS system and generally were not privy to the networking that helps programs as they attempt to make their way through the broadcasting maze of funding, scheduling, critical reviewing, and other stages necessary to meet with success.

Production units within PBS stations did not do any better. PBS stations, especially smaller stations whose principal focus was broadcast and not production, did not necessarily see their role as assisting minority productions. Since funding was generally unavailable from PBS-CPB, productions came to an end at the conclusion of government funding.

Public broadcasting stations that had received the benefit of lucrative grant budgets usually made no fiscal provisions to incorporate minority production personnel into their core staffs when the soft monies ended, even though it was unrealistic to expect whole integration of personnel into existing operations.

In the case of the *Carrascolendas* staff, the vast majority of its ethnic and racial minority employees were regarded as having insufficient broadcasting experience to warrant line jobs at KLRN, even though some of them had as many as six years experience working in a national multimillion-dollar production. I was the only minority person, out of a multiethnic staff that at times totaled as many as one hundred, who was offered a position by the KLRN management when the *Carrascolendas* monies ended. The position called for a cut in pay and fell short of the amenities offered to other recently hired vice presidents, the position I held at the station in 1976. I declined the offer.

I had no customary industry contract with the station specifying any creative rights for the work I was originating, nor was I considered a permanent station employee, even though I worked for KLRN for thirteen years. People in this category were also given retirement benefits, which I never received. Although eventually the *Carrascolendas* budget exceeded the entire station budget, and I was the executive producer and the project director responsible for obtaining the funds and managing the entire operation, I largely functioned outside of the station's other ongoing business.

Toward the end of the *Carrascolendas* production years, at the instigation of two of our national advisory board members, Gus García, a longtime Austin political activist and city council member, and Severo Gomez, the director of bilingual education at the Texas Education Agency, KLRN management reversed its long-standing practice and asked me to attend station board meetings. But this was not before I had a lively discussion with a leading member of the KLRN board about discrepancies in the management of the *Carrascolendas* staff versus other station personnel, a claim he discounted with, "Oh, Aida, that's not possible. Don't be such a Mexican jumping bean."

The discussion did little to change KLRN's practices during the course of our production years.

Minority television productions such as *Carrascolendas* did not do any better in forming alliances with schools and other educational agencies connected to school systems. While schools initially saw the virtues of receiving largely subsidized television programs, when funding stopped, school institutions could not or were not willing to sustain productions through any special efforts or to make production budgets a part of the funds which these groups already received for their minority classroom programs.

A conservative educational establishment, generally unconvinced at the time of the value of media vehicles, saw any moves to incorporate productions into their already existing projects as not only expensive, but as diminishing the limited dollars they had which otherwise could be used for projects more clearly affecting direct classroom instruction. Furthermore, programs of this sort were produced outside of their control by minority producers whose educational credentials were sometimes dubious.

At the national level, the jealously guarded terrain of local school system funding precluded the possibility of subsuming these productions within programs being developed as part of what by then had become the U.S. Department of Education, some of whose projects, including bilingual education, were becoming increasingly controversial. Bilingual programs, subjected to an assault of criticism, were scrambling to justify their own existence and had little time or desire to provide the leadership required for such endeavors. Coproductions that might have included educational as well as television groups usually needed an institutional base that was missing from what were essentially rudderless, isolated ventures. Television's potential for providing beneficial elements outside the scope of a typical classroom, especially with respect to multicultural education, became a moot point.

By the end of the 1970s, other governmental agendas had replaced desegregation issues, and eventually the discontinuation of funding brought this era to a close. The few ESAA-TV programs produced in the early 1980s had such limited runs that broadcast distribution was difficult, even in those areas which would have benefited the most from multicultural programming.

But the needs of ethnic and racial minority populations did not end, and, in a way, grew more pressing as the decades progressed than they had been in the 1970s. Regardless of demographic projections indicating increasing numbers of Hispanics, this segment of the population remained largely excluded from television. Indeed, twenty years after the ESAA-TV programs, there were fewer multicultural programs on PBS than there had been in 1976, and no long-running series focusing on language and cultural diversity was on the air. If Hispanics had progressed from the television and movie portrayals of the 1950s and 1960s, when they were generally portrayed as servants, gang members, and criminals, they were still not doing very well.

For the generations of young children who during the next two decades would watch the mix of bilingual characters populating the fictional village of Carrascolendas, the bureaucratic and broadcasting problems of minority television producers were as fanciful as the comedic and musical vignettes which they saw on the program. The world of who did what in government agencies or what power plays were involved in what would finally become the program content were as foreign to them as they were to me when I first contemplated translating the idea of doing a program for Mexican American children into reality.

Survival for me in those early days of *Carrascolendas* often meant doing almost constant battle. For the children viewers, doing battle meant surviving whatever challenges were inherent in their ethnic and racial mix. The hope was that *Carrascolendas* would contribute to the solutions necessary to answering those challenges. Although the specific effects on these children cannot be quantified by any valid social science measure, by virtue of their longevity, at the least, the programs provided one of the few consistent examples of Mexican American or Hispanic cultural identification on television.

But in 1969, when the story was beginning, these events and projections were far off in a future that at best seemed hazy and uncertain. When I left that Denver meeting with the promise of two hundred thousand dollars, I scarcely envisioned the things that were to come in the years that followed. The dominant feeling I had as I boarded the plane the next day for Austin was panic.

If I had been foolhardy at having made the request to go to New York and Washington to chase after funds for what I thought would be a good television program in two languages, I was now awestruck at the prospect of the reality facing me. I was about to start a television production for which I seemed to have ample imaginative resources but few real-world capabilities.

CHAPTER SIX

■ The Mythological Mosaic

ALTHOUGH I KNEW what the proposed television project should accomplish, I had given little thought to what I would call the program. I knew that the name should be symbolically significant. It had to capture the meaning of Mexican American culture and encompass the sense of the program's larger purpose.

If the series was to address the needs of Mexican American children encountering Anglo school culture, the title of the show had to be symbolic of a time of cultural wholeness for Mexican Americans that did not exist in an everyday multicultural system dominated by Anglos. Consequently, it became crucial for the program to be based in a mythical and historical past in which the cultural values of Mexican Americans were dominant. After much soul searching, the name came from my own personal and cultural mythology.

As far back as I can remember, words fascinated me. I was four years old when the talk in my family centered on the announcement we received from New York telling us that Tía Chabela's daughter, Bernice Danelli, was going to marry a young man whose last name was Napodano.

I heard the news, held the invitation in my hands, and asked my mother, who was teaching me to read my first words, to tell me exactly where the word "Napodano" was.

"Napodano," she pronounced carefully.

"Napodano," I repeated slowly.

I could feel the sounds roll around in my tongue. The syllables followed a different order, like nothing I had heard before. "Napodano" sounded foreign and faraway, like the aunt and cousin I had heard about but never seen.

I went around the house for days repeating the name, and, when no one in the family could stand it any more, I made the announcement that I was changing my name from Aida Nydia Barrera to Aida Nydia Napodano. My father, who took special pride in the Barrera heritage, smiled but was not pleased.

Early on, I had displayed definite name likes and dislikes, especially where my own name was concerned. My mother's name for me had been Aida Nydia, but this had been questioned when preparations were initiated for my baptism. Father Gustav Gollbach, the German priest who directed the parish of the Immaculate Conception Church in Rio Grande City, had said that the Barrera baby who had been born on Christmas Day could not be named only the non-Christian combination of Aida Nydia. My mother, whose leanings were more toward poetry than religious tradition in these matters, refused to name her children after their *santo*, the saint's day commemorated on the birth date of the newborn child. If she followed Spanish and Mexican custom, she would have named me after the inscription which appeared on the Catholic calendar for Christmas Day. In this case, my name would have been Natividad (Nativity). A known name in the Hispanic world, Natividad was a legitimate name, but it was not the name my mother had chosen for her second daughter.

Although we are now far more accepting of cultural differences in names, this was not the case when I was growing up. Anyone whose name deviated from the norm heard taunts from their classmates. English translations of Spanish religious names like Concepción (Conception), Angel (Angel), Santos (Saints), and Jesús (Jesus) were met with skepticism and oftentimes ridiculed by those unfamiliar with Hispanic customs. My mother was adamant in her stand against the priests of the Immaculate Conception. Her resolve did little to deter Father Gollbach and his assistant.

My mother was not pleased when she was told she had to add a third name or change the name altogether. She felt she had come up with the perfect combination of sounds, in harmonious symmetry to my sister's name, which was Alma Nelda, and these would lose their lyrical quality if a third name was added. The permission granted for my sister's name had been a fluke, given in a weaker moment in church policy, but in my case, the situation was not to be repeated.

An impasse was reached. My baptism was postponed.

Father Gollbach was a man of note in South Texas and ordinary people did not trifle with his decisions. I grew up hearing about his ingenuity and talent. He was a combination amateur pharmacist and architect who brought innovative health care and European design to South Texas. He blended his knowledge of medicine with the *remedios caseros* (home remedies) indigenous to the area and often came up with judicious combinations, which further enhanced his reputation. He also constructed a replica of the Lourdes Grotto in France, giving the parishioners of Rio Grande City cachet in the nearby small towns and ranches.

A man of formidable appearance, Father Gollbach cut quite a figure in the Rio Grande Valley when he went riding on his horse Kaiser, creating a persona for the priest that reached almost mythic proportions.

In spite of his obvious worldly sophistication, Father Gollbach was a conservative when it came to religious matters. At baptisms, he permitted the use of "heathen" names only when cleansed by the addition of saintly ones. My Tía Tencha, who had some of the same aspirations toward modernity that my mother had, named her daughters Lesbia, Minerva, and Leticia, but she added María to each of their names. In adult life, these cousins were called Lily, Minnie, and Letty. No such solutions were available for me.

After lengthy debate, when the absence of my baptism was becoming a family embarrassment, my father and his sisters convinced my mother to add Isabel to my name. The famous Tía Chabela (Isabel) was also born on Christmas Day, and adding Isabel to my own name seemed the perfect solution. The impasse ended, and after friends and relatives alike were convinced that my soul was going to be doomed to eternal damnation, I was finally baptized.

Either my mother transmitted her distaste for the name, or I intuited the situation in some other fashion, because I never became an Isabel. When I could barely talk, I rejected the name by declaring, "*Chabel no.*"

My own personal mythology began with this one decision. If there is a symbol for our origins, it is in the name that we carry with us throughout our lives, the label presenting us to the world. The family story of my name gave me the beginning of a sense of self.

I was Aida Nydia, without the Isabel.

My intention for the television series I was proposing was that it, too, should have a label signaling its origins. But it was one thing to imagine a series of images. It was quite another to give the images concrete form. At times, not only did I not have the skills for the task, but I had doubts that what had worked for my own personal mythology and my mother's stories in a very individualized home setting and for those shoestring budget Spanish–English programs I had done early on would work in a program that was to satisfy a larger constituency. Again, the resources I thought were so limiting ended up giving me more than I envisioned.

At thirteen, I was hired for an evening and weekend job at El Teatro Juárez in Edinburg, which provided me with an entire set of mythical metaphors, much as my mother's stories had. On one of our family trips to the movies at the Juárez, the theater manager, Jimmy Longoria, a friend of my parents, said he needed someone to sell candy and popcorn and wanted to know if either my sister or I was interested. The likely one to get the position would have been my sister Alma since she was older; but, being the pushier of the two, I quickly said I wanted the job. The only problem was that the age requirement for working was sixteen, and I was only thirteen. Although none of this was discussed openly, I knew the age requirement would not be an issue; the obstacle was in getting a Social Security number so I could be legally employed.

I told no one, least of all my parents, when I decided the only way to get the job was to lie about my age. I prepared a strategy which I considered fairly foolproof. I took special pains with my appearance the day I went to the Social Security office. I wore my gingham green and white dress with the sash and bow in back and the ruffle across the bottom of the skirt, thinking surely this was the dress that made me look the oldest. Although we were not permitted to wear makeup at the time, I took my mother's Tangee lipstick mini-tube and, using my little finger like she did, applied it very carefully to my lips. I combed my hair in an upsweep which I felt added the requisite three years, and carefully rehearsed the story I had decided to tell.

I thought surely the way to go was to change my name and the name of my parents to English ones, concluding that the people who did the Social Security transactions wherever they did them would never link my very Mexican family to one that liked to anglicize their names. I chose my parents' wedding day as the date of my birth, giving me enough years to make the sixteen I needed. I said my name was "Ida" and gave it the English hard "d" pronunciation. My parents Margarita and Fadrique were changed to Margaret and Fred. My story was complete.

Once in the office, I looked straight in the eye of the tall, sallow-skinned clerk and in my best angel-declamation voice, I repeated the facts of my story as if I had known them from the time I had started talking. I pronounced each name in my best Anglo pronunciation, camouflaging the Spanish syllables to such a degree that I knew the clerk would have no recourse but to conclude I spoke no Spanish whatsoever.

I was about to turn and leave when the puzzled man gave me the form with the facts I had given him and told me to sign it. I tried to write where he had indicated, but my hand was shaking so uncontrollably that I struggled to hold the pen upright long enough to scribble the letters.

I knew the clerk was about to press me for proof of age, so, hoping to deflect the situation, I blurted out, "You see, sir, an aunt of mine died recently, and I've been very nervous ever since."

My father's youngest sister had indeed died shortly before, and although her death had not been sudden, like my brother Enrique's, it had nonetheless affected my entire family. Tía Chenda Dreumont had died at forty-one from cancer of the colon and she had been a loving aunt to all of us. I felt a special kinship to her because everyone said I looked like her, but only in my jumbled logic did this have anything to do with getting a Social Security number. The clerk looked confused, must have thought Mexicans were strange and Mexican young girls even stranger, but he asked no further questions. I walked out of the Social Security office with the required paperwork, and, once I had turned the corner and was out of sight of the clerk, I ran all the way home.

El Teatro Juárez was on Harriman Street, around the corner from the Citrus, which faced both Twelfth Street and the central square, site of the Hidalgo County Courthouse, where my father worked as a young man during his short-lived administrative job. The Citrus acted as main headquarters for Dr. L. J. Montague's theater chain of the Juárez, the Citrus, and the Aztec, as well as for his medical offices, since these were located above the Citrus.

Because my job at the Juárez was selling candy and popcorn, I picked up replacements at the Citrus and, loaded with boxes of candy, walked down a long block that included some of the leading Mexican businesses in Edinburg. Chapa's Dry Goods, Estela Lane Treviño's Beauty Shop, Dr. Gilberto Guerra's office, and La Farmacia Garza were almost a blur since the challenge during those daily runs was to walk fast enough that the hot afternoon sun would not melt the chocolate candy before I got from one theater to the other. El Teatro Juárez catered to Mexican Americans and Mexican nationals ("*con pepeles o sin pepeles*"—with papers or without—as we said at the time, mimicking the mispronunciation of the word "*papeles*" common to Anglo customs officers). The crowds packed the two narrow aisles of hardback seats for the showings of the standard Spanish-language films representing the best from Mexico's golden age of cinema. There were comedies parodying "*los turistas gringos*" (the gringo tourists), "western" musical *rancheras*, and passionate melodramas. Pedro Infante, Jorge Negrete, María Félix, Mario Moreno Cantínflas, and countless other Mexican stars paraded across the black-and-white screen to the delight of viewers from all over the Rio Grande Valley.

My work at the theater not only fed a healthy teenage appetite for junk food, but also gave me my first lessons in the value of a work ethic and earning a salary, as well as grounding me in the hidden secrets of feminine makeup. My mother, whose concession to makeup included a dash of Coty face powder and the lightest shading of Tangee lipstick, believed her daughters should keep their complexions free of any artificial adornments. The mothers of my girlfriends at St. Joseph generally subscribed to the same philosophy, so no one I knew ever experimented much with makeup.

Such was not the case with Elia Sanchez, the ticket seller at the Juárez. Elia had long, wavy light brown hair, a huge bosomy front and tiny waist, and the longest lashes I had ever seen, which swept up and down over lined hazel eyes. She immediately became my role model and I secretly made a pact with myself to watch her every move whenever she freshened her makeup. I never quite succeeded in my attempts to copy everything she did, although I did learn one invaluable trick from her. Elia curled her lashes with a long needle, a practice I religiously followed for years afterward even though I knew I was running the risk of gouging out my eyes. Of course, after my mother found out what I was doing, she became convinced her daughter had taken leave of her senses.

The biggest bonus in working at the Juárez, however, was the vantage point I had as I stood behind the counter in the concession area. Immediately adjacent to the popcorn machine, and just before the stairs leading to the projectionist's perch, was a small square window which permitted free and virtually continuous viewing of the movies. I not only could see the films but I could watch them over and over until I had memorized the dialogues and plot lines.

I saw every movie that showed in Edinburg, including the American films that came to the Citrus and Aztec theaters. I traded extra work for unlimited entry to these other places. Going to the movies became a ritual. When I was not in school or working, I was at the movies. And, of course, when I was working, I was also at the movies.

I saw the same features over and over. The American films were enjoyable enough and taught me the subtleties of characterization and dialogue, but the impressions created by the Mexican films were the most memorable, for these were the productions we discussed at home, these were the dramatic vehicles that included the expressions, the jokes, and the songs that were reinforced in casual family exchanges.

I developed a strong visual sense; an appreciation of picaresque, broad, and self-deprecating street humor; and a scriptwriting style that, although knowledgeable of American movie-making techniques, relied heavily on the poetic and theatrical devices of Spanish and Mexican cultural traditions. It was also here that I first became conscious of the antiheroic style of storytelling.

The movies created a world of myth and metaphor for me, and I filtered my vision of the world through the images I was seeing on the screen. I used those movie stories partially as a way of coming to terms with the world around me and partially as a way of escaping that world. In the world of the movies, I could retreat into a world of my own making, like I had retreated in those earlier years into the world of Rio Grande City. But the world of the Mexican antiheroic movie plotlines greatly expanded that world, forming a landscape of familiar points of reference, told and retold in a multiplicity of visual dissolves. Drawn with the broad strokes of caricature, the stories were readily identifiable, easily recognized by young and old, rich and poor, literate and illiterate.

Because the characterizations were highly simplified, they were easy to assimilate and internalize. I, along with the audience, was receptive to the images and to the scripting and dialogue techniques, which incorporated rather straightforward slapstick devices.

The caricatures of the Mexican film screens of the 1940s through the 1960s featured the exploits of comics who appeared in one ridiculous situation after another. They became archetypal models, analogous to trickster figures found in myths and fairy tales, but with enough virtues to elevate them into a heroic realm in spite of their antiheroic origins.

Although these devices have been widely written about in literary and theatrical accounts, as well as the more traditional studies of mythology, the importance for me was not the scholarly documentation but rather the experience I had of participating in what were largely unschooled popular performances.

The christening of *Carrascolendas* was no less of a struggle than my own baptism had been many years before. If the choice of my name was the beginning of my own personal mythology, then the name for *Carrascolendas* had to go through similar mythological and cultural filters. My ancestral heritage had originated in Mier and Rio Grande City, so these provided the logical symbolic centers for the series, portraying Mexican American culture in what I perceived to be its most original form.

I grew up hearing about "Carrascolendas," and it was as much a part of my personal mythology as my own name. The word was an oral transposition of "Carnestolendas" (literally, carnival, the masquerade festival before Lent), the name given in 1753 to one of the earliest ranches on the north side of the Rio Grande River. Carnestolendas, across from Camargo, in northern Tamaulipas, later became Rio Grande City. These settlements, along with others such as Mier, Reynosa, Laredo, and others on both sides of the river, formed the bicultural beads of my mythological past, a past shaping the very essence of Mexican American culture.

When I was faced with the problem of choosing a name for the television program I was creating, my mother came to my rescue. "*Ponle* Carrascolendas, *hijita*," (Call it Carrascolendas, dear,) she told me, instinctively selecting the exact and appropriate symbol. And although she reminded me that "Carrascolendas" was not the "proper" word, as it was written in history books, she, like me, fancied the more colloquial expression that people actually used.

I decided on "Carrascolendas" because it was far more fanciful and childlike in sound than "Carnestolendas" and analogous in lightness and tone to a name like *Rumplestiltskin*. In addition, the term symbolized the unique linguistic plight of the Mexican American. "Carrascolendas" was the result of an oral transmission, considered a deterioration in the language, akin to a *pochismo*. It was not "Castillian," and some Americans would have said it was "Mexican" and not "Spanish."

At the time *Carrascolendas* came to be, many classroom teachers referred to Mexican American students as "nonverbal," remarking that the children could speak neither Spanish nor English. I was always baffled by such remarks, considering the chatterbox Mexican

American children I knew and the lively Mexican American gatherings I had attended all my life.

Our perception of ourselves was just the opposite of the prevailing attitudes held by those teachers. We always thought it was the Anglos who were quiet and the Mexicans who were raucous. What those classroom teachers meant was that Mexican American children did not verbalize Spanish or English according to some narrowly conceived set of norms.

Carrascolendas was intended to speak against that set of norms. In choosing the name, I wanted to give value to the language people actually used. By choosing "Carrascolendas" over "Carnestolendas," I wanted to grant a validity to the former which would alter the reality of the latter. For those of us who grew up in that part of South Texas, "Carrascolendas" was an archetypal symbol, representative of the Mexican American or Hispanic ethos. It was symbolic of what we were as individuals, over and above what others thought we were.

Like fairy tales and myths, *Carrascolendas* appealed to fantasy and not to reality. The reality of the majority of Mexican American children was they were poor, their families had little or no education, they had trouble speaking English, and they did not do well in school. A television program could not change the actuality of those circumstances. What a television series could do was influence the content of children's imaginations. It could open avenues for their creativity, and by providing this impetus, could encourage the children to become the instigators of their own change.

The "fairy tales" I heard at home did not tell me about Hansel and Gretel, Snow White, or Little Red Riding Hood. Rather than the Brothers Grimm, my mother told us "real" stories about Carrascolendas. My mother's fairy tales were populated with a colorful cast of characters worthy of the best of books.

We heard about the adventures of Canuta, *cabeza de explosión* (Canuta, whose head "exploded" with hair ornaments), who was beloved not only for her panache in costuming but also for her good deeds.

There was Bessie (pronounced in Spanish as Beh-seh) whose shotgun approach to ailments was, "If one pill is good for you, five will be better." Bessie combined her talents as an unlicensed pharmaceutical guide with reporting on the doings of the local citizens, and occasionally contributed to amorous match-matching intrigues in the best tradition of La Celestina, the famous go-between of sixteenth-century Spanish literature.

Doña Jenara, who must have been born a wise old woman since no one could remember that she had ever been a young girl, mixed an unrivaled knowledge of anatomy with fancy. When Doña Jenara was faced with a sprained ankle, she would pour urine on a red hot brick, holding the injured foot directly over the brick to steam the ligament into place, a remedy which everyone swore was a fail-safe method of insuring that all muscles would heal properly.

Other accounts were more gripping and told of apparitions or of visits from divine messengers or perhaps God himself. These recurring images always served to rescue the heroes or heroines in the stories, who were caught in hopeless and desperate situations. Indeed, the apparitions invariably alleviated the problem and brought solace which otherwise was not available. But the protagonists of the stories were real people who were able to verify the "facts" of the accounts.

One such story told about Doña Herminia, who came to the Valley from Mexico in the early 1900s and married an American, Don Carlos Smith. Unaccustomed to living in Texas, the young bride was beside herself with sadness because she didn't see or hear from her family in over a year.

One day, as Doña Herminia stood crying by the side of the road, she suddenly saw a man appear on the horizon. He came toward her as if he knew the road and the house and the people who lived there. He stopped in front of her, and as if by some preordained motion, he reached in his pocket, took out a letter, and handed it to her.

As she fumbled to open it, the man kept on walking and disappeared from view. The letter brought news from Doña Herminia's family.

No one saw or heard from the man again and Doña Herminia could never explain who the man was or how he had been able to find her.

Everyone swore the facts of the story were true, including Doña Herminia, whose reputation for veracity was never questioned.

People may or may not have actually lived in Carrascolendas, but this was almost irrelevant to the "fairy tales" about the place. By the time the stories about the leading players were told, they had transcended their historical reality and become folk heroes who either participated in fragments of events or populated full-blown dramas.

The characterizations and dialogues were so vivid that years later, in conversations I had with the noted scholar and folklorist Jovita González, she mentioned people's names I readily identified. When she described the details of their physical characteristics as these had changed through the years, she assumed I had seen the people, knew what they looked like, and had an ongoing relationship with them. But I had never met any of them and only knew them as they lived in my mother's imagination and, subsequently, as they lived in mine.

I met Jovita in 1981, when as president and founder of the Southwest Center for Educational Television, I was directing a series of ethnographies on folk culture and music in a program I called *Sabor del Pueblo* for National Public Radio (NPR) in which I wanted to feature her. When I first spoke with her, Jovita asked me who my family was and immediately "placed" me. For her, this meant that I, along with her, came from those families who were "*originarios de Mier*" (originators of Mier, the northern town in Tamaulipas where our families once lived). Jovita, like Albar Peña and a host of others I knew from South Texas, took special pride in saying she was a descendant of the original founding families of the area.

A small, slender woman with a fragile look that hid what must have been a strong intellectual determination, Jovita was a pioneer in the field of Hispanic ethnographic research in South Texas in the 1920s—long before the scholars who are now recognized as icons in the field. She received a master of arts degree from the University of Texas at Austin in 1930, and as a protégée of J. Frank Dobie, went on to become president of the Texas Folklore Society.

Jovita participated in the same cultural tradition as I had, and as a young woman collected many of the stories common to her South

Texas Mexican upbringing. Jovita was born in Roma "*para vergüenza de la familia*" (it was the "shame" of the family that she was born on the Texas side rather than the Mexican), she said half in jest. Jovita, who was proud of being a Texan, wanted everyone to know she was also proud of having a Mexican heritage. As a young woman, she lived in Rio Grande City and knew my father's family well.

Although the stories she documented differed in specific content from those I had heard as a child, the mythological motifs were familiar. Jovita heard her stories at gatherings in the ranches of Starr County, which serves as the state's geographical legal jurisdiction for Rio Grande City. In the conversations we had shortly before she died in 1983, she immediately related to the perceptions I had about the area.

People having common cultural characteristics, she said, transcend whatever physical distance might be between them, to the extent they could identify each other in a group, "*por la pinta*" (by their stripe), even though they had never actually met. As it turned out, this actually happened the first time I saw her.

Jovita was living in Corpus Christi at the time, and we had spoken on the phone several times in preparation for her bus trip to Austin. She did not like airplanes, she said, and refused to travel in them. I was hesitant about being able to recognize her without some identifying markers and told her so, but her voice didn't miss a beat as she replied, "You don't need to wear anything special. I'll know who you are."

Indeed, she spotted me in the crowded bus station almost immediately; and, to my surprise, I also accurately identified her. If I had to explain how I did this, I don't think I would be able to do it.

Jovita assembled her own cast of fairy-tale characters in the ranch dwellers she described. Among them were Tío Julianito, *el pastor*, with his brood of half-starved children; Alejo, the fiddler; Juanito, *el inocente* (the innocent or idiot), whose mind was being kept in heaven by God; and Pedro, the hunter, who had seen the world and spoke English. There was even a *celestina*, antedating Bessie of Rio Grande fame, except in this case, the amorous go-between was male. Tío Esteban, the mail carrier, did not limit himself to carrying love letters but also embellished his trips with news of other scandalous affairs as he traveled from one ranch to another.

Like the stories I heard as a child, Jovita's tales were filled with the dramatic elements that made the retelling all the more effective. Her versions of spirit stories were populated by the host of witches, buried treasures, and ghosts familiar to my own upbringing. One such account told of a moonlit night with everyone sitting on a large canvas hand-shelling ears of corn. Tío Julianito, *el pastor*, was the narrator. A limping ranch hand and a shadowy figure in a black cape were the lead characters. The setting was a remote ranch outbuilding on one of the overcast, starless nights common to South Texas. The insistent knocking on the door of the hut interrupted the moaning of the wind and the howling of the coyotes. The limping ranch hand crossed the room and opened the door, but the blast of cold air pulled the door from his hand, sending the flickering lone candle in the room into darkness.

To the ranch hand's "*¿Quién anda allí?*" (Who goes there?), the stranger answered, "*Un peregrino perdido*" (a lost pilgrim).

The spectre in the black cape entered and asked for shelter. Trying to warm the sudden coldness with his voice, the ranch hand asked if the man wanted to take off his hat and cape. "No," the man answered, "but I shall take off my head." As he spoke, the man took his head off, which had been transformed into a skull. The spirits of penitent souls as balls of fire engulfed the room and the figure of the stranger.

Jovita originally wrote about this story in 1932, but it is unclear when the account was first told. The tale has the characteristics of the legends told about the Mexican revolutionary hero Pancho Villa. Jovita was privy to the rumors circulating about Villa, who was assassinated in 1923 and was decapitated in his grave three years after that. Stories of Villa's escapades as he eluded both American and Mexican officials are common to both sides of the Texas–Mexico border, and his appearance as a ghost holding his head in his arms has often been linked to his pact with devils.

Whether Jovita's version was fact or legend was unimportant. What did matter is that Jovita's ghost and lost pilgrim—like the story of Doña Herminia's man, which I heard—are symbolic, rather than personal, and serve to teach the listeners about human behavior. In my case, as in Jovita's, they also taught us the components of drama and narrative, as well as the effective use of suspense and other theatrical devices.

Although the time of Jovita's stories preceded my own experiences by several generations, we shared in the cultural communal bonding that the stories about Carrascolendas and its surrounding region brought to us. And it was this sense of community which Mexican American and Hispanic children were beginning to lose and which I hoped partially to restore through the medium of television.

Jovita told me that hearing these stories had a significant impact on her, just as hearing my mother's and others' stories had had on me. The fact that real people like Tío Julianito, Doña Herminia and her husband, Don Carlos, and Pancho Villa himself were the principal characters made them all the more effective.

As a cultural center, the imaginative space of Carrascolendas represented a true symbolic archetype, providing the link with my own as well as Jovita's Texas Mexican heritage. The connection was enhanced because we *heard* the stories rather than having read them. It was my hope that the series of television programs I was planning would be able to at least emulate, if not replicate, this process.

Apart from the mythical and imaginative space, the physical terrain of Carrascolendas carried with it the additional emotional energy of *mi tierra y mi pueblo* (my land and my town). The land and the sense of place had special significance for anyone associated with the original geographical jurisdiction called Carrascolendas. As children, we knew the land was important because our parents and relatives told us so, but it was not until I was a young adult that I began to see the meaning of those many family stories lamenting the loss of the land.

The loss of the land involved a loss far surpassing the changing of land titles of pieces of property from one group to another. With the founding of the first settlements and ranches of northern Mexico and South Texas had come an establishment of a patrimonial system binding the people participating in that system into a community, complete with the norms, traditions, and values inherent in that community.

As more American settlers came to the area, so did new attitudes toward the development of the territory, along with the inevitable clashes and divisions attending that development. The splitting up of the ranches followed, sometimes in legal sales but often under questionable circumstances which caused the Texas Mexicans to lose their properties—losses which included the loss of heritage and community which was part of that ownership.

Many of the original families who had come to the area of South Texas had done so with Spanish/Mexican land grants. There was a concept of a ruling class, as exemplified in the family stories I had heard and the ones Jovita González documented. But if there was an attitude of snobbery, there was also a sense of political leadership and social responsibility that came with being *patrones* or landowners. The stories about my grandfather and those family members who had come before him were prime examples of this.

Under Spanish and Mexican legal customs, landowners were not individuals but families and lineages. By preserving the land in common, Mexican families hoped to do more than contain the perimeters of ranch boundaries. Families like the Barreras, Guerras, and Hinojosas regarded land ownership much like they did intermarriage. Their goal was to keep things within the families. The impulse to contain property and familial connections went beyond elitism into a realm that was deeper and more complex. If maintaining a ranching business operation was important, so was holding on to the semblance of unity and the cultural system of values that went along with that unity.

This patrimonial ethos and the personal and community mythological systems it created, with its basis in the preservation of a traditional lifestyle, eventually contributed to the erosion of properties. In the case of my grandfather and his brother, fighting for a political ideal had superseded logical economic wisdom. Going back to Mexico because they were needed in the revolutionary struggle took precedence over remaining in Texas, where their lifestyle and properties were already established.

Retaining a strong sense of place even when legal ties to a specific plot of land ceased to exist was one of the underlying messages in those family stories about *las tierras* (the lands). As *mestizos* with a claim to both Spanish and Indian heritage, one part of us identifies with people who came here from somewhere else. In this respect, we are like other Americans, although the Spanish/Mexican legal system we inherited does not support complete identification with mainstream values. The other side of us, however, relates strongly to the people who were already here, and so we have a solidity with place that sometimes takes precedence.

Although not an exact duplicate, this attitude about the land has vestiges of the spiritual-familial concept of the land which is part of Native American culture. In speaking about the cultural conflicts besetting the Pueblo Indians of New Mexico, Jemez Pueblo Indian Joe Sando pointed out in an interview for a film we produced as part of our work at the Southwest Center for Educational Television that one of the truths about the Pueblos is that "they understand themselves to be a part of nature, and, for that reason, they, like nature, change but ultimately remain the same." Living harmoniously with the land, which gives maternal sustenance, is part of this relationship.

I had heard endless family conversations about the litigation attendant on the loss of properties that was carried on in Texas courts across a number of generations. The loss of lands for South Texas Mexicans represented more than the changing of names on title deeds. It had to do with the loss of heritage and the loss of self. It had to do with the confrontation of historic forces that were taking them from being among the many to being among the few. It had to do with going from a majority to a minority.

On these levels, Carrascolendas was symbolic of a loss, of the cultural conflicts that had brought about that loss, and of a yearning for the retention of something that was no longer there.

If Carrascolendas represented a sense of loss and a love of place, it also represented the confusion inherent in that duality. In selecting Carrascolendas as the fictional television village, I was returning to those elements which were fundamental to my own makeup, the love of what my mother called "*las campanas de mi pueblo*" (the [church] bells of my hometown). She always coupled that reference with the saying, "*no puedes negar la cruz de tu parroquia*" (you cannot deny your parish cross [where you come from]). She was trying to tell us that what was important about who we were was not necessarily written down on a piece of paper. It went beyond that, into the world of the spirit. It transcended the physical and encompassed the mythical.

I remember as a young woman reading Thomas Mann's *Tonio Kroger* and seeing echoes of my mother's earlier admonitions in Mann's fictional creation. Mann drew a portrait of a young man who left the bourgeois trappings of his hometown for an artistic life in Munich, only to discover the love he had for his place of origin.

I was sympathetic to Tonio's feelings of isolation, which in some measure were akin to the minority experience. Tonio felt the difference between himself and the people surrounding him. He struggled to communicate with them. In the presence of that distance, Tonio lost and then found himself in his life as a creative artist.

With the artistic skill that Mann possessed, he composed a portrait of a man who lived only for his work. Stripped of that context, the man was like an actor without makeup whose only reality comes from performing. At the core of Tonio's character was a duality, inherited from a father with a northern, puritanical temperament and a mother who was sensuous, impulsive. The duality brought the precariousness of infinite possibilities as well as infinite dangers, leaving Tonio stranded between two worlds and at home in neither.

Although contextually different, Tonio's predicament spoke to my own situation. My own dual heritage came from being a border kid and growing up in what essentially were two worlds. In Tonio's words were vestiges of the pieces of the narrative I had heard in my own childhood. "We are a people between two worlds," my mother always said. "We are a people without a flag. We are wanted neither by the Mexicans nor by the Americans."

Like Tonio, I wanted to reawaken Hispanic children to the possibilities encompassed in their dual heritage. I envisioned doing so through an artistic television creation which required their active participation. I had seen children's responses to television and knew the kinds of connections which the medium could bring to viewers. Those connections could help to reestablish a sense of community with an identifiable language and a commonality of ideas. A television series was a way of providing a semblance of mythological instruction, a way of bringing back the group to its central, unifying core.

Seen from this perspective, the television program was meant to highlight the values in Mexican or Hispanic culture. It was intended to create a new mythological paradigm, one that spoke directly to Mexican American children in a way that had not occurred before on television.

The creation became *Carrascolendas*.

The decade that launched *Carrascolendas* saw an unprecedented transferring from what was taught in the home to what children were having to learn in school, from movies, or from television. Minority mothers, like women in other segments of the population, were facing increasing economic pressures. They were having to leave their families and work outside the home. The interpersonal connectedness I had received from those fairy-tale sessions with my mother was diminishing for the majority of Hispanic children who were going to be viewing *Carrascolendas*.

Television, with its increasing viewership, was providing that connectedness, however. It was the purveyor of cultural mythologies which were not being transmitted through interpersonal relationships. Although lacking in the one-on-one interconnectedness occurring in the kind of familial settings I had known, television nonetheless was serving as the purveyor of powerful mythological symbols. It was creating the simulacrum of the cultural situation, in much the same way that the stories around the campfire in Jovita González' time had done. But the distance in the electronic transmission had now changed the complex of the communication, placing limits and greater demands on the imagination of the child as well as on the television storyteller or narrator.

If television had become the narrator of fairy tales, though, it was doing a poor job where Mexican American and other Hispanic children were concerned. In the 1960s and 1970s, the media models Mexican American and other Hispanic children saw either had no specific relationship with their cultural situation or diminished whatever positive impressions they may have had of their cultural origins.

The movie representations of earlier decades filled the airwaves in reruns, becoming the norm for Saturday morning and after-school viewing. The stereotypes of the "Tony the Greaser" films, as well as the overblown antics of characters like Pancho López, Cisco Kid, and José Jimenez, were not exactly worthy of emulation. Spanish-style *caballeros* like Zorro did not improve the situation. Nor did the Speedy González series, produced in the 1950s but still seen in 1975, featuring Speedy and Slowpoke Rodríguez, the two mice who spoke English with typical Spanish accents and whose big hats and white cotton clothes placed them squarely in the Hollywood Mexican peasant tradition.

The women didn't do any better, when they were seen at all. Portrayals still centered around the perennial hot-blooded *señoritas* or the pious women with the downcast eyes. If Carmen Miranda was one of the highest paid performers during the 1940s, she still was the woman with the hat of fruits on top of her head. *West Side Story* in 1961 provided little improvement with its portrayals of gang rivalry, irrespective of its Romeo-and-Juliet theme.

The most popular Latino television personality in the 1950s and 1960s, and in reruns ever after, was Desi Arnaz, Lucille Ball's husband in *I Love Lucy*. Desi was Cuban-born Ricky Ricardo, the king of the *babalú* with his bongo drums, ruffled shirt, and torrents of Spanish whenever Lucy's escapades aggravated him. He was the prototypical Latino turned to stereotype, and his image was so pervasive that Cuban writer Oscar Hijuelos makes Ricky and the *Lucy* show the mythological television metaphor for his 1989 Pulitzer Prize-winning novel, *The Mambo Kings Play Songs of Love*. Ricky actually becomes a character in the novel-turned-movie and is the focus for the immigrant ethos that Cubans aspire to when they come to America.

In the literary myth which Hijuelos spins, the heroes are two musicians named Nestor and Cesar Castillo, their hair slicked down and parted in the middle, and sporting thin mustaches and butterfly-looking lace bow ties. Their moment of splendor comes when they live the American dream, Cuban style, and do a bit appearance on the Lucy show. The stereotypical Cuban Americanism of the Lucy program comes to be the definition of Cuban Americanism in general, almost as if one feeds upon the other, to the exclusion of whatever other reality may exist

The importance in the Hijuelos portrayal is not only that Cubans are presented as stereotypes but that Cubans can only see themselves in the context of being stereotypes. Even more critical, they aspire to be stereotypes. They want to be Cubans who play the castanets, shake the maracas, and dance the flamenco.

The use of stereotype can be a useful theatrical device, and the entire Lucy series, like other television situation comedies, does not limit its satirical portrayals to one group. One Lucy episode, Sue Carter has pointed out, shows how Lucy and Ricky met in Cuba. Lucy is dancing and her Cuban partner says something to the effect that "foreigners have strange steps." Lucy replies: "I'm not a foreigner. I'm American." While Lucy's reply stereotypes the American tourist, and indeed the Lucy character is a stereotype, television and other theatrical portrayals of Americans are generally varied. Audiences have the benefit of being exposed to this variety. The opposite is true for dramatizations of Hispanics, whose inclusion in television, even today, is extremely limited, so the use of stereotype where Hispanics are concerned takes on a magnitude that is far more egregious in its consequences.

In 1970, the year *Carrascolendas* went on the air, the Frito-Lay Corporation canceled its advertising campaign featuring the Frito Bandito. He was removed from television commercials after protests from Latino groups, particularly Chicano activists who felt the representation was demeaning to Mexicans. The cartoon bandit, sporting the traditional mustache, six-gun holster, and big *sombrero*, was the protagonist in scenes where he stole corn chips.

Even public television of the period was not exempt from injudicious portrayals, such as the early segment that showed Luis and María eating hot peppers on *Sesame Street*, a depiction that carried with it a far more serious implication, since the intent in a prosocial program like *Sesame Street* was not to sell tortilla chips but to model behavior which presumably a young child could understand and imitate.

If the intention was for *Carrascolendas* to present a new television mythology, then its central design had to create its own unique cultural flavor. In a way, the creation of the new *Carrascolendas* environment reprocessed the old Carrascolendas and in so doing came up with its own cultural forms and corresponding mythology, allowing the children who watched it the possibility of living mythically.

The antecedents for the program design came from Spanish/Mexican and Mexican American cultural elements which translated to television to form this new cultural reality. As an archetypal cultural system, it had its own meanings, values, rituals, and activities which contributed to the creation of its own mythology. On conscious and subconscious levels, its field of operation included the full complexity of language as well as the use of place and story.

If television was to become the transmitter of cultural norms and archetypes, then programming, especially programming for children, had to address specific cultural situations in a significantly symbolic way. I concluded that there was no more authentic models to go to for the creation of a television program than those that had come to occupy center stage in the Carrascolendas of my imagination. These models, in turn, had developed from the amalgam of stories and movies I had heard and seen.

Many of the characters I had seen at El Teatro Juárez echoed mythological characters from Spanish literature. The progenitors for the trickster escapades I had seen in those Mexican movies were the characters in the picaresque novels (the novels of roguery) developed in sixteenth-century Spain. The protagonist for this literary form is the *pícaro*, the young rascal who uses his wits to survive. Traditionally a poor outcast, the *pícaro* lives by ingenious tricks, which he plays on a series of masters who employ him. The picaresque tradition centers on this lowly, solitary individual who finds himself pitted against a hostile world. In the course of his misadventures, the *pícaro* comes to know a great deal about the nature of humanity, its strengths and weaknesses.

The picaresque stories are told with low-brow satirical humor. The genre, and its variations, begins with the anonymous *Lazarillo de Tormes* and reaches exemplary achievement in Miguel de Cervantes' *Rinconete y Cortadillo*. Cervantes' artfulness extends even to his characters' names. Names such as Rinconete (Corner or Nook), Cortadillo (Cutter), Ganchuelo (Little Hook), Centopiés (Centipede), and Narigueta (Snub-Nosed) immediately place their characters in antiheroic postures and communicate an entire world of information to the reader.

I read these novels while I was developing *Carrascolendas* and saw their ancestral connection to the Mexican films I had watched earlier. As dramatic and artistic vehicles, picaresque stories seemed especially appropriate for translation to a television model for young Mexican American children. They were larger than life and were filled with a spirit of fantasy that appealed to the imagination. They valued the ordinary and made heroes of those who were unheroic. The antiheroic becomes the heroic. The stories brought laughter to otherwise somber situations and, in so doing, resolved problems through humor rather than through didactic sermonizing.

Most critically, picaresque stories share a key characteristic with fairy tales; both show that the person at the bottom (the antihero, the servant) can struggle against life's problems and hardships, emerging victorious in the end.

The Chaplinesque tricksters of the Mexican screen that were so familiar to me were comics whose names were as symbolic as the roguish adventures in which they appeared—Cantínflas (a combination sound using the word "inflate"), Tin Tan (Ding Dong), Resortes (Springs), Mantequilla (Butter). Those names, appealing at several different levels, immediately communicated a sense of humor, a common person's perspective, and an inventiveness necessary to overcome any number of vicissitudes.

The *pícaros* for *Carrascolendas* did not become the main characters in the program. Rather, they set the tone for the entire series. In almost direct imitation of Cervantes and the Mexican movies I had seen, I named the tricksters Caracoles (Snails or Curls) and Campamocha (Praying Mantis). The *Carrascolendas* characters were not intended to mirror the thieves and *pícaros* of their earlier Spanish models, although a figure like Benito Vendetodo (Benito Sells All), one of our more malevolent figures, was reminiscent of Cervantes' Monipodio (Underworld Gang), the leader of the gathering of bullies that populates *Rinconete*.

Cervantes' Señor Monipodio was a middle-aged man with a crudeness of face and figure matching his generally shady behavior. His tall stature and dark skin, overpowering eyebrows, heavy black beard, and deeply hollowed eyes helped to define his character as the antithesis of Cervantes' antiheroes, who, unlike Monipodio, struggled against great societal odds for their survival.

Monipodio's *Carrascolendas* counterpart, Benito Vendetodo, did not follow Cervantes' exact portrayal, especially with respect to skin color. If Cervantes' Monipodio appeared to follow the dark/light dichotomy common to a prominent aspect of Western iconography which equates physiognomy with malevolence/virtue, *Carrascolendas'* Benito Vendetodo did not follow this stereotype. Although Benito's hair was dark, his skin tone was among the fairest of the *Carrasclendas* actors. But regardless of his coloration, Benito was the program's unscrupulous merchant who tried to unload such technological flops as an automatic broom and a fantastic table-setting robot on Caracoles, who owned the restaurant "El Nopal." Caracoles, stung at being duped, decided to trick Benito into buying a money tree, a small bush which bore gold coins instead of flowers. Naturally, the tree was a fake. The Benito-Caracoles morality tale, given musical form by Raoul González, closed with an admonition about tricksters and the value of handling money:

You've got to be careful with money;
handle it well from the start.
A fool may be holding his money,
but soon they'll be far apart!

The trickster was not the only archetypal metaphor for *Carrascolendas*. The mythology of *Carrascolendas* was multicultural, and, as such, had to accommodate images that defined the Mexican American or Hispanic child against the variety of ethnic groups in the larger society. Although we made a practice in *Carrascolendas* of including characters from different cultures, the most dominant position was occupied by the Anglo.

The *gringo* is an essential component of the definition which Mexican Americans have about themselves, for it is the *gringo* that dominates the Mexican American's exterior world, and, by implication, his or her interior world as well. It is the *gringo* who creates the standard by which Mexican Americans are measured and by which they measure themselves. In this sense, the *gringo* becomes part of the essence of Mexican Americanness. This reality is so pervasive that much of the scholarship dealing with the Mexican American does so from the standpoint of the American, at times to the virtual exclusion of whatever Mexican models may have gone into that definition.

Coming to terms with the Anglo, or what is perceived as the mainstream image, is basic to the minority experience. Without the Anglo, the concept of the Mexican American as we know it today would not be. What we would have, instead, would be groups of people with no identification against any particular central model.

The identity of the Mexican American is an Anglo–Mexican composite in which the skew that goes toward one side or the other of that duality is determined by the degree of assimilation that each individual person happens to have experienced.

The use of the word "Anglo" itself implies a unity of ethnicity that has no basis in reality since "Anglo" can be applied metaphorically to anyone who is Caucasian, but non-Hispanic. "Anglo" is the English word that is used for *gringo* in much of the Southwest. Although a misnomer, "Anglo" reflects the concept of the other that is so critical for the Mexican American.

Breaking down the word "Anglo" into separate components allows one to gain greater respect for the cultural richness of the society and the individual, making stereotyping virtually meaningless and foolish. In spite of this, many Mexican Americans and "Anglos" still persist in seeing themselves in the context of this dichotomy, and it is this dichotomy that is crucial for whatever concept each group has about the other.

Paradoxically, the relationship which Mexican Americans have with Anglos is one which Mexican Americans have with themselves. It also corresponds to the relationship which they have outside of themselves. This duality between oneself and the other is a two-way process. If the Mexican American has the Anglo as a point of definition, the Anglo in turn also is defined by the Mexican American, or, in the larger society, by minority groups in general. Each group struggles to understand the other. In the multicultural setting of the society which surrounds us, comprehending this other becomes vital to whatever truths we know about ourselves, for the delineation of our own identities can only exist in terms of those others.

For young children, the definition of this other is even more crucial than it is for adults, for the definition which children have of themselves will come out of this other and will give children the initial impetus for coming to terms with whatever they will be in the future. This identification of self can determine productivity, impetus for learning, and general attitudes toward limitations and potentialities. In *Carrascolendas*, this understanding was particularly significant, for many of the difficulties facing young Mexican American children originated from the concept of this other.

The *Carrascolendas* mythology had to accommodate this confrontation and resolve it in a language that children could readily accept. Thus, a dominant motif in *Carrascolendas* was that everyone is someone special, especially those who may seem different from ourselves. This motif served as a lesson both for Anglo children, who would view Mexican Americans as different from themselves, and for Mexican Americans, who might hold up Anglos as the standard-defining model for themselves.

In one scene, a pink, polka-dotted horse comes to the village, and after some initial reticence because of the difference in his physical appearance, he comes to see that to be different is simply that; it is no cause for undue consternation. The resolution of the horse's problem (his perception of his difference) in this particular program is made at a level that children can understand.

The other cast members reassure the horse that in spite of his pink polka-dots, he is no different from anyone else. Each person is different in his or her own way, they tell him. Agapito the lion has a paunch; Uncle Andy the shoemaker has gray hair. His confidence restored, the polka-dotted horse realizes that he will be accepted by the others, just as he himself accepts them and as he now accepts himself.

The horse completes his transformation by breaking into a song-and-dance routine. Raoul González reiterates the message with a song:

Have you ever met
a pink, polka-dotted horse?
Well, my friends,
I'm something to see!
Oh, you won't forget
a pink, polka-dotted horse,
and that's what I'm so proud to be!

Another instance of treating the other in *Carrascolendas* involved a humorous cartoon portrayal of the *gringo*. Using the traditional bilingual children's song "El Ratón Vaquero" by the Mexican composer Cri Cri and the flexibility of animation, the sequence portrays a cowboy mouse with blond hair and the requisite big feet that all Mexicans know *gringos* have. The song does a satirical take on the American cowboy icon, whose seldom-recognized progenitor is the Mexican *vaquero*. In the *Carrascolendas* version of the cowboy myth, the Western-movie scene comes complete with a *gringo* who obliterates his enemies.

In a reversal of the John Wayne good guy who kills all the Indians and Mexican *bandidos*, the cowboy in the song is a not-very-manly mouse, and the Mexican is a sheriff-cat who traps the mouse in a cage. The scene has a voice-over bilingual musical track that ends with the cat saying he is not going to free the mouse even though the mouse is a *gringo* and speaks English. Since our goals in *Carrascolendas* were to improve intercultural relationships rather than create additional tensions, we felt no justice would be served by leaving the poor mouse imprisoned. In our more benevolent epilogue, the *gringo* cowboy escapes, albeit without having fully vanquished his foe, since the cat is alive and well at the end, with only a swollen nose as evidence of what would surely have been labeled as a Mexican standoff by the more insightful cartoon critic.

The animated sequence we developed began with an establishing shot that showed a small, stylized Western town. The camera, positioned from what could have been a hill-top, does a paced zoom down the dirt-filled street. A slow dissolve parts the swinging saloon doors and continues the descent into a section of an interior wall with a small mouse hole having its own set of swinging doors.

A large cat, wearing a sheriff's badge and holding a cage, is poised in a hovering stance outside the hole. A blond mouse, in full gunfighter's costume complete with large, prominent boots, comes out of the hole. In one quick movement, the triumphant cat slams the cage down over the mouse. For a moment, the mouse stands frozen in the cage, looking up at the gloating cat. Seeing some cheese that has been placed in the cage to attract him, he eats the cheese and, Popeye fashion, immediately sprouts huge muscles.

The mouse looks at the cat and nonchalantly bends the bars of the cage. He proceeds to climb out of the cage and, drawing his two guns, confronts the startled cat. The cat grabs the mouse and puts him back in the cage. The mouse comes out again and, this time, shoots the cat. Two corks come out of the guns and hit the cat on the nose. The cat runs off, clutching his swollen nose. The mouse walks out of the saloon and into the street. The last view is a low-angle shot as the mouse, gunbelt swinging, walks off into the sunset.

Although the multicultural setting of *Carrascolendas* was not the place for specific refutations of stereotypical myths held about ethnic groups and the vast number of messages concentrated on positive rather than negative actions, it was nonetheless important to have a few instances of the *gringo*, even momentarily, being on the defensive.

The cowboy mouse sequence was done so children could see that talking about *gringos*, or any other culture, could be done in a way accepting of differences, at the same time that those differences could be treated with humor.

In addition, the sequence spoke, albeit lightly, about the nature of stereotypes or caricature. Stereotypes will invariably arise between groups, and it is in the nature of dramatic presentations in video or film to make use of stereotypes; but this is not to say stereotypic portrayals should guide human relationships or the opinions one group holds about another.

Stereotypes, especially in comedy, can be a rich theatrical device. We should take them for what they are, artistic devices which we can use like we would use any other creative production device. Stereotypes call attention to human foibles and exaggerate them for our enjoyment and not so we can use them to the detriment of one group or the other.

The relationship with the other does not stop with the *gringo*. Critical to the definition of Mexican Americans is their relationship to Mexicans that are born and still live in Mexico, those *mexicanos del otro lado* (Mexicans from the other side) who were so familiar to me as I was growing up. At a personal level, this was an aspect of the more intimate relationship which I had with Tío Abrahán and his family and those feelings of not quite measuring up because of inadequacies in the Spanish I spoke. Extended to a global dimension, this relationship included the connection that Mexican Americans have with others in the larger Hispanic community, a consideration which became critical in *Carrascolendas* once the program became a national series encompassing Hispanics from different groups.

In *Carrascolendas*, we wanted the children viewers, whether they were Mexican American, Puerto Ricans, Cubans, or members of some other ethnic or racial community, to know that their larger identity included those other groups and that these relationships could be positive rather than negative. We dealt with these situations by having characters in the series that came from different countries. Their conversations explored the subject of distinct national origins, as well as what this meant in terms of vocabulary, foods, or customs. We had Tío Cheo, a Cuban toy store owner acted by the comic actor Roblán, whose rivalry with Anglo Uncle Andy, the shoe repair man played by Joe Bill Hogan, included more musical repartee than actions. In addition, there was a Puerto Rican vendor, a Chilean radio announcer, and a couple of Puerto Rican teachers. Their respective national identities became the subject of the dialogues, including discussions of words that were common to Mexicans but not to Puerto Ricans, such as *raspa* and *piragua* for snowcones, as well as words that had different meanings for different groups, such as *tostones*, which for Puerto Ricans and Cubans refers to a common dish of fried plantain discs, but which for Mexican Americans refers to fifty-cent coins.

Doing a mythological television recreation, even one that was culturally specific like *Carrascolendas*, was not necessarily a question of consciously choosing production elements that fit against preconceived archetypal patterns. Certainly, there were such instances—like the selection of the name for the program or the development of the trickster characters, which came directly from influences I consciously thought of at the time I was creating the series. At other times, though, things just happened, and it was instinct rather than rational choices that took me in certain directions.

A production of the magnitude of *Carrascolendas* was frequently an overwhelming task, and in the hurried pace of trying to meet deadlines and broadcasting schedules, there was little time for studious reflection about what we were doing. Sometimes we did things because it "felt" right to do so. Other times, we had the best intentions but what was finally translated on screen just did not work, so we scratched it and started anew.

If I had an overriding concern, however, it was that we do justice to what was uniquely Mexican American or Hispanic, and I wanted to do this by metaphorically bringing Mexican American or Hispanic children back to a cultural home base, whatever that may be. I wanted to solidify the child's cultural moorings in a way that was not occurring through movies or television and, in so doing, restore something of the mythological wholeness the original Carrascolendas had come to mean for me.

CHAPTER SEVEN

▪ Carrascolendas

I KNEW THE central character in *Carrascolendas* had to be a child, but how to do this in a television production was difficult. Bringing a child into a studio situation was not easy, especially in a public broadcasting situation, where resources were more limited. Placing the burden on a child of carrying an entire program was even harder. Considering the multicultural goal of the series, choosing the ethnic identity of a central character also became problematic. And, if the child was designated as Mexican American, then the choice with respect to gender would have to be made. If the program was for children, I reasoned, it should also be about them, but designating a group of children as the central leads, even a small grouping, would diffuse the focus that a main character could have.

I wanted a universal symbol, something that would be attractive to all children and not necessarily be so culturally specific that we could not retain the flexibility needed for appealing plotlines, whether the message was intended for Mexican American or for non-Hispanic children. The main character had to serve as a pivotal point in the stories, enhancing the image of the Mexican American child but not alienating any viewer from what were to be entertaining and instructive concepts for all children, regardless of their ethnic background.

The solution was Agapito, an archetypal figure representing the spirit of a child and embodying childlike characteristics without having to be bound by any of the limitations that an actual child had. Agapito was a lion who conversed and got into trouble in two languages and who went from one ethnic group to another, without necessarily being ill at ease in any. He could profess ignorance to any custom or idea and be "told" the correct answer and no one needed to take offense. Whether as bungler or avid learner, he could tread the fine line that frequently makes relationships between ethnic and racial groups such a delicate matter.

Agapito was intended to transcend the specific nature of his character. He had to be more than a lion. But his very creation had evolved from the intimate and specific setting that was my own childhood, so his character had to be a combination of these two elements, plus enough other characteristics so his appeal to children would go beyond ethnic boundaries.

In order to be faithful to the overall concept and goal of *Carrascolendas*, it was important to root the main character in the same cultural base that had initiated the central idea of the series. That, again, had to be those elements in Mexican American culture that represented the wholeness and values that were important to transmit to Mexican American children, even at a subliminal level. Certainly, lions had been useful foils as characters in children's stories across different cultures, and the intention was that Agapito could draw from these traditions without necessarily being overwhelmed by them. But the vision for Agapito had to have more than what those images could provide.

Agapito had to have the fancifulness of the image of the not-so-kingly Lewis Carroll lion, whose propensity for being drummed out of town did little to enhance his royal demeanor. But he also had to have the American indigenous quality of Dorothy's Cowardly Lion, whose quest for courage finally makes him see that he already has the confidence in himself for the roaring confrontation with the Wizard of Oz.

Apart from these influences, Agapito had to be pure, down home, Texas Mexican.

As I finally developed his persona, Agapito had the bombastic bluster of his Anglo Saxon and American forebears, but with the ingenuity of the Mexican folk hero Juan Oso, who was half man and half bear and who could turn himself into a lion so that he could protect his goats from a wild boar.

On a more immediate level, Agapito was Texas Mexican, faithful to my own South Texas background. His name came from the stories I heard of my mother's Tío Agapito, whose trips in the 1910s and 1920s were a legendary part of family lore. I never met my famous great-uncle but had always been intrigued by the sound of a name which struck me as having a combination of rustic and fanciful qualities.

Tío Agapito lived at a ranch called El Arroyo, ten miles from Rio Grande City. Every Saturday, Tío Agapito would come to town in his horse-drawn wagon to load up on provisions for the week. A portly man whose reputation preceded him wherever he went, he was known for his eccentricities. His horse doubled as his surrogate persona and, to emphasize his point, he had named the animal, Agapo, giving the horse added pomp by retaining the root of his own name and eliminating the diminutive, *ito*.

Whenever Agapo could not make the trip, Tío Agapito would harness his two mules to the wagon, and, although at a slower pace, the trek was still made. Tío Agapito had named the mules Las Hermanas Craig, Rosa y Mereh (The Craig Sisters, Rose and Mary), after his first cousins, my mother's mother and her sister. The Craig sisters had found no humor in the matter, but Tío Agapito had ignored their pleas to change the names. He painted his wagon a bold spring mesquite green and accented the spokes and the hubs of the wheels by painting them lemon yellow, a combination appealing to his love for overstatement.

His colorful arrival into Rio Grande City was anticipated by everyone, but especially my mother and the other children her age looked forward to these weekly visits, for not only did Tío Agapito have tales to tell about the happenings at the ranch, but his trips invariably meant goodies would come from the relations at El Arroyo for the city relatives to enjoy.

Tío Agapito always had a large pillow case, held together with a row of buttons across the middle of the cloth in the style of a sham or duvet, which was filled with packages of the sugared cinnamon *pinole* (pinole) and the *panecitos de apretón* (squeeze cakes), which everyone knew as *bastimento*, hard cornmeal snack cakes that were made by taking your thumb and pressing on the small balls of dough, the equivalent of giving the dough a squeeze or a hug. Opening the pillow and distributing the treats were invariably part of the theatricality of Tío Agapito's arrival into Rio Grande each weekend.

Animal archetypes with human characteristics have been recurrent symbols throughout the history of humankind. As a literary motif, the character of the helpful animal is found in fairy tales, cartoons, and animated movies. Children are especially responsive to theriomorphic symbols and can share a psychic identity with animals or animal symbols which sometimes baffles adults. This is why animals are effective in children's programs, as evidenced by the overwhelming popularity of the Disney cartoon characters Big Bird, Barney, and others.

Children can easily pretend to be an animal, and they are convinced they are that animal. In contrast, adults maintain a distance generated by the years they have spent reaching maturity. The gulf those years created at times threatened to overwhelm the goals I envisioned for the central character in *Carrascolendas*.

My own affinity for animal characters was instinctive, and it was this feeling for what young children liked that caused me to choose a lion as the main character for *Carrascolendas*. The educational consultants when we first began production of the series were not so convinced. They felt the lion was silly and dumb. One memorable comment was, "Can't we have another kind of character? That one looks like it has a mop over its head."

The remark referred to the lion's mane and distinctly un-Hollywood-style costume. Designed and executed by Bunny Thompson, the wife of KLRN producer Bill Thompson, the costume fit our budget and time constraints. After the initial funding was in place, we had to develop the characters, write the scripts, find the actors, produce the shows, and be ready to broadcast the series within a period of some four months. A congenial and bubbly Italian American who had grown up in New York, Bunny Thompson was willing to drop all tasks and family demands in order to design and sew the first costumes we did for *Carrascolendas*. After coming up with a suitable composite pattern for what we all thought a lion should look like, Bunny had scoured Austin fabric stores for the necessary felt and yards of yarn necessary to make the costume. I was satisfied with the suitability of the costume, but the educational skeptics were not so convinced.

Analogous remarks were made about the name, Agapito. "Where did you get a name like that?" one administrator wanted to know. "I've never heard that name before," said another.

In the crush of trying to get those first programs on the air, I felt foolish about going into explanations about my mother's Tío Agapito, but by the time the criticisms were made, it was too late to make any substantial changes in the character. When it became obvious that the lion was to remain, the group of consultants came to the studio, previewed the segments we had produced, and remained silent after the tape stopped rolling. I thought the silence was worse than the comments, and for those few months before our first broadcast date, I lived in panic that they were correct in their evaluations.

Agapito proved the consultants wrong. Yarn and all, he had immediate audience appeal. Furthermore, he was meant for the camera. In time, as budgets increased, his homemade Austin costume was transformed into a Hollywood designed, overblown Disney-style "skin," with a rotund belly, stuffed giant paws for feet, a voluminous feathery mane colored in light and dark shades of gold, and a long tail tipped with a fluff of gold feathers. In creativity and splendor, we thought his costume rivaled the best that was ever offered in children's television.

But even with this transformation, Agapito was not to see the end of his critics or the resulting political intrigue that his costume would elicit. As the budgets for *Carrascolendas* surpassed the million dollar mark, so did the bureaucratic hassles we had to undergo to obtain expenditure approvals.

In 1975, review of the budget for *Carrascolendas* was taken over by a new political appointee who had just joined the Public Affairs Office of the U.S. Department of Health, Education, and Welfare, which had jurisdiction over the awarding of the funds for the productions. These funds were monitored by the submission of line-item budgets which specified exactly how the money was to be spent. Generally, the budgets were reviewed by others within the Department of Education, who by the fifth year of production were more or less versed in the funds required by such an undertaking. But such was not the case with the new appointee.

We had submitted the customary budget, calling for the purchase of two lion costumes. A red flag was placed on the item and we had to stop whatever purchase orders were in the process of being transacted. Weeks passed, telephones calls and messages went back and forth to Washington and, again, back and forth to Los Angeles where the costume was being refurbished. Eventually, we were given the go ahead to proceed.

Years later, Dave Berkman, the project officer assigned to oversee the *Carrascolendas* contracts, would talk about his frustrations with what at times seemed like an incomprehensible system. He would support us when he could, but sometimes the governmental restrictions predominated regardless of the illogical nature of the conclusions. One such incident centered on the red flagging of funds spent for two lion suits when only one costume seemed to suffice. Of scant relevance was the fact that two suits were needed to give a sweaty Agapito respite from one while the other was being cleaned.

In one of our many conversations about our project, Dave told us that establishing what office was to have jurisdiction over television project budgets took the actions of a politically well-connected Democrat who was also an ACLU activist, staffers of two senators and representatives, and an orchestrated campaign on Capitol Hill.

Oblivious to these maneuverings, Agapito continued to create the fantasy that was part of the original intention for the character and certainly fulfilled all the aspirations I had created in my own imagination for the Tío Agapito I had never met. As eccentric as his progenitor, the Agapito of *Carrascolendas* captured the essence of caricature without creating a distance with his audience. Agapito's costume restricted his movements and gave him enough of a clumsy yet comfortable look to make him approachable, childlike, and lacking in adult maturity. He moved about the sequences with enthusiastic conviviality, relating to both young and old alike with equal proportions of candor and mischief, eliciting exasperation and affection.

Agapito's face was his own human one, perfect for articulating whatever language lessons were to be incorporated into the programs, but the full-blown persona of the character was a composite that went beyond those limits. A humanized lion personified everything that was important to have in a main character. He could be a child and be imbued with all the innocence a child could have, yet be the adult we needed for the logistical realities of the production.

Agapito became the most popular character in the series. He was awkward and appealing, trying to act mature where he really was not and happiest when he was in the company of the children who were regular visitors in *Carrascolendas*. He was often mystified by the complexities of life, but approached the problems that faced him with hopeful naiveté. He was cooperative, trusting, and enthusiastic. The children loved him.

The lion's ethnic look had not been an issue, at least not initially. In fact, his creation was intended to have no ethnicity at all. The best actor for the part turned out to be Harry Porter, a tall, Anglo Texan with large, friendly eyes, a substantial nose, a strong chin, and a rubbery face which had the capability of breaking out into an enthusiastic roar, a broad smile, or a look of chagrin if he was caught in some gaffe.

Harry had an affinity for Mexican American culture that caused him to learn perfectly unaccented Spanish. Harry lived his life from a Mexican and Mexican American perspective, a fact not lost on members of his own family. His sister Catherine Lusk once remarked that when Harry was born, someone forgot to tell him that he wasn't Mexican American. Harry soon became the favorite, not only of the production company but also of the children viewers. Harry was fair skinned, had green eyes, and looked like a typical Anglo, but his portrayal as Agapito was so convincing that he transcended his ethnic origins to the point that we had reports of intense arguments among adult viewers as to whether or not Agapito was an Anglo or a Hispanic. The conclusion in at least one debate we heard of was that Agapito was a Mexican American because his face had Mexican American features.

This, of course, pleased the Chicanophile Harry no end, as it did the rest of us. I was especially glad the execution of a *Carrascolendas* character had succeeded in transcending the boundaries of ethnicity and racial composition. Agapito had achieved what the majority of us were all hoping to have in our own lives and the lives of the children viewing the television programs.

Not quite on as grand a scale as Agapito, but equally fanciful, were some of the other characters in *Carrascolendas*. These characters became abstractions for the combination of human characteristics which we wanted to present in the story lines. One of the design motifs we used in *Carrascolendas* was related to size and was in some measure analogous to Lewis Carroll's Alice, who alternates between being ten inches small and nine feet tall. The absurdity with growing smaller or larger is central to the definition of Alice and enhances the attraction of the character.

The preoccupation with size is a recurrent theme in children's stories and may echo the ambivalence some children feel with a world that is either overwhelming or beyond their control. But it can also strike a humorous note. By inverting the logic on size and introducing an element of the absurd, an ordinary situation changes into one of fantasy with more appeal to children.

In *Carrascolendas*, the dolls Berta and Dyana, played by Natalia "Berta Cruz" Dowd and Dyana Elizondo, and the oversized props that were used as part of their central set created skewed spatial relationships. Utilizing a technique reminiscent of Lily Tomlin's character of the little girl who sits in the giant rocking chair, the dolls' play area in *Carrascolendas* was filled with giant blocks and larger-than-life toys. The props were designed to create the illusion that the dolls were indeed small and childlike, creating a point of identification with the children viewers but also contributing to the fantasy that the dolls had come to life. The same stylized approach was taken with Thomas (played by Terry Tannen), a life-size marionette who sings and dances as his strings are manipulated in tune to the music.

In other *Carrascolendas* sequences, excessive size was an abstraction necessary to the medium of television. Large props were used either to overemphasize a concept or to compensate for the smallness of the television monitor. The largeness of an object was especially important since the viewing for the program frequently occurred in crowded classrooms and the children sitting in the back of the room did not have the same viewing advantage as those in the front. One of these occasions was a program featuring a mystery letter addressed to "The Special Person in Carrascolendas." In this television mini-thriller, Pepper, the detective, erroneously kept delivering the letter to different characters, thinking she had now found *the* special person in Carrascolendas. The sequential action not only introduced the principal characters in the program but also came to the obvious conclusion that the characters, and by extension, the children viewers, were all special in some way.

But the dolls attracted attention not only because of their size. Initially, I had gravitated to doll characters because I knew children loved playing with these make-believe little humans and because of the visual possibilities two such characters could bring to the series. Unlike Barbie, Berta and Dyana were designed as typical, old-fashioned baby dolls. They had painted faces with prominent lashes and circles of red rouge on their cheeks. Their ruffled dresses and hair ribbons were coordinated with the colors of their knee-length socks and round-toed shoes. The dolls appeared in their own play area, which was filled with giant toys and blocks. They sang, danced, and told riddles.

Rhyming riddles are traditional to growing up in Spanish/Mexican culture, so we built in recurring sequences on riddles. Our goal was to reinforce traditional forms for Hispanic viewers as well as introduce non-Hispanic children to an aspect of the culture which they did not know. We also decided to capitalize on the traditional cultural forms by writing new riddles and using rhyming devices, adapted to fit specific curriculum requirements.

A riddle such as the following one introduced and reinforced traditional Spanish-speaking cultural forms:

Redondito, redondón,
Que no tiene tapa ni tapón.
¿Qué es? (El Anillo)

A little round, a lot round,
It has neither lid nor stopper.
What is it? (The Ring)

The riddle on "potato" was written to introduce a vocabulary word which was part of an entire curriculum sequence on food:

De color café y un poco gordita,
Sabrosa yo soy y muy rechonchita.
¿Qué es? (La Papa)

Brown colored and a bit chubby,
I am tasty and very chunky.
What is it? (The Potato)

Whenever possible, we tried to use culturally relevant techniques to enhance the cognitive content areas of the program. We wanted to provide a cultural base that was familiar to certain children in the viewing audience at the same time that we hoped to assist in building cultural bridges with those children who were seeing these cultural forms for the first time.

The characters of the dolls were created innocently enough, but Berta and Dyana, like Agapito, became the objects of political debate. As the years progressed and gender issues became prominent in the greater society, one of the younger Anglo women in our production team felt the dolls had an unduly stereotypical feminine look and that their portrayal betrayed sexist leanings in the series.

I was taken aback by the comment. I mistakenly thought that since I was a woman, had created all the central characters, and was the project director of the entire enterprise, gender bias could not exist in any of the portrayals. I tried to find reasons for my sentiments and searched in my own upbringing for an appropriate defense.

I had always thought of myself as growing up in a family of strong women and always took pride in saying I was the product of a mother who had brought up her daughters with the *redondillas* (Spanish metric form) of Sor Juana Inés de la Cruz, the sixteenth-century Mexican nun who had written the poem "*Contra las injusticias de los hombres al hablar de las mujeres*" (Against the injustices of men as they talk of women), the first known manifesto in the New World of the intellectual rights of women.

Recognized as a preeminent literary figure and perhaps the greatest poet of Mexico, Sor Juana's intellectual vision and creative talents left an enduring literary legacy within the Spanish-speaking world. Certainly I had been nurtured on her poetry and in later readings came to know of her library of four thousand books and her proficiency in several languages, as well as her knowledge of philosophy, astronomy, theology, painting, and music. In addition to her poems, Sor Juana wrote meditations, allegorical and religious plays, comedies, letters, and other texts. Her words resonated with me, as indeed they did throughout the Spanish-speaking world.

Hombres necios que acusáis
a la mujer sin razón,
sin ver que sois la ocasión
de lo mismo que culpáis.

Bothersome men, you who accuse
women without reason,
without seeing that you are the occasion
of the same thing that you are blaming.

I had heard my mother recite these lines over and over as I was growing up. The knowledge of Sor Juana and what she stood for contributed to my formation as a woman, irrespective of the constraints of any *macho* traditions within Hispanic culture. Both my parents had encouraged our professional and intellectual development. The echoes of Sor Juana's words not only reinforced that encouragement but caused me to go beyond the level of kindly parental admonitions. Sor Juana's legacy was as much a part of my childhood as the nuns of the Incarnate Word and the Sisters of Mercy had been. It was difficult for me to see how I could have created characters who would be considered sexist by women in the general population.

In examining the roles the dolls had in *Carrascolendas*, we found they played substantial roles, and, in another era or in Spanish/Mexican culture, would probably never have been taken for passive or stereotypical. But the realities of a period in which there was greater consciousness of women's issues meant I had to recognize that ruffles and bows could be misinterpreted, especially in the overall society.

And, indeed, I had to remind myself that television has a greater responsibility in the portrayals it presents. Sometimes a representation can have an effect simply because it is seen in isolation and not necessarily because it is inherently bad. I concluded that this was the case with the dolls' ruffles and bows.

Since my goal was to expand the aspirations of girl viewers and create new options for them in the roles they saw portrayed in the program, I decided to make some changes in the dolls. I resolved the dilemma by giving one of the dolls mechanical abilities and creating dramatic situations designed to illustrate this side of her character. Dressed in coveralls, the doll showed that girls can excel in traditionally male-dominated areas.

I had grown up with concepts of femininity that had nothing to do with mechanical ability, and in our family there were women who were quite capable in tasks traditionally considered the domain of men. A woman's abilities had no relationship to what she wore or whether or not she adorned herself with ribbons and lace.

In Rio Grande City, Canuta, Bessie, and Doña Jenara were capable women who functioned in the outer society as much as they did in their homes. Although my mother's contemporaries were largely housewives, there were other Valley women of the time who were entrepreneurs and business owners. My mother's best friend, Conchita Cantu, owned and operated a tortilla factory. Her sister, Esther Ruenes, had a chain of theaters. Sofía Vela managed a department store.

In contrast to the much-touted dominance of Spanish/Mexican *machismo*, the women I grew up with were as proficient and as strong in character as any of the men. I always found the submissive *señorita* movie and television portrayals unrealistic and was resentful that these roles were the usual ones given to Spanish/Mexican women; or, characterizations went to the other extreme and showed the *señorita* spitfire and sexual bombshell. But in a production like *Carrascolendas*, there was no time for explanations of the sort that were needed, so rather than risk further misinterpretations, we made the necessary adjustments.

Some of our efforts evidently provided the desired results. In 1975, the Corporation for Public Broadcasting issued the Report of the Task Force on Women in Public Broadcasting. An analysis of children's

PBS programs showed that *Sesame Street* had the smallest proportion of females (78 percent male versus 22 percent female) while *Carrascolendas* had the highest (49 percent male versus 51 percent female). But we were not absolved completely. The report said that the males in *Carrascolendas* were shown in occupational roles twice as often as females. As capability for additional productions increased, we increased the variety of female portrayals, although some of these characters either lacked the personality development that the dolls had or simply did not resonate with the audience in the same way.

We experimented with an Anglo female character who was a roofer, but she met with little success with viewers, although we couldn't see anything wrong with the portrayal. Another Anglo female was Pepper, an enterprising detective. Pepper, acted by Elizabeth "Lizanne" Brazell Nichols, appeared in a number of sequences and some of these were among the best we had in *Carrascolendas*. Because of time constraints, however, the character of Pepper did not have the same opportunity of establishing an identity with the viewers that the dolls did.

In responding to the legitimate concerns of showing more and varied roles for women characters, we may have shifted the focus away from more effective dramatic characters. But our discussions did have an effect on all of us, including me, as we became ever more conscious of the subliminal messages we were communicating to our young viewers.

Caracoles and Campamocha, the tricksters in *Carrascolendas* portrayed by Pete Leal and Mike Gómez, also came in for their share of criticism. Decidedly Mexican, the two benevolent picaresque comics had touches of Chaplin, Abbott and Costello, and the Marx brothers. Bilingual educators objected to the initial look which we created for them, and although I did not feel the comments were justified, their costumes were altered to avoid any possible misinterpretations.

Originally, the two had rather disheveled looks and behavior. They were modeled on the *pícaros* of the novels of roguery of sixteenth-century Spain, the antiheroes of the *carpas* that toured South Texas during the 1920s and 1930s, and the Mexican film comedies of the 1950s and 1960s which I had seen in my first job at El Teatro Juárez.

They resembled Mexican comics such as Cantínflas, Tin Tan y su Carnal Marcelo, and other similar characters. Their look was scruffy.

Although the immediate precursors of Caracoles and Campamocha were the Mexican comics, they owed a great deal to universal picaresque figures and American comedic models. By the time that comics like Cantínflas became popular, the prevalence of American films had seen the universalizing of comedy figures like Charlie Chaplin and the Marx brothers. This influence was obvious in early *carpa* comics like Lauro Guerra, whose costuming and makeup followed the Chaplin look. Others, like Don Catarino, the Dueto Cinema, El Niño Fidencio, and Don Lalo, wore highly stylized disheveled costumes and distorting makeup and wigs, enhancing their roles as *pícaros*. The *pícaros*' look derived from these basic stylized characteristics. Their costuming had the bold look of caricature and did not reflect any practical vision of the real world.

My intention was to follow the *pícaro* tradition with Caracoles and Campamocha, and certainly their costumes reflected this tradition. With scattered hair, unshaven faces, and tattered clothing, Caracoles and Campamocha appeared as the lowest of the low, but their aspirations and actions were in sharp contrast to that look. Although they got themselves into one scrape after another, they always emerged victorious and, by extension, taught the child viewer that outward trappings were not necessarily indicative of the inner efforts a person was willing to make. In the process, they were supposed to be funny and make children laugh, and in this they succeeded.

But at least some critics among educators thought otherwise. If Mexican men were to appear in *Carrascolendas*, the word came down, they were supposed to be upstanding, exemplary, and, above all, upwardly mobile looking. Mexican American children were surrounded by enough role models that were negative and scruffy looking, the comments continued. They needed to look at males who wore suits and ties and who preferably belonged to white-collar professions.

I sympathized with the comments, although I thought the characters had been misinterpreted altogether. Again, the sociological intentions interfered with the creative ones, and, again, I felt that launching into explanations of comedy, caricature, and even the very nature of stereotype itself in theatrical portrayals was more than one television series could accomplish. In the end, I felt that the greater goal of influencing Mexican American children was more important, and that educators, if mistakenly ignorant of comedic styles, were well meaning in their criticisms. Caracoles and Campamocha cleaned up their act and became more "educationally" acceptable, if less true to their own picaresque heritage. They became entrepreneurial and working business owners, but we stopped short of giving them white-collar professions. Caracoles owned a restaurant and Campamocha a fixit shop. We heard no more comments.

Benito Vendetodo (Benito Sells All) portrayed the malevolent trickster and his character also received some educator criticism. Benito's was an even more exaggerated style, and his look was intentionally meant to match his personality. Benito, whose antecedents came not only from the Spanish literary picaresque tradition but also from the familiar villains in vaudeville melodramas, had a long handlebar mustache and exaggerated fly-away hair which easily betrayed his antagonistic intentions, making it easy to use him as a foil in certain plots.

Unlike Caracoles and Campamocha, whose antics usually turned positive, Benito was as evil as we ever dared to get in *Carrascolendas*. Our mistake was that we chose a Cuban American actor to portray the role, and at least some Cuban American educators felt that Benito's character implied that all Cuban American men were this way. The fact that he was so unrealistic did not matter, nor did the fact that we had other Cuban characters in the series who were positive (but not necessarily funny). What was important was that one segment of the viewing public was vocal enough to make its objections felt. The vocal outcry against Benito, perhaps because the Cuban population was much smaller than the Mexican American, was not at the level of the comments we received about Caracoles and Campamocha, and our response to these objections was to tone down Benito's malevolent side and make him more mischievous than outright bad.

A host of other secondary characters also populated *Carrascolendas*. Their personalities were designed to heighten the overall sense of caricature and fantasy, without necessarily connecting them to a specific culture. In fact, our intention was the opposite. We wanted to draw from a variety of cultural forms and, in some instances, the dramatic potential of a theatrical technique was the sole overriding factor which determined whether or not we would include it in a script. A number of these roles were given to members of different ethnic and racial groups to enhance the cultural diversity of the program. The members of the cast, including myself, assumed different roles in a variety of skits, giving each person a multiplicity of "faces" without having to bring in additional performers.

Running gags or sequences would utilize sets over and over again in order to do scenes which were then "stripped" in a number of different shows. In this way, we could use a given piece of scenery or concentrate the usage of certain costumes, actors, and musical requirements, making productions far more cost-effective than they otherwise would have been. These segments were edited as inserts to separate programs, giving any one show a great deal more variety.

One particularly successful "strip" was "The Days of the Week." Done as an ongoing comedy routine, the segment had the look of 1940s radio and featured Uncle Andy, a regular character, doubling as a zany announcer who had a question-and-answer call-in program. A trio of singers, whose performance, style, and dress parodied the Andrews Sisters, provided musical interludes intended to reinforce the content objectives. Uncle Andy maintained a steady stream of scattered, high-speed chatter, while the three singers in 1940s pompadours, clunky shoes, and streamlined dresses repeated the three-part harmony as they rocked in unison with forefingers gesturing in the air to Raoul González' song:

> This is the way, the way we say
> One of the days of the week.
> Monday's the day, and the way we say
> One of the days of the week.
> Monday. Monday. Monday.

Some characters were simply drawn, playing on the theatricality of stereotype, and had few or singular identifiable items of clothing or makeup. One wore an outlandish straw hat, another a pair of bold plaid trousers with suspenders, and another ordinary, everyday clothing. One of the many bit parts I played was a takeoff on the Carol

Burnet cleaning lady character. As the woman with the mop and pail and old-timey ruffled cap, I could break the more formal distance which Señorita Barrera had to maintain. I could also give myself opportunities for slapstick, ridiculous behavior which was not permitted of the other, more serious, role.

Another role I had was that of a gray-haired, spectacled teacher, a broad caricature set up as a separate, modular sequence, complete with a small wooden table which passed for a desk with the requisite apple on top, a chalkboard in the background, and a stool for the student. The nutty teacher was played as a duo with Juana, a "kid" whose dress matched her ding-y manner and who simply could not learn. The character of Juana was a variation on the "Juana, La Loca" rhyming chants and stories I had known as a child, but the version we preferred as children was not exactly appropriate for educational television.

> *Juana, la loca,*
> *Tiene una moca,*
> *Llena de caca,*
> *Para su boca!*

> Juana, the crazy one,
> Has a mug,
> Filled with excrement,
> For her mouth!

Our cleaner version of the character of Juana had to have things repeated over and over again until she finally was able to see the point of the sequence. The technique was designed to give us additional opportunities for the repetition of curriculum content.

If the true origin of the Juana character was an inside joke for adult Hispanics, other comedic devices appealed to all viewers and came from more generalized models which cut across cultural boundaries.

"Curiouser and curiouser," said Alice, and for the moment the young girl forgot how to speak "good English." The verbal faux pas was childlike and forgivable, for Alice, confused and surprised by the looking-glass dreamworld of Wonderland, could hardly be expected to observe the rules of good grammar.

Words, pronounced Humpty Dumpty, were to be mastered and managed and given any meaning you chose, "neither more nor less," although even the philologist philosopher cautioned Alice about the proud and temperamental verbs.

Humpty Dumpty's "mimsy" and "mome raths" may have sounded like so much nonsense, but his nominalistic position was clear. His approach to words was to manage the whole lot of them, and if he had to pay words extra for extra work, he would. "The quest is," Humpty Dumpty said, "is to be master—that's all."

Lewis Carroll's famous jabberwocky world of "brillig" and "slithy toves" has a universal appeal that transcends cultural boundaries, and on certain levels, the lessons we learn from Carroll are analogous to the task of creating a successful television program for children. Carroll took metaphors and images and came up with an abstract composition that captured the relationship between a child's imagination and the world of words. He made that world go beyond the nonsense to a plain where the garbled syllables made a great deal of sense. In freeing the child from traditional everyday boundaries, he facilitated the composition of a new world which in many ways had no boundaries. It was almost as if the child had control of those new dimensions.

Through the use of the imagination, the child could stop, follow, make connections, or go off in an entirely different direction from what the author anticipated. The use of Carroll's technique is especially evident in the scene with Alice and the Kitty in Looking-glass House, where the furnishings and the words in the books go the wrong way. Alice suggests a pretend game and succeeds in "getting through" into Looking-glass House. The "magic" of the game melts the glass into a silvery mist and before Alice knows what is happening, she has jumped down into the looking-glass room.

Carroll knew that a child's limits of size, lack of knowledge, and absence of control can be overwhelming when contrasted with an adult world. The hours he spent being around children taught him that a child's world is a physical world. A child interprets everything in physical terms because he or she is largely controlled by physical limitations. Carroll knew that to appeal to children he must liberate them from those limitations. He did this by resorting to verbal trickery and creating a child's world with a different set of rules.

The intent in *Carrascolendas* was to create an analogous jabberwocky world, but the verbal trickery had to be multicultural, done with humor, and presented in two languages. This was best accomplished by the symbolism found in folklore, myths, legends, popular sayings, and jokes, which established a commonality with the Hispanic viewer without causing these children to feel they were participating in an isolating experience and without resorting to lengthy programming presentations which would lose non-Hispanic or non-Spanish-speaking viewers.

The strength of words was especially evident in the popular bilingual knock-knock jokes. Based on a combination of known cultural forms, the jokes were understood by a variety of viewers. Children who were knowledgeable in the subtleties of Spanish, English, and assorted bilingual plays or mispronunciations common to people who must communicate in both languages readily captured their meaning. But because the jokes were brief and simple in content, they were accessible to viewers who were not bilingual.

The majority of the jokes used throughout the series were part of traditional Hispanic popular culture, although at times, especially for the knock-knock jokes, we wrote new material utilizing both English and Spanish traditional cultural forms.

Dyana Elizondo, the young woman who played the role of Dyana the doll, had a flare for writing bilingual jokes styled like many in Texas Mexican popular culture. The jokes provided an easy device to break the pace of other, longer segments. Since they were repeated frequently throughout the programs, they were easy to learn and understand.

Knock-knock.
Who's there?
Jam.
Jam who?
Jam [exaggerated pronunciation
for *Ya*] *me voy a acostar.*
(I am going to bed.)

Knock-knock.
Who's there?
Cinco. (Five.)
Cinco who?
Sin comida me muero de hambre.
(Without food, I will die of
hunger.)

Knock-knock.
Who's there?
Hueso. (Bone.)
Hueso who?
Hueso [i.e., What's the]
matter, honey? [Delivered
in Spanish-accented English.]

But the world of "slithy toves" affected more than the language. The trickery created the television simulacra, those physical elements that form the images you finally see on screen. This composite is made up of the people that take part in the production either as actors or non-actors, the clothes, makeup, furnishings or buildings, camera angles, and editing effects which highlight or underscore certain items. This physical component requires that the program have a specific image, one that first originates with an idea, which somehow must go from story board outline, to set, and then eventually to whatever we will see on the television monitor.

A variety of techniques can be used to achieve this final physical simulacrum. The look can originate with the program's cultural content and be juxtaposed with it in such a manner that it enhances the overall intent of the production. If the physicality of the program is effective, it can set multiple levels of subliminal messages in motion, causing either conscious or unconscious responses in viewers. This can be done with a television commercial, a movie, or even a children's television program.

In a program like *Carrascolendas*, the message at one dimension dealt with ethnic and cultural values. We included cultural subjects in the scripts because they were Mexican American or Hispanic in content. We wanted to say certain things because we hoped that this would change the attitudes of non-Hispanic children about Hispanics and the opinions which Hispanic children had about themselves. At another level, we wanted to present specific cognitive content that went beyond any cultural goals. These were the things all children could learn simply because they were appropriate developmentally for children of certain ages. How to strike the balance between these different categories of messages is the challenge of any production team. The best television and film production designers know the power that subtle nuances can make.

The mise-en-scène for *Carrascolendas* included a multiplicity of designs. Especially at the beginning, we came up with abstract, multi-level structures which made use of geometric cutouts of circles, squares, and triangles through which actors could emerge and retreat. The intention in these particular pieces of scenery was to create angles, distance, and dimension without sacrificing the speed of production time. I wanted to give actors with minimal or no professional experience physical anchors by giving them a "performing frame" and reducing their area of operation. In this fashion, nervous hands or self-conscious feet could be hidden behind the larger wall connecting the various openings. Another safeguard was that relatively amateur camera operators could abruptly change the camera angles without running the risk that they would leave actors out of the shots because the latter might be slow in following their position cues and place themselves out of camera range. The geometric cutouts also became perfect staging devices for delivering bits and pieces of isolated Hispanic culture such as short rhymes and jokes, which were difficult to translate or transfer in any meaningful way to larger or all-English settings.

The overall effect of these geometric forms was that we could manipulate the eye of the viewer by putting images in relief, one against the other. And in so doing, we took advantage of the value of the closeup, the importance of background, and the critical tension between the two.

These visual manipulations of fantasy and reality became dominant themes in the design used in other scenery, costumes, makeup, graphics, and typography which made up the sequences. The illusion was of a three-dimensional mosaic played against a cyclorama shaded by the tones of a variety of multicultural elements.

The beginning title of *Carrascolendas* had irregularly shaped, skewed letters signaling the viewer to something fanciful and cartoonish. The animated sequences followed this graphic style, both in content and artistic design.

"Thelma, the Hippopotamus," the animated musical story of a hippo in a pink bikini whose objective was to provide a linguistic exercise in the /e/ sound in such words as "thick," "thin," "think," and "thing," was a typical example of the lyrics I wrote, which in turn took its design style from the story line I had originally created for the sequence:

Thelma was a hippopotamus,
She had an o-so-fat-so bottamus.
She ate throughout the whole day long,
She even ate as she sang this song.

One day poor Thelma tried to sit,
But oh her bottamus didn't fit.
Oh Thelma, you've just got to stop.
If you don't stop, you'll surely pop!

Her middle got so very thick,
It even passed the measuring stick.
Oh to be thin, poor Thelma thought.
I just won't eat; I'll play a lot.

Now Thelma runs and jumps and skips,
And not a snack goes through her lips.
She's thin, so thin, you'd hardly think,
That Thelma is that thing in pink!

Although the influences of those plays on perspectives so common to our initial sets remained a part of *Carrascolendas*, eventually, as budget permitted, the town itself came to have a defined look that had as much to do with abstraction as it did the things that were part of Mexican American or Hispanic historical memory. The overriding concern was that the look should transcend any particular environment the Hispanic children knew, especially if that environment was limited economically.

It was important to root the Hispanic children viewers in their own architectural heritage as well as expose the non-Hispanic audience to a Spanish/Mexican look even if this originated in fantasy.

During later years and after we had moved to one of the buildings in the new Communication Center on the University of Texas campus, we constructed an entire village, designed by Wayne Higgins, in a 5,400-square-foot studio where the set could be left standing during the production months. The buildings in the central part of the town fronted on an old plaza, in the style common both to Spanish and Mexican city squares. The floor of the plaza was laid out in a circular design of varying sizes of cobblestones.

The architectural look generally followed the Moorish/Mexican construction reminiscent of the eighteenth and nineteenth centuries, when the historical Carnestolendas and other Texas and Northern Mexico towns and missions were in existence. The predominant building materials resembled plaster, adobe, or stone, with architectural motifs such as balconies, grill work, indigenous totems, pilasters with capitals, simulated bands of moldings (or entablatures), decorating walls, doorways, and windows.

The original Carnestolendas at one point in its history became a riverboat landing and its name was changed to Rancho Davis or Davis Landing. Steamboats carried freight and passengers from the mouth of the Rio Grande at Brownsville-Matamoros as far as Roma-Rio Grande City-Camargo.

As befitted an area that derived its sustenance from a river, and duplicating some of the mills that existed in Texas missions, the central structure in the village of Carrascolendas became a mill house. The mill house, with a fifteen-foot-high wheel that churned water in a pond, housed several Carrascolendas teachers who alternately came to live in the village. It also provided living quarters in the attic for Doña Paquita, the grandmother, and a couple of her grandchildren.

The television town had a restaurant called "El Nopal" (The Cactus), owned and operated by Caracoles; toy and shoe shops belonging to rival uncles Tío Cheo and Uncle Andy; a clubhouse for kids that declared adults off limits; a lion's "den" for Agapito; and a barber/shop radio station with the call letters KLIP. Other features incorporated the humor seen in many Mexican towns or Mexican American neighborhoods. A typical example was the mechanic's corner which housed Campamocha, the fix-it man, and his assortment of tools. The shop was called *La Palanca: Lo que no se arregla se arranca* (The Lever: What Is Not Fixed Is Pulled), a rhyming motto that betrayed the goals of the establishment and captured the essence of Mexican street humor.

But at other times, the situation called for a complete departure from any cultural connections. In these instances, the scenery was essentially functional and followed the dictates of the plotlines. The settings for these purposes were varied. A fanciful pirate ship or a circus tent interior served to visualize scripts written to emphasize some particular point in a story. A bench in front of a stylized park setting served as the minimalist backdrop for a vaudeville routine. An elaborate pumpkin patch transformed the two dolls into pumpkins "planted" in the ground.

Whatever the specific goal, the scenery, like other production techniques and physical elements, was used as an imaginative device to evoke an expressionism that was meant to capture the overall meaning of *Carrascolendas*, and this meaning had more to do with a state of mind than it did with whatever was put together with hammers and nails or captured with the camera and reduced to an editing track of cuts and dissolves. The hope was that the *Carrascolendas* mosaic eventually would transcend the realistic dimensions of the television screen and be able to reach out intimately to the viewing children, as only this particular medium could do.

CHAPTER EIGHT

▓ Cookies and Tortillas

IF THE "SPEEDERS" incident those many years before at St. Joseph in Edinburg started the whole process of *Carrascolendas*, then the children in the San Antonio classroom that hot September morning in the early 1970s symbolically brought me full circle to the meaning of the *Carrascolendas* mythology. This was true no less for the kindergartners who were waiting to regale me with their artistic composites of the television program than for those other children elsewhere whom I never met but who through the years formed their own imaginative versions of what they saw on television.

Unbeknownst to me or the children who were facing me on that day, the initial grant in 1970 of two hundred thousand dollars for thirty black-and-white shows started a sequence of events which would have an impact both on me and on many groups of children like those in that classroom who would view the programs in years to come. In 1976, after 220 programs, *Carrascolendas* lost its last competition for funds and productions came to an end. Because of the nature of the funding it had received and how this funding had affected its definition, options for its revival were virtually nonexistent. Twenty years after that and many audiences of children later, *Carrascolendas* was still in sporadic reruns, perhaps speaking less to its virtues than to the absence of suitable and newer productions designed to address the goals which the program initially intended to meet.

Its shelf life thus extended well beyond the period of its production. *Carrascolendas* received accolades from some of the major film festivals, and reports surfaced occasionally of unauthorized distribution into countries like the Dominican Republic, Venezuela, Argentina, and even Canada, but in these cases broadcasts were too scattered for any accurate documentation. Still another report indicated that portions of the series were given to Belize as part of a global media distribution system designed to assist emerging countries which were in the process of setting up educational television and audiovisual facilities.

But the "magic lamp" of the children in San Antonio could not envision what would happen to the television programs which they were watching with such enthusiasm. They were oblivious to the multiculturalism buzz that surrounded them, the debates about language and its effects on instruction, the political consequences of government initiatives, and the fluctuations within the public broadcasting market, all increasingly bringing newer agendas to the forefront and causing programs such as *Carrascolendas* to have brief and precarious lives.

For those children who were among the first audiences of *Carrascolendas*, such as the kindergartners surrounding me on that hot September morning, the important thing was they were reaping the benefits of the wave of minority educational broadcasting that was blossoming at the time, irrespective of how long the flurry of interest might last or whether the need for programs like these would still exist in the decades to come. The children then knew they were seeing something they had not seen before, and they were as anxious to give me their impressions as I was to hear what they had to say.

I had barely begun to address the class when almost in unison, a series of hands went up in the air as the students vied for the privilege of asking about the program's characters or of telling about a particular *Carrascolendas* segment. One girl with hair the color of Crayola yellow was anxious to be recognized, and when it was her

turn to speak, her voice came out in a squeaky breathless rush, "Siñ
. . . reedah Barr . . . eh . . . ah . . ., I liked it when . . . Aghg . . . peetoe
. . . when he . . . he made the cookies."

"Oh . . . h," I replied, in my best I'm-going-out-to-meet-the-public
voice. I had seen some adults speak to children in the overfriendly
tone you might use if suddenly the munchkins of *The Wizard of Oz*
materialized before you, and I always told myself I would never do
that. But here I was, flustered by the little girl's outburst, and coming
perilously close to doing the same thing.

I had no idea what the child was talking about, but I did not dare
admit it for fear of sounding insensitive or forgetful about what was
going on in *Carrascolendas*. In the first three years of the series, I had
written the majority of the scripts for the programs and had come up
with the idea for all of the characters; but, after dozens of scenes,
they all tended to merge together.

I was reticent about watching the finished program, particularly
any sequences in which I appeared. I was never happy with the results and concluded we could have done so much better. When I
viewed the final product, I had a tendency to be overly critical and
this, in turn, affected the general morale of the cast and crew. So once
we taped a show, I blocked it out and went on to the next production.
There were scripts which had not been bad, and I sometimes remembered these. But there were those others I wished I had been given
the wisdom to discard after the first draft, and these I found I remembered even better.

I thought surely the little girl was talking about one of the scripts
that should never have made it to production. "Why don't you tell
the rest of the boys and girls the story?" I urged, recovering as much
of my natural voice as possible.

The little girl started to recite in huge detail a sequence which I
recognized immediately. She was talking about one of our more controversial segments, one which became a battleground of how educational concepts should be presented on television.

At our end we called the sequence, "When Agapito Made the Flour
Tortillas."

The funds *Carrascolendas* received during its first three years were awarded through the Elementary and Secondary Education Act, which restricted funding to schools and school-related institutions. Because of those stipulations, and regardless of who had created and initiated the project, *Carrascolendas* was first produced as a subcontract with an agency having the appropriate classification under the federal guidelines. This bureaucratic maneuvering, instigated by the U.S. Office of Education, predisposed the management of the project to a multiplicity of complications and almost doomed it to failure.

We found out early in those first grant negotiations that the only way KLRN could be awarded a contract was to funnel the money through an official local education agency—a school district, an educational service center, or a group having this official designation. As a public broadcasting operation, KLRN was not a local education agency, nor was it eligible for this classification. But the Office of Education was interested in the idea I had presented, and officials there wanted to find a way through the bureaucratic maze to give us the money to do the bilingual television programs I had proposed.

Originally, Office of Education personnel indicated that we would get the money through a San Antonio school district with an ongoing bilingual education program whose staff could facilitate the curriculum planning for our television program. The funds for our project would be added to their grant, with the understanding that the extra money would be awarded as a subcontract to the station, minus a small portion for the district for their participation in the project. I was told that arrangements like these were done in order to accommodate limitations of the original legislation which otherwise might not have permitted the development of innovative ideas.

The district chosen by the Office of Education officials as our contractual conduit had a bright and energetic superintendent who readily agreed to receive the funds. The only problem was that he felt that of the two hundred thousand dollars we were to get that first year, he wanted the district to get half since his understandable primary interest was in getting much-needed additional funds into his school. At one point, he even wanted the production to be done in the district television studios—not exactly an operation on a par with a PBS broadcast facility—so that more of the money could be retained by the district rather than go to KLRN in the subcontract.

Since the original strategy was to devise a way to have the television station receive the funds, the Office of Education personnel proceeded, in a rather tense session, to tell district representatives the grant would be assigned elsewhere. I was caught in the middle and did not want to tell the Washington people what should be done, since I hardly had the authority or expertise to do so. I also had an interest in retaining as much of the grant funds for the production itself rather than have the monies be dissipated for administrative costs or for some other local school use. Although the district people did not know of the KLRN grant until the moment the Office of Education approached them with the idea, they were nonetheless unhappy at almost having received a windfall and at the last minute having it taken away from them. More misery would come our way because of the local education agency situation.

The Washington officials finally determined we should go with an alternative local group, one that, in their opinion, also had an existing exemplary bilingual program. At least theoretically, this group accepted the terms and the budgetary divisions stipulated by the Office of Education project officers.

The agreement was that the agency would do the initial curriculum planning for the project and the production group at KLRN would be subcontracted to do the rest. The evaluation component was to be done by Frederick Williams, a communications scholar at the University of Texas. The agency receiving the original contract was to hire personnel who would write behavioral objectives; I would then take those objectives and write suitable scripts and produce the programs. The bulk of the monies went to KLRN since the production costs far outweighed hiring people to do the educational component. In theory, this all sounded well and good, but in practice it was another matter.

Once the local education group was awarded the contract, the agency staff took a more proprietary attitude towards the project. Part of it was understandable, but part of it was not. Essentially, the agency officials felt the responsibility for executing the work was theirs since they were the ones who had actually signed the contract, and KLRN was there to follow their direction. The perception transmitted to us was that although KLRN television crews and I had production capability, we did not have backgrounds in education and knew nothing about what made up a good bilingual program, nor did we really know children all that well. Hoping to counteract these deficiencies, the agency officials hired people they thought combined these skills. We didn't know it, but our troubles had just begun.

The initial months of the project were filled with difficulties. Some of the people at the local school agency did not like the name *Carrascolendas*. One senior executive could not pronounce it and said the name was not in the dictionary. A mini-evaluation was done with a group of children, and we found out that the future audience readily pronounced the name.

Problems with the name resurfaced from time to time, but not from the children, who accepted the name, as they did other names which often were incomprehensible to adults. These critics, including a prominent television writer, echoed some of these attitudes by saying the name of the program was a "corruption" of an authentic Spanish word.

The implication was that the legitimacy of the word resided with the definition decreed by Spanish lexicographers rather than with the point I was trying to make by choosing a name that was not in the dictionary in the first place. The comments, especially those which came early in the production period when there was still uncertainty about the program, produced concern. I concluded that I should have called it something easier to pronounce.

Two other administrators for the local agency came to the studio, looked at a kitchen set, in which we had a green refrigerator, and retreated without comment. During a restroom break, I overheard the two women saying the program was going to stereotype Mexican Americans because the refrigerator was the color of *guacamole*, a Mexican salad made with avocado. I couldn't believe this was a serious comment. The choice of the appliance color was dictated by production requirements; the cameras of the period had difficulties reproducing the starkness of black and white. Our choice of appliance colors was dictated by the shades in vogue during the 1970s; "avocado green" and "harvest gold" were our options. On the recommendation of the technical crew, we had chosen the "avocado green" refrigerator.

Initially, the project had an advisory committee, a federal requirement, made up of local parents, teachers, and other educators who gave guidance during the grant year. The local agency decided that since I was a production person, I could not attend the committee meetings. After some discussion back and forth, permission was finally granted for me to attend these sessions.

As the productions increased in size, the relationship with the original contracting agency grew more and more difficult since in the organization's view, the contractual origination engendered a proprietary interest in the series, while I, at the television station, felt a stronger and stronger need to sever those ties in order to develop the programs as I had originally envisioned them. Eventually we ended the relationship with the local school agency, but not before we went through the flour tortilla episode.

At the time *Carrascolendas* began, behavioral objectives formed the basis for the prevalent pedagogical theory. Behavioral objectives described the expected outcomes which were to result from instruction on specific topics. The objectives were the criteria utilized to evaluate educational practices, and during the 1970s formed the methodology employed to assess federally funded classroom programs of bilingual education as well as television productions like *Sesame Street* and *Carrascolendas*.

As applied to *Carrascolendas*, behavioral objectives served as the structural curriculum units guiding the scripts and eventual production of segments of the program. Curriculum specialists at the local educational agency wrote the behavioral objectives, and I then translated the objectives into a script in response to stated particular needs. In theory, we were supposed to work together in coming up with workable solutions which would be appealing to children because it would have been counterproductive to stipulate behavioral objectives which could not be translated into a television program. In practice, there was much stumbling around. The cookie or flour tortilla story was one red flag example.

The behavioral objectives for this story originated with teachers reporting that Mexican American children often came to school, and seeing what the other children were eating for lunch, did not want to eat the rolled-up tortilla bean tacos they carried to school in brown paper bags. This created a problem since the children opted to go hungry rather than eat food that in the home setting was perfectly acceptable. Severo Gomez, the chair of the *Carrascolendas* advisory board, along with other adult advisors we had at the time, indicated that their childhoods had been marked by this dilemma. Severo remembered hiding behind a tree to eat a lunch he felt did not measure up to the white bread with the neat edges the *gringo* children ate.

In their enthusiasm to become a part of the creative process, the staff at the local agency had written a script corresponding to this cultural dilemma. The segment featured a Mexican American puppet who, with eyes downcast, was embarrassed because he had brought bean tacos in a brown paper bag for his school lunch. A little *gringuito* puppet with a peanut butter and jelly sandwich in a sporty lunch box appeared on the scene. The puppet was perky and happy at the fact that lunchtime had finally arrived. The two characters talked about the lunches, with the Anglo puppet convincing the Mexican one that both lunches had merit and both were equally good.

I objected to the script because it showed Mexican Americans, even Mexican American puppets, who were ashamed of being what they were. I thought surely there were other ways of saying to children, "Look, tortilla bean tacos are part of what you are all about, and it's okay to eat them—whether you are at home or at school." We had several rounds of heated discussions, and in the end I decided to take an alternative route. I ignored the puppet suggestion and wrote the sequence in which Agapito made the flour tortillas.

As with so many other instances in *Carrascolendas*, the flour tortilla segment originated with my childhood. I did not go through any experiences with school lunches the way Severo Gomez recounted, nor did I remember taking bean tacos to school. What I did remember was that flour tortilla making at our house was an event the children in the family looked forward to with a great deal of anticipation.

My mother had a reputation as *una cocinera que tenía muy buena mano* (a cook who had a very good hand/a very good cook). The term "*buena mano*" was used for anyone who could knead dough to the right consistency, a critical skill in baking.

In making flour tortillas, the kneading is crucial and so is the rolling out of the dough and the final cooking of the flattened pancake-like circles on the griddle. Kneading too long can turn the dough stringy; rolling excessively or bringing down the rolling pin too hard on the dough can also destroy the consistency of the dough. And turning the tortilla on the griddle too often or not often enough can produce a hard tortilla instead of a pliable and almost flaky round product that will dissolve in your mouth.

As children, we always knew the tortillas were made to perfection when they'd puff up like small turtles as they were cooking on the griddle. Hot off the griddle, we would slip a piece of butter inside and watch as the steam melted it into liquid. We knew a turtle tortilla meant we would be able to scoop up the last morsel and lick the dripping butter from all the fingers we could manage to put into our mouths.

My brother, sister, and I knew each and every one of the steps to making tortillas, although coming up with perfect tortillas was another matter. We went through the frustrating experience of trying to duplicate the exact procedure and could recount the string of failures, with the inevitable piles of worthless tortillas that were produced as a result.

Of course, no one wanted to eat these miserable products, and what invariably happened was that we started making up stories to describe the outlandish shapes. My mother was tolerant of these occasions and generally joined in the hilarity, although at times I know she wished we would leave the tortilla making to her. As it happened, my sister and I never learned to make flour tortillas, and, as adults, the best tortilla maker in our family turned out to be my brother.

The significant thing about flour tortillas was that they were a source of childlike fun and were representative of whatever notion I had grown up with of Mexican American culture and, by extension, Mexican American family unity. Communicating this sentiment to a young child may not provide the solution to the tortilla bean taco problem, but at least it would show Mexican American children that flour tortillas were not sources of embarrassment. Tortillas were important as cultural symbols and whatever segment we presented on television needed to explore the virtue of the culture itself, and not necessarily by contrasting it to what Anglo children did or did not do.

What was almost beside the point was telling Mexican American children viewers that tortilla tacos were better, worse, or even just as good as peanut butter and jelly sandwiches, because, in the future, they might very well encounter other situations in which Mexican American food was worse from a nutritional viewpoint than whatever alternative American food they might be able to have.

Implicit in the puppet segment as it had been scripted was the fact that Mexican American cultural issues could be resolved only in relation to Anglo culture or Anglo cultural symbols. Far too many ethnic and racial difficulties were resolved in this manner and not simply independent of whatever problems the Anglo component brought to them.

The segment as I finally scripted it showed Agapito trying to make flour tortillas and failing at the task, in much the same manner as we had done as children. In true lion fashion, Agapito tried time and time again but instead of rolling out nicely rounded crepe-like pancakes, he produced, first, a muddle of flour and water that looked like an ill-shaped star and then another that resembled the sole of the typical Mexican *huarache* (sandal). These were the shapes my brother's creations used to take when we were children, and I transferred those two notions into the script.

Undaunted, Agapito persevered and solved the problem by spreading a large amount of dough and making cutouts with an empty coffee can, something that was pure Agapito slapstick ingenuity and had nothing to do with Mexican American culture. At the end, we decided to incorporate the concept of the circle into the script since geometric figures appeared in other sections of our curriculum goals.

The five-year-old blond girl in San Antonio, together with her classmates, had seen the segment as it was finally produced. She had picked the incident as her favorite and recounted almost verbatim the sequence of events which had occurred in the program, even though the scene was presented in its entirety in Spanish.

The girl spoke only English, yet she knew the most minute details of the story of Agapito and the flour tortillas. Evidently, neither she nor any of the other English-speaking children in the class seemed to be concerned by the absence of English in the scene.

Although I had been immersed for some years in exploring techniques for the teaching of a second language to children, I was continually surprised by the capacities young children showed in this area. The little blond girl was no exception. It was not her comprehension of the segment from a linguistic viewpoint that was so significant. Rather, it was her understanding of what essentially symbolized a Mexican American cultural experience that placed the incident at a different level.

Although the theories of bilingual education at the time were undergoing an initial process of development, there were certain overriding philosophical concepts that were important for the interplay of languages and cultures which we wanted to accomplish with *Carrascolendas*. When I first thought of the series, I did not think of abstract educational theories since I had scant background in these areas. Instead, I wanted to produce a program that spoke to Mexican American children about themselves and the experiences and values that defined them as Mexican Americans.

One of those defining elements was language, and the way Mexican Americans communicated with each other was important. Because of the particular experience I had had with language, a situation I knew existed for many Mexican American children, I wanted to capture the essence of that experience in whatever programming we did.

As a Mexican American kid growing up in Texas, I was part of a dual linguistic world, and initially my intention was to show that world in dramatic televised form. But how I handled this bilingualism in scripts was a subject of considerable debate among the scholarly consultants for the program. I wanted to present a variety of speaking styles, reflecting the community I knew. Some Mexican Americans spoke in a mix of the two languages, like many of my contemporaries. Others had problems with Spanish and either intentionally or unintentionally rejected the language altogether, like some of the younger people I knew. Still others had problems with English, like my aunts and uncles and my own mother. They retained Spanish as their principal language because it was the language of their ancestors and the language of the homeland they had shared with those ancestors. These older family members had never learned to speak English with a great deal of fluency.

Regardless of the language or combination of languages used, it was important to show its acceptability. Acceptability was the key. Acceptability would change situations such as the one I had gone through in remaining silent at Tío Abrahán's house in Monterrey or being laughed at in a classroom because the word "spiders" had been pronounced as "speeders."

While I was not naive enough to think these linguistic dilemmas would be eliminated altogether, my hope was that the program would begin the process in changing perceptions about how Mexican Americans were regarded by those "others" in the society. And once this process started, it, in turn, would be instrumental in helping to change the way in which Mexican Americans regarded themselves, of far greater importance than what specific speaking style you happened to have.

Acceptability of speaking styles did not necessarily mean that the formal, grammatical structures of the language would be ignored. Quite the contrary. As important as showing an awareness that language is a thing that is alive and constantly changing is the recognition of the fact that the purpose of an educational endeavor is to educate and improve literacy and linguistic abilities. Throughout the years of the *Carrascolendas* productions, we employed a Spanish language specialist whose sole duty was to review scripts for language usage and advise us on the best solutions to follow with specific language problems.

Oftentimes, we had to carve out our own linguistic path since during this early period, the speaking style of bilinguals was still in dispute. Mixing the two languages as it was done naturally by bilinguals was not considered a good thing for children to emulate, so I was encouraged to write scripts in either Spanish or English depending on the subjects to be treated. We then alternated the placement of these sequences in the finished program to balance the two languages.

The intention was to vary the style of presentation in the sequences without changing the content. In this manner, the children did not tire of the material, yet were able to have repeated exposures to the same core curriculum, thereby increasing the opportunity for learning. Alternating the language without changing the content also meant that children with varying degrees of proficiency in either language could follow the overall content of the program. We knew that not all children understood everything in a given program, yet assumed that children who captured bits and pieces of summarized content would be able to maintain an interest in what they were watching.

As the attitudes in language relaxed and the natural mixing done by people who speak two languages became more acceptable among language theorists, we devised a system of script writing that presented all information in both languages within one segment, without resorting to direct translations. Instead, we asked questions or brought in comments from different characters which made the conversations natural and served the purpose of telling viewers of different language capabilities what was happening in the sequences.

A challenge throughout the years of *Carrascolendas* was not only in trying to find cast and production staff who reflected the cultural, ethnic, and racial diversity of the program but also in finding the linguistic combination considered ideal for the tasks we had to accomplish. I reasoned that if we were trying to reach a certain segment of the population, the best way to start was to hire representatives from that group to help produce the endeavor. It turned out that nothing illustrated the complexity of the Spanish language and the linguistic dilemma besetting many Hispanics like the people we eventually hired to work for the program.

Once *Carrascolendas* achieved national stature and we had the budgets to afford it, we tried to import staff into Austin from other parts of the country where Hispanics from other Spanish-speaking groups lived. But convincing Puerto Ricans and Cubans, the other two large Spanish-speaking constituencies at the time besides Mexican Americans, from leaving places like New York, San Juan, and Miami was not easy. When our first recruiting efforts via long distance proved a failure, I convinced Graciela Rogerio, who was already part of our production staff at the time, to go with me to New York to interview potential candidates. Joe Aguayo, a Puerto Rican who worked for the Children's Television Workshop, the producers of *Sesame Street*, had promised to assist us in identifying people who might be willing to work in our program.

The evening we arrived awakened us to the realities of Hispanic stereotyping prevalent in New York. Graciela, a Mexican American with a caramel-colored skin who had grown up in Laredo and who had been an elementary school teacher prior to working for me, was as awestruck as I was by the magnitude of New York.

Exhausted from our trip, we decided to go for a snack to a coffee shop around the corner from our hotel and didn't realize the place was a hangout for ladies of the evening until we were approached several times, including one of the pimps, who wanted to enlist us to work for him. We didn't know whether to laugh or be insulted and instead beat a hasty retreat back to our hotel room.

The next day, as Graciela was shuffling interviewees in and out of the hotel room where I was conducting auditions, she was mistaken as one of the maids and asked to bring towels into an adjacent room. One of the aspiring actors, who was anxious to say the right thing at the audition, insisted he could speak with a Spanish accent. Noting his flawless, unaccented English, I interpreted his comment to mean that he was completely fluent in Spanish and said this was a good thing since we were looking for bilingual actors. What he meant was that he could fake a Spanish accent; this is what New York casting call directors required once they saw he was Hispanic.

In the course of the productions, we hired a number of Puerto Ricans and Cubans such as Frank Marrero, Leslie Colombani, Ray Ramirez, Erich Santamaría, Raul Julia, Elsie Rodríguez, Luis Avalos, Iraida Polanco, Luis Santeiro, and Armando Roblán, among others.

After returning to Austin, I kept hearing about a talented New York composer and singer, Raoul González, who could write compositions in Spanish and English. I was immediately interested since up to that point I had written whatever bilingual songs were needed for the program, and I thought of myself primarily as a scriptwriter and not a composer. I called Raoul and he agreed to come to Austin for an interview.

Raoul had an engaging, easygoing manner and we had immediate rapport. A handsome man, Raoul had the honey cinnamon skin tones of his African and Spanish heritage. He also had the ready wit of the streets of Brooklyn, where he had spent much of his youth, and the easy banter of night spots like Ocho Puertas of old San Juan in Puerto Rico, where he performed regularly. Once Raoul showed me how quickly he could spin a melody (he composed the theme song to *Carrascolendas* on a ten-minute bus ride through the streets of Austin), I was ready to talk seriously and offered him a job.

A long-time city dweller, Raoul laughed and told me it would be difficult for him to consider leaving New York for out-of-the-way Austin, Texas. I laughed back and told him if I really wanted him to join our project, all I had to do was sprinkle *un polvito* (a little powder) in his direction and he would have no recourse but to succumb and say "yes."

Raoul burst out laughing and said I didn't know what I was saying. He added, "When I get to know you better, I'll tell you what you just said."

Raoul eventually joined our staff and went on to compose some two hundred original bilingual songs for *Carrascolendas*. It wasn't until much later that I found out what had elicited his laughter.

When I was having the joking interchange with Raoul, I had told him I'd "sprinkle a little powder on him," implying that once I did this, he wouldn't be able to say "no" to my offer of a job. Mexican Americans who believe in witchcraft sometimes casually refer to "sprinkling a powder" to either cast a spell or control another person's behavior. I did not know the reason Raoul laughed so heartily was that among Puerto Ricans, the word "*polvo*" is the street term for having sex.

I never used the word "*polvo*" around any Puerto Ricans again. But the added mix of different Spanish speakers into our production staff gave us an automatic edge on linguistic diversity. These language perspectives were reflected in the programs we produced and in the multiplicity of audiences we could reach.

The theme song written for the series by Raoul González reflected the mixture of Spanish and English necessary for our language goals without resorting to a word-for-word translation.

Have you ever been to Carrascolendas,
Carrascolendas, Carrascolendas?
If you've never been to Carrascolendas,
Come along, come along,
come along, come along,
to Carrascolendas.

Vamos a estar en Carrascolendas,
Carrascolendas, Carrascolendas.
Te va a gustar Carrascolendas.
Vámonos, vámonos,
vámonos, vámonos,
a Carrascolendas.

The translation of the second verse of the song is not part of the original song lyrics:

We're going to be in Carrascolendas,
Carrascolendas, Carrascolendas.
You're going to like Carrascolendas.
Let's go, let's go,
let's go, let's go,
to Carrascolendas.

In another sequence, Chuchin (played by actor Ray Ramirez), a Puerto Rican/Cuban teacher who was a newcomer to the village, demonstrated the easy flow that can occur when you mix English and Spanish. Although the languages are used to avoid translation, they are not used as authentically as bilinguals would do it. In other words, there is no mixing of languages within a phrase or sentence.

We avoided lengthy language explanations in *Carrascolendas*, but there were instances such as the example given here when we talked about what happens when people speak two languages. This particular sequence was presented through another of Raoul's songs to make it more appealing to young children. The translations in parenthesis were not part of the original script and are included here to facilitate reading.

CHUCHIN: *Es un placer vivir en* Carrascolendas (It's a pleasure to live in Carrascolendas). Forgive me if my speech is in English and Spanish, but when I get excited, I speak the two languages at the same time. *Así soy* (That's the way I am). You see, I come from a place in New York called Brooklyn, and I've lived with my family in Puerto Rico, so I am the two things.

Chuchin sings to the traditional Puerto Rican *plena* rhythm:

Yo vengo de Brooklyn *y de* Puerto Rico,
Yo soy una rara y buena combinación.
Yo quiero a Brooklyn *y a* Puerto Rico,
Y a esos dos sitios, yo le he dado mi corazón.

Yes, I come from Brooklyn and from Puerto Rico,
I'm what you might call a combination of the two.
I love good old Brooklyn, I love Puerto Rico,
And if you could go there, you'd feel the way I do.

The translations in parenthesis were not part of the original song lyrics:

I speak Spanish, I speak English,
A mí me gusta hablar los dos.
(I like to speak the two.)
I say, "How are you?"
Yo digo, "¿Cómo estás?"
(I say, "How are you?")
I say, "Good-bye," *y a veces digo,* "Adiós."
(and sometimes I say, "Good-bye."

"Code switching" is the term language specialists use to refer to the natural linguistic flow among bilinguals. A person who has familiarity with two languages can easily go from one to the other, and sometimes this happens in mid-sentence or mid-thought. Traditionally, code switching was denigrated among language purists, who felt that changing languages mid-stream was indicative of poor language habits and reflected verbal poverty rather than linguistic acuity. Code switching was not encouraged. Rather, students were admonished to speak either one language or the other because this was indicative of a disciplined and literate mind.

Since Hispanics in the United States lived in a combination of linguistic worlds, they were particular language transgressors and, indeed, the derogatory terms "Tex-Mex," "Spanglish," or "*pocho*" demonstrated that the easy flow of going from one language to another was a drawback rather than an advantage. Those feelings of language inadequacy when I was young stemmed from the attitudes I heard around me, and during the production years of *Carrascolendas*, the children who were viewing the programs were subjected to the same array of language biases.

"*El* desk *alto*" (the high desk), the phrase I had used on that visit to Tío Abrahán's in Monterrey, was an example of code switching. My chagrin at having committed the linguistic gaffe reflected my awareness of knowing that the combination of words I had used was not appropriate.

Language theorists now concede what many bilingual specialists have known all along. Code switching is not arbitrary and indeed does not indicate that the code switcher is changing languages in willy-nilly fashion. Code switching follows specific linguistic rules, in the way any language does. For example, someone who is bilingual generally would not say, "*el escritorio* high" (the high desk).

Code switching was not perceived as legitimate at the time we were doing *Carrascolendas*, and even if it had been, our linguistic guideline probably would have been to avoid code switching in our dialogues since the time of a television program was limited. The goal in any language program is to elevate the level of the student's linguistic proficiency, with the implication being that at a certain educational stature, code switching is no longer appropriate. The distinctions here are between speaking styles that differentiate professional versus personal language situations rather than a speaking style that is stigmatized, as is the case with Tex-Mex speech.

In *Carrascolendas*, we devised a system of writing dialogues that allowed for language to flow back and forth. We had one short sequence between two characters in one language followed immediately by another sequence in perhaps a different setting with one of the first characters and another new character. In the second scene, the gist of the first dialogue was presented in the second language, but with new twists in the plot, so that the script did not become bogged down in a word-for-word translation.

The added plotline kept the story going at a reasonably fast pace, and in this manner, we hoped to let the alternate language repeat the description of the action. We used slapstick and other comedic devices to maintain the tempo, trying to make the entire program interesting enough for those viewers who understood both languages, yet also trying to keep the plot developing for children who spoke one language or who only had a sketchy knowledge of the second language.

The only *pochismos* we ever permitted in the programs were the names of objects or other colloquial expressions which were in common usage among Spanish speakers in the United States. By including a word such as *huila* (kite), a common word in the Southwest, in addition to *cometa* and *papalote*, which are the dictionary words for kite, we came as close as we could get at the time to granting legitimacy to a Tex-Mex word. As language rules relaxed, Hispanics and the way they spoke gained stature, and linguists began to study the intricacies of people who are bilingual. Code switching came to be considered a legitimate form of communication, with the easy back-and-forth flow of language which bilinguals have reflecting a systematic word order that has its own internal linguistic logic, like any other language.

The imposition of other language rules on *Carrascolendas* not only reflected the language bias some people had but, in certain cases, showed a naivete about language and the complexity of producing a program in two languages. Because *Carrascolendas* was a bilingual television series, federal officials reasoned that the programs had to adhere to strict language divisions which would prove that indeed the federal requirements had been met. We had to follow a specific language ratio of English to whatever second language was being used, and in our case that was Spanish. This rule was operational regardless of the linguistic demands of the situation being portrayed.

Since the task of actually measuring the percentage of language components was astronomical in a series like *Carrascolendas* and did nothing to prove the validity of the concept behind the rule, we concluded we could ignore this guideline; we figured nobody in the U.S. Department of Education was going to take the time to watch every program and spend hours counting words. Evidently nobody ever did, because nobody ever called us on it.

At the time of the flour tortilla segment, I separated the use of Spanish and English by writing entire sequences in either one language or the other. I wrote the segments in this manner hoping that the pacing and action rather than the verbal explanations would carry monolingual children from one scene to another, with the assumption being that certain children would miss some details and only bilingual youngsters would understand everything that was presented. Since the objective in the flour tortilla segment was to present a cultural concept having special value for Mexican American children, I wrote that script in Spanish.

The little blond girl in that San Antonio classroom had understood the transmitted cultural message. The only "mistake" the girl made in summarizing the gist of Agapito's adventures with the flour tortillas was in calling the tortillas "cookies," a detail which she could easily learn later. The word "tortilla" had cultural value, but had she learned that as an isolated vocabulary word, the impact on the little girl would not have been as significant. In that case, she would have been able to repeat the word, give its definition, and perhaps even learn to spell it. But she would not have been able to capture what essentially was a Mexican American experience as well as its corresponding cultural value.

It was possible in a television program to speak directly to a Mexican American five-year-old and say, "Look, there's nothing wrong with flour tortilla bean tacos. They're good at home and they're just as good at school. The only reason you don't think so is because you feel inferior about being a Mexican American. What you have to do is think differently about yourself and then it won't matter whether you eat flour tortilla bean tacos or peanut butter and jelly sandwiches." The puppet idea as it had been scripted by the local education agency told the children viewers to change their attitudes, and it showed them the reason: one food was as good as the other. The same thing could be accomplished if the two sets of children sat at a common table and ate both foods.

What the Agapito flour tortilla segment did was quite different. It gave the non-Hispanic children the opportunity to participate in a Mexican American experience, and it showed Mexican American children that the experience of being a Mexican American relative to flour tortillas was a positive and not a shameful one. This was distinct from what would happen if the non-Hispanic children went to a Mexican restaurant and ordered flour tortilla bean tacos, or if the school cafeteria served the food and both non-Hispanic and Mexican American children sat down and had a common and joyful eating experience.

This last is akin to ethnic observances, intended as cross-cultural celebrations, which came into vogue in the 1970s and continued in the decades that followed. There is some cultural value in celebrating Mexican Independence Day on the sixteenth of September or in telling students, the way we used to be told, that the Spaniards had brought the oranges to South Texas. These practices provide some community connections and enhance the feeling of a larger, global Spanish-speaking family, positive endeavors worthy of maintenance.

But as good as these practices are, they contribute little to the experience of being Mexican American and the definition of self which Mexican American children must develop in order not to have situations like the one that initially led to the writing of a behavioral objective about flour tortilla bean tacos. The hope was that a culturally specific television program like *Carrascolendas* would be able to contribute to that definition of self and make it possible for children of different backgrounds to share in a cross-cultural experience.

Carrascolendas could not transplant non-Hispanic children into Mexican American kitchen settings of the kind I had grown up with, nor could it take Mexican American children and make them go through a cultural grounding that was firm enough to withstand whatever ill feelings they might develop later on about their ethnicity. But what

Carrascolendas could do, because it was presented via the unique medium of television, was to create a participatory cross-cultural experience that could be shared by children viewers from different ethnic and racial groups.

At first, I was impressed by the blond girl's absorption of the flour tortilla segment, as I was by the enthusiasm which the class showed toward the sequence, but on reviewing it further, I came to see the full meaning of what occurred in that classroom. As far as the young girl was concerned, both tortillas and cookies were accorded the same status in that special world she, the television, and Agapito created. But the significance of the flour tortilla segment went beyond what those kindergartners saw or almost anything I consciously intended to do in writing the scene. I concluded that television had brought the special component into the mix that caused the various reactions from the children. If I had any doubts about this initially, the poster the children drew eliminated them.

That altered world was readily visible in the poster art they created for my visit to their classroom. By drawing themselves into the poster, they created a landscape that merged their world with the one they found coming out of the television set. They knew the magic of the box brought them appealing characters such as bilingual lions who made flour tortillas or flour tortilla cookies. At a subconscious level, the children had already started to change their cultural assumptions about the ingredients in those round pieces of dough. The blond girl began this process by selecting the segment as her favorite and by giving her impressions of what had taken place.

Incidents in other classroom visits reinforced the idea that television is an interaction between what is being seen and who is doing the seeing. One student was convinced that I had come from the television set to his classroom via a magic lamp; countering another child's skepticism about my identity, he pointed to a v-shaped ring I always wore. "It's her, all right," he said. "She's the *real* Señorita Barrera. Look at her crooked ring."

Another time, a teacher greeted me at a conference during the period of my earliest productions with a "I just knew you were going to wear red. I've always seen you in red." Embracing me with an exuberant hug, she wanted to know if I was married and if not, why not, and if I had any possible prospects for marriage lined up. I was indeed wearing a red suit the day I met that teacher, although she had only seen me on black-and-white television, yet her intimacy and effusiveness cut across whatever layers of unfamiliarity and absence of color there may have been between us.

The same phenomenon was occurring with the first-grade child whose comment on the magic lamp and crooked ring transcended the television distance between us. These viewers were seeing more than the programs had ever intended. They were imbuing the visual images with their ideas or interpretations, and they were responding in a unique and individual fashion to the "Señorita Barrera" they had come to think about in terms of their own experiences.

The blond girl related the television segment on the making of flour tortillas to her personal consciousness, not like an object but like experience. She may not have lived the experience in the same manner I had as a child or in the same way some of her Mexican American classmates may have done, but she participated in the experience in a far more significant way than if she had merely been told about it.

Seen from this perspective, the scene became a part of her past succession of thoughts, part of her history. In reaching back to what she knew, she had naturally identified those round objects of dough as cookies because she knew about cookies and cookie making, and not tortillas.

Through this concept of past succession, the Anglo girl was able to become a part of the communal consciousness which she shared with the other children in the classroom, including the Mexican American children, whether or not they had the same experience making flour tortillas that I had. The children had been connected through the experience of television, sharing an immediacy that was analogous to a belonging together in a common self. That common self was evident in the poster art in which they had all participated.

The children viewers had control of the *Carrascolendas* image the day I went into that Texas classroom. They had reconfigured the *Carrascolendas* program into their own abstract work of poster art, and in that artistic mosaic they became villagers of the town of

Carrascolendas as much as the characters who appeared regularly on the show. To use the terminology of one of the students, they had taken the "magic lamp" of their imagination and placed themselves in the town.

The girl with the yellow hair who so vividly related the tortilla-cookie story needed no culturally specific language abilities in order to understand virtually all the details of the story. She spoke only English and yet she related to what Agapito did in the segment. By absorbing what she saw, this child participated in a Mexican American cultural activity. And by selecting this as her favorite among all the sequences in the program, she had elevated it in her mind to a stature that went beyond the more didactic sections of the program.

This participation gave this student a kinship and a similarity of experience with the Mexican American children who sat alongside her in the classroom. Her involvement with the television program served as the catalyst for the experience of getting to know the children whose cultural backgrounds were different from hers.

The children who watched *Carrascolendas* were involved with each other in a way that had not happened before they went through the television viewing experience. The resulting connections departed from whatever cultural situations they brought with them into the mix, but critical to the new combination was what they saw in the program.

This dynamic was evident in the encounters I had with children during the times the programs were being broadcast. It was also obvious among those adults I met incidentally during the next twenty to twenty-five years who had watched *Carrascolendas* as children. Whether it was a child who was relating the story of the experience of viewing or whether it was a young adult recalling the effects of the program, the reactions followed a similar pattern.

On one of these occasions, I was beginning my introductory remarks on another class visit when a seven-year-old stood up and made an impatient bid for attention. Given the opportunity to interrupt, he hurried with his observation, "Now that I've seen you on TV and that I've seen you here . . . I think you're prettier on TV."

At another time, a six-year-old boy who came to our studios to participate in a production sequence kept following Agapito, the lion, around the set. Harry Porter, who was already in full costume for his

Agapito performance and who was trying to go over his lines for the taping, could do nothing to elude his tiny shadow. Finally, the boy could contain himself no longer. Tugging at Agapito's leg, he stood on his toes, and blushing with some embarrassment, blurted out in a half-whisper, "Agapito, Agapito . . . do you have a pee-pee?"

Some ten years later, I was shopping at a vegetable market and the Anglo cashier recognized me from the programs. She could not contain herself and said she would have to tell her brother she'd met me because both of them had seen *Carrascolendas* as children. On a follow-up trip to the same market, she reported she had told her brother about our meeting. "Is she still alive?" he had questioned. "She must be at least fifty!" I hasten to add that I was nowhere near fifty at the time.

Nearly twenty years after the production of *Carrascolendas* ended, I was attending a student gathering at the University of Illinois at Urbana-Champaign and David Arroyo, a first-generation Latino graduate student from the suburbs of Chicago, came and introduced himself to me. He did not know me, nor did he recognize my name. We made small talk and I asked him if he spoke Spanish. Embarrassed, David confessed he spoke a little. Knowing the dilemma of many young Hispanics who are still plagued by what remains an emotional issue in this country and often think they know much less Spanish than they actually do, I hastened to reassure him that many people of his generation have lost a great deal of fluency in the language. We continued chatting for a bit about Latino issues, and there was a momentary pause in the conversation. Suddenly, he started singing the theme song of *Carrascolendas*.

I was taken aback and asked him if he knew the program. David grinned and said when he was a kid, he and his brother had found the program by flipping channels while watching television. A buddy of his would join them and through the years they had joked about watching the program and the Spanish they had learned there. He said that although they could not articulate concepts of ethnicity at the time, they thought *Carrascolendas* related to them in the same way members of their family or close friends did. "We thought of it as *normal*," he said, "and some of the other programs we saw weren't *normal*."

When I told David who I was and what my relationship was to

Carrascolendas, he was as surprised as I had been to hear him singing the theme song at the particular moment he did.

For these children and young adults, the television illusion had invented its own reality. In that reality, Señorita Barrera was better looking than in the reality of the classroom. Agapito, who ran around *Carrascolendas* without resorting to the need for bodily functions, suddenly had to have an additional explanation for his body parts once he was seen in the incongruous reality of a television studio. The timeless television reality of the childhood years of the cashier and her brother had taken a leap into what must have been ancient history for them and a whopping accumulation of years for me. And what was normal for David Arroyo was only normal as far as the sequences he was seeing on that television program.

The question of my prettiness was not significant to the students who only saw me on television, nor were Agapito's physical attributes of importance to the children who considered him as their favorite television character. My being alive began and ended at the beginning and end of the television program for the cashier and her brother, and they had never thought to question my age or longevity in that context. Nor had David Arroyo, his brother, and his friend considered the normal definition of their own lives in relation to the normal trappings of a bilingual lion and his coterie of friends.

These anecdotal incidents illustrate the degree to which the television reality took on a personal and social implication which suddenly became critical because it was transferred to the physicality of a classroom, television studio, vegetable market, or university campus. The program had introduced a dimension in which a prettiness existed which did not occur in real life, the reality of one's own bodily requirements was not of consequence, age did not matter, and the ambiguity of one's own ethnicity with the corresponding ability to speak the language of that ethnicity was made normal.

The children in that Texas classroom gave symbolic value to their poster art. They manipulated the space on the paper, producing child-like, colorful forms constructed more in the realm of fantasy than of reality. But in recreating their own version of what they saw on television, they went through a process of liberating their imaginations into the representational world of images. They produced their own visual palette of symbols and provided their own aesthetic against which the television mosaic was seen. And it was against this aesthetic that both television producer and television viewer mutually created their own mythology.

If a mythology provides us with a guide for what is valuable and gives us a set of cultural norms with which we can be productive, then the responsibilities for whatever we show on television increase in magnitude. If our task is to help children find deeper meaning in their lives, then it becomes important to provide them with the requisite storytelling vehicles that develop their inner resources and imagination. It is only in this way that children will be able to build their own myths and construct their own illusions, limited only by the boundaries of their imaginations.

But the task of creating mythologies on television in a multicultural age is even more complex. A culture dominated by homogeneity could conceivably have a common ethos. In a heterogenous society, the challenge is in finding a common ethos in difference. Television has the capacity to provide that ethos, if it would only do it.

The children who drew the *Carrascolendas* poster in the Texas classroom I visited those many years ago had indeed created a common ethos. By extending their world, the children reached an understanding of things that transcended the mere lessons they were seeing in a television program. They became involved with each other in a way that went beyond anything I ever imagined with the storytelling devices I tried to place before them.

The magic of the medium of television took those incidents from my upbringing and translated them to that classroom, liberating the children's imaginations and making it possible for them to create their versions of the tortilla-cookie story. If the story lost something in the translation, it gained a measure of significance. The recreation went beyond the limits of any one culture. In a world composed of the nuances of multicultural dimensions, this has its own virtue.

The children in that Texas classroom came up with their own interpretations of what they had seen in the *Carrascolendas* programs. They were reacting as a creative force to the television they watched, and they were prepared to integrate that new composition into their lives and the setting of their classroom. History and the television program placed them in the middle of several cultural landscapes, but their manipulation of the television images liberated them from that space.

In their own creative execution, they followed the dictates of their imaginations, using the medium as a conduit for their artistic expression, but doing so according to the medium's own peculiar characteristics and their previous cultural conditioning. This dictated whether they saw cookies or tortillas in the story about Agapito.

The flour tortilla segment was included in the series in the hope of alleviating the cultural dilemma facing thousands of Mexican American children whose home values conflicted with those of the school or mainstream society. When faced with the task of producing a television segment addressing this problem, I remembered my own childhood experiences and tried to integrate them into the segment I produced. In recreating the familiar memory, I wanted to demonstrate the acceptability of flour tortillas to everyone, including bilingual television lions. And in writing the script for the flour tortilla segment, I set up my own interrelationship with those children who were going to view the program.

My initial experience came as a result of my own cultural situation, and it was the translation of that cultural context into the cultural dilemma which the Mexican American children were facing which brought another dimension to the television experience. The children viewers and I became a part of that televised translation, stemming from similar as well as different experiences across cultures. Our interaction transcended the events that occurred in that Texas classroom, as well as the set of circumstances that had taken me there in the first place. For me, this was satisfaction enough.

Bibliography

Addams, Jane. *Twenty Years at Hull-House*. New York: Signet Classics, 1981.

Anderson Imbert, Enrique, and Eugenio Florit. *Literatura Hispanoamericana*. New York: Holt, Rinehart and Winston, 1960.

Ball, Samuel, and Gerry Ann Bogatz. *The First Year of Sesame Street: An Evaluation*. Princeton: Educational Testing Service, October 1970.

Bandura, Albert. *Social Learning Theory*. Englewood Cliffs, N.J.: Prentice-Hall, 1977.

Barcus, F. Earle. *Television in the after School Hours*. Newtonville, Mass.: Action for Children's Television, October 1975.

———. *Weekend Commercial Children's Television, 1975*. Newtonville, Mass.: Action for Children's Television, October 1975.

Barrera, Aida. *Active Spanish*. Austin: Southwest Texas Educational Television Council, 1963–1964.

———. "Carrascolendas." *PTR, Public Telecommunications Review* 4, no. 4 (July/August 1976a): 20–25.

———. *Carrascolendas III: Scripts*. Unpublished manuscripts, 1972.

———. *Carrascolendas: 100/200: Teacher's Television Guide*. Austin: Southwest Texas Public Broadcasting Council, 1976b.

———. *Elementary Spanish Guide*. Austin: Southwest Texas Educational Television Council, 1966–1967.

Barthes, Roland. *Mythologies*, trans. Annette Lavers. New York: Noonday Press, 1972.

Baudrillard, Jean. *America*, trans. Chris Turner. New York: Verso, 1989.

Baum, Frank L. *The Wizard of Oz*, ed. Michael Patrick Hearn. New York: Schocken Books, 1983.

Bedell, Sally. "A Generation without Cultural Hangups." *TV Guide* (May 21, 1977): 37–41.

Berkman, Dave. "Minorities in Public Broadcasting." *Journal of Communication* (Summer 1980): 178–188.

———. "Confessions of an Ex-Bureaucrat." *Public Telecommunications Review* 8, no. 6, (November/December 1980): 14–16.

Berry, Gordon L., and Claudia Mitchell-Kernan, eds. *Television and the Socialization of the Minority Child*. New York: Academic Press, 1982.

Bettelheim, Bruno. *The Uses of Enchantment: The Meaning and Importance of Fairy Tales*. New York: Knopf, 1976.

Blanco, Andrés Eloy. *Obras Completas, Tomo 1: Poesía*. Caracas: Ediciones del Congreso de la República, 1973.

Blume, Wilbur T., and Paul Schneller. *Toward International Tele-Education*. Boulder, Colo.: Westview, 1984.

Brown, Ray. *Children and Television*. Beverly Hills: Sage, 1976.

Calvert, Robert A., and Arnold De León. *The History of Texas*. Arlington Heights, Ill.: Harlan Davidson, 1990.

Campbell, Joseph. *The Hero with a Thousand Faces*. Princeton: Princeton University Press, 1973.

———. *The Power of Myth*, ed. Betty Sue Flowers. New York: Doubleday, 1988.

———, ed. *The Portable Jung*. New York: Penguin Books, 1976.

Carrascolendas: Bilingual Education through Television. Interim Report. Austin: Southwest Texas Public Broadcasting Council, 1971.

Carrascolendas: Bilingual/Multicultural Television Project. Funding Proposal. Austin: Southwest Texas Public Broadcasting Council, May 1975.

Carrascolendas: Teacher's Guide I, 500 Series. Austin: Southwest Texas Public Broadcasting Council, 1975–1976.

Carrascolendas: Teachers Guide II, 600 Series. Austin: Southwest Texas Public Broadcasting Council, 1976–1977.

Carrascolendas: Writers' Notebook. Austin: Southwest Texas Public Broadcasting Council, 1975–1976.

Carroll, Lewis. *Alice's Adventures in Wonderland and through the Looking Glass.* New York: W. W. Norton, 1971.

Carter, Thomas P. *Mexican Americans in School: A History of Educational Neglect.* New York: College Entrance Examination Board, 1970.

Carter, Thomas P., and Roberto D. Segura. *Mexican Americans in School: A Decade of Change.* New York: College Entrance Examination Board, 1979.

Cater, Douglass, and Stephen Strickland. *A First Hard Look at the Surgeon General's Report on Television and Violence.* Washington, D.C.: Joint Program of Aspen Institute for Humanistic Studies and Academy for Educational Development, March 1972.

———. *TV Violence and the Child: The Evolution and Fate of the Surgeon General's Report.* New York: Russell Sage Foundation, 1975.

Catholic Archives of Texas, Austin. *Papers for St. Joseph and Sacred Heart Schools, Edinburg; Incarnate Word Academy, Brownsville; Immaculate Conception Church, Rio Grande City.*

Center for American History, University of Texas at Austin. *Collections for Starr County, Rio Grande City, Mier Expedition, Mier, Tamaulipas, Mexico.*

Cervantes, Miguel D. *Six Exemplary Novels*, trans. Harriet de Onís. Great Neck, N.Y.: Barron's Educational Series, 1961.

———. *Rinconete y Cortadillo.* New York: Las Americas Publishing, 1960.

Chapa, Jorge. "The Myth of Hispanic Progress: Trends in the Educational and Economic Attainment of Mexican Americans." *Journal of Hispanic Policy* 4 (1989–1990): 3–18.

Clark, Richard E. *Children's Television: The Best of ERIC.* Syracuse: ERIC Clearinghouse on Information Resources.

Committee on Children's Television, Inc.: The Peaceable Kingdom: A Dis-

cussion of the Report and Policy Statement on Children's Television Programs Issued by the Federal Communications Commission. San Francisco: Committee on Children's Television, Inc., 1975.

Communicating with Children through Television. New York: CBS Economics and Research, May 1977.

Comstock, George, Steven Chaffee, Nathan Katzman, Maxwell McCombs, and Donald Roberts. Television and Human Behavior. New York: Columbia University Press, 1978.

Crawford, James. Bilingual Education: History, Politics, Theory, and Practice. Trenton: Crane, 1989.

———, ed. Language Loyalties: A Source Book on the Official English Controversy. Chicago: University of Chicago Press, 1992.

Crèvecoeur, Michel-Guillaume Saint-Jean de. Letters from an American Farmer and Sketches of Eighteenth-Century America, ed. Albert E. Stone. New York: Penguin, 1986.

CTW Research Bibliography: 1968–1976. New York: Children's Television Workshop.

Darío, Rubén. Poesías Completas, ed. Alfonso Méndez Plancarte. Madrid: Aguilar, 1961.

Davidson, Cathy N. Revolution and the Word: The Rise of the Novel in America. New York: Oxford University Press, 1986.

Dedericks, Sister Joseph A., and Sister Rose Mary Cousins, eds. Catholic Schools: Dawn of Education in Texas. Beaumont: Beaumont Printing and Lithographing Co, November 1986.

De León, Arnoldo. The Tejano Community, 1836–1900. Albuquerque: University of New Mexico Press, 1982.

———. They Called Them Greasers: Anglo Attitudes toward Mexicans in Texas, 1821–1900. Austin: University of Texas Press, 1983.

Dos Novelas Picarescas: El Lazarillo de Tormes y El Buscón. Garden City, N.Y.: Colección Hispánica, Doubleday, 1961.

Eliade, Mircea. Myth and Reality. New York: Harper Torchbooks, 1963.

Ferguson, Clara P. Preadolescent Children's Attitudes toward Television Commercials. Austin: University of Texas, 1975.

Fighting TV Stereotypes: An ACT Handbook. Newtonville, Mass.: Action for Children's Television, 1983.

Franklin, Benjamin. Autobiography and Other Writings, ed. Kenneth Silverman. New York: Penguin, 1986.

George, Eugene. *Historic Architecture of Texas: The Falcón Reservoir.* Austin: Texas Historical Commission, December 1975.

Glazer, Nathan, and Daniel Patrick Moynihan. *Beyond the Melting Pot.* Cambridge: M.I.T. Press and Harvard University Press, 1963.

Gleason, Philip. "American Identity and Americanization." In *Harvard Encyclopedia of American Ethnic Groups,* ed. Stephan Thernstrom, pp. 31–58. Cambridge: Harvard University Press, 1980.

González, Jovita. "Among My People." *Publications of the Texas Folklore Society* 10 (1932): 99–108.

———. "The Bullet-Swallower." In *Puro Mexicano,* ed. J. Frank Dobie, pp. 107–114. Dallas: Southern Methodist University Press, 1975.

———. "Don Tomás." In *We Are Chicanos,* ed. Philip D. Ortego, pp. 48–52. New York: Washington Square Press, 1973.

———. "Folk-Lore of the Texas-Mexican Vaquero." In *Texas and Southwestern Lore,* ed. J. Frank Dobie, pp. 7–22. Dallas: Southern Methodist University Press, 1967.

———. Interviews, *Sabor del Pueblo,* Austin: Southwest Center for Educational Television, 1981.

———. "Social Life in Cameron, Starr, and Zapata Counties." Master's thesis, University of Texas, 1930.

———. "Stories of My People." In *Texas Folk and Folklore,* ed. Mody C. Boatright, Wilson M. Hudson, and Allen Maxwell, pp. 19–24. Dallas: Southern Methodist University Press, 1954.

Goetzmann, William H., and William N. Goetzmann. *The West of the Imagination.* New York: W. W. Norton, 1986.

Grimm, Jacob. *Fairy Tales of the Brothers Grimm, 1785–1863.* New York: Metropolitan Museum of Art, 1979.

Gunning, Mother M. Patricia. *To Texas with Love: A History of the Incarnate Word and Blessed Sacrament.* Austin: Von Boeckmann-Jones, 1971.

The Hebbronville Story. Hebbronville, Tex.: Hebbronville Chamber of Commerce, Jim Hogg County, 1958–1963.

Higham, John. "Multiculturalism and Universalism: A History and Critique." *American Quarterly* 45, no. 2 (June 1993): 195–219.

Hijuelos, Oscar. *The Mambo Kings Play Songs of Love.* New York: Harper and Row, 1990.

Hunt, Peter, ed. *Children's Literature: An Illustrated History.* Oxford: Oxford University Press, 1995.

Huston Stein, Aletha, and Lynette Kohn Freidrich. *Impact of Television on Children and Youth*. Chicago: University of Chicago Press, 1975.

Isber, Caroline, and Muriel Cantor. *Report of the Task Force on Women in Public Broadcasting*. Washington, D.C.: Corporation for Public Broadcasting, October 8, 1975.

Johnson, Henry Sioux, and William J. Hernández-M. *Educating the Mexican American*. Valley Forge, Penn.: Judson Press, 1970.

Johnston, Jerome, James Ettema, and Terrence Davidson. *An Evaluation of FREESTYLE*. Ann Arbor: Center for Research on Utilization of Scientific Knowledge, University of Michigan, 1980.

Jung, C. G. *The Archetypes and the Collective Unconscious*, trans. R. F. C. Hull. Princeton: Princeton University Press, 1990.

———. *The Basic Writings of C. G. Jung*, trans. R. F. C. Hull. Princeton: Princeton University Press, 1990.

———, ed. *Man and His Symbols*. New York: Dell, 1968.

Kanellos, Nicolás. *A History of Hispanic Theatre in the United States: Origins to 1940*. Austin: University of Texas Press, 1990.

Katzman, Nathan I. *Violence and Color Television: What Children of Different Ages Learn*. East Lansing: Michigan State University, June, 1971.

Kaye, Evelyn. *The Family Guide to Children's Television*. New York: Pantheon Books, 1974.

Kelly, Hope, and Howard Gardner, eds. *Viewing Children through Television*. San Francisco: Jossey-Bass, 1981.

Krauze, Enrique. *Mexico, Biography of Power: A History of Modern Mexico, 1810–1996*, trans. Hank Heifetz. New York: HarperCollins, 1997.

Laosa, Luis M. *Carrascolendas Formative Research Report*. Los Angeles: University of California, December 26, 1973.

Lesser, Gerald S. *Children and Television: Lessons from Sesame Street*. New York: Random House, 1974.

Liberty, Paul G. Jr., Frank Gerace, Raymond Koegel, and Paula Gwinn. *Carrascolendas: Final Evaluation Report, Fall, 1975*. Austin, Tex., February 2, 1976.

Liebert, Robert M., John M. Neale, and Emily S. Davidson. *The Early Window: Effects of Television on Children and Youth*. New York: Pergamon, 1973.

Mann, Thomas. *Tonio Kroger and Other Stories*, trans. David Luke. New York: Bantam Books, 1970.

Maule, Randy William. "A History of K–12 Instructional Television." Ph.D. diss., University of Florida, 1987.

McDonagh, Sr. Kathleen. *Mother Teresa Solis, IWBS: First Incarnate Word Vocation in the New World.* Unpublished Report, 1998.

McLuhan, Marshall. *Understanding Media: The Extensions of Man.* New York: Signet, 1964.

McNamara, Jo Ann Kay. *Sisters in Arms: Catholic Nuns through Two Millennia.* Cambridge: Harvard University Press, 1996.

Melody, William. *Children's TV: The Economics of Exploitation.* New Haven: Yale University Press, 1973.

Meyer, Manfred, ed. *Children and the Formal Features of Television: Approaches and Findings of Experimental and Formal Research.* New York: K. G. Saur, 1983.

Mielke, Keith W., Rolland C. Johnson, and Barry G. Cole. *The Federal Role in Funding Children's Television Programming: Volume I: Final Report.* Bloomington: Institute for Communication Research, April 30, 1975.

Miller, Hubert J. *José de Escandón: Colonizer of Nuevo Santander.* Edinburg, Tex.: New Santander Press, 1980.

Montejano, David. *Anglos and Mexicans in the Making of Texas, 1836–1986.* Austin: University of Texas Press, 1987.

Moody, Kate. *Growing Up on Television: The TV Effect.* New York: Times Books, 1980.

Morris, Norman S. *Television's Child: The Impact of Television on Today's Children.* Boston: Little, Brown, 1971.

Moynihan, Daniel P. *Maximum Feasible Misunderstanding.* New York: Free Press, 1969.

Muller, Werner, and Manfred Meyer. *Children and Families Watching Television: A Bibliography of Research on Viewing Processes.* New York: K. G. Saur, 1985.

Murray, John P. *Television and Youth: Twenty-five Years of Research and Controversy.* Stanford: Boys Town Center for the Study of Youth Development, 1980.

Murray, John P., Eli A. Rubinstein, and George A. Comstock, eds. *Television and Social Behavior, Reports and Papers, Volume II: Television and Social Learning, Report to the Surgeon General's Scientific Advisory Committee on Television and Social Behavior.* Washington, D.C.: U.S. Government Printing Office, 1972.

Nelson, Bernadette, Joseph Zelan, Susan Brighton, Daniel Sullivan, and David Napior. *An Evaluation of the Emergency School Aid Act TV Programs Focusing on the Following Categories of Potential Impact or Effect: Management/Administration, Production, Distribution, and Financial Issues.* Cambridge: ABT Associates, July 31, 1980.

Nelson, Bernadette, Daniel Sullivan, Joseph Zelan, and Susan Brighton. *Assessment of the ESAA-TV Program: An Examination of Its Production, Distribution, and Financing: Executive Summary.* Cambridge: ABT Associates, 1980.

Nobel, Grant. *Children in Front of the Small Screen.* Beverly Hills: Sage, 1975.

O'Connor, Robert F., ed. *Texas Myths.* College Station: Texas A&M University Press, 1986.

Olson, David E., ed. *Media and Symbols: The Forms of Expression, Communication, and Education.* Chicago: University of Chicago Press, 1974.

Paine, Thomas. *Common Sense and Other Political Writings.* Indianapolis: Bobbs-Merrill, 1953.

Palmer, Edward L., and Aimée Dorr. *Children and the Faces of Television: Teaching, Violence, Selling.* New York: Academic Press, 1980.

Paredes, Américo, ed. and trans. *Folktales of Mexico.* Chicago: University of Chicago Press, 1970.

———. Interview. *Sabor del Pueblo.* Austin: Southwest Center for Educational Television, 1981.

———. *"With His Pistol in His Hand:" A Border Ballad and Its Hero.* Austin: University of Texas Press, 1958.

Pattison, Walter T. *Representative Spanish Authors.* New York: Oxford University Press, 1951.

Perales, Alonso S. *Are We Good Neighbors?* New York: Arno Press, 1974.

Pettit, Arthur G. *Images of the Mexican American in Fiction and Film.* College Station: Texas A&M University Press, 1980.

Prescott Webb, Walter, ed. *The Handbook of Texas.* Vol 1. Austin: Texas State Historical Association, 1952.

Rodriguez, Richard. *Hunger of Memory: The Education of Richard Rodriguez*. Boston: David R. Godine, 1982.

Romo, Ricardo. "George I. Sanchez and the Civil Rights Movement: 1940–1960." *La Raza Law Journal* 1 (1986): 342–362.

———. "Mexican Americans in the New West." In *The Twentieth Century West*, ed. G. Nash and R. Eulain, pp. 123–145. Albuquerque: University of New Mexico Press, 1989.

Ruiz, Ramón. *The Great Rebellion: Mexico 1905–1924*. New York: W. W. Norton, 1980.

Salazar, Veronica. *Dedication Rewarded: Prominent Mexican Americans*. San Antonio: Express-News Corp., 1976.

Sando, Joe. Interview. *The End of the Race*. Austin: Southwest Center for Educational Television, 1981.

San Miguel, Guadalupe Jr. *"Let All of them Take Heed": Mexican Americans and the Campaign for Educational Equality in Texas, 1910–1981*. Austin: University of Texas Press, 1987.

Schramm, Wilbur, Jack Lyle, and Edwin B. Parker. *Television in the Lives of Our Children*. Stanford: Stanford University Press, 1961.

Scott, Florence Johnson. *Historical Heritage of the Lower Rio Grande*. Rio Grande City, Tex.: La Retama Press, 1965.

———. *Royal Land Grants North of the Rio Grande, 1777–1821*. Rio Grande City, Tex.: La Retama Press, 1969.

Seeking Solutions to Violence on Children's Television. San Francisco: Committee on Children's Television, Inc., February 1977.

Serrano Martínez, Celedonio. *La Bola Suriana: Un spécimen del corrido mexicano*. Secretaría de Desarrollo Social, Gobierno del Estado de Guerrero, 1988.

Singer, Jerome L., and Dorothy G. Singer. *Television, Imagination, and Aggression: A Study of Preschoolers*. Hillsdale, N.J.: Erlbaum, 1981.

Smith, Ronald L. *Sweethearts of '60s TV*. New York: St. Martin's Press, 1989.

St. Joseph Catholic Church, Edinburg, Texas, 1942–1977. McAllen: Outreach Publications.

Television and Growing Up: The Impact of Televised Violence. Report to the Surgeon General, U.S. Public Health Service. Washington, D.C.: U.S. Government Printing Office, 1972.

Television Research Committee: Second Progress Report and Recommendations. Leicester: Leicester University Press, 1969.

Terrace, Vincent. *Fifty Years of Television: A Guide to Series and Pilots, 1937–1988.* New York: Cornwall Books, 1991.

Van Wart, Geraldine. *Carrascolendas: Evaluation of a Spanish/English Educational Television Series within Region XIII.* Austin: Education Service Center, Region XIII, June 1974.

Williams, Frederick, Robert LaRose, and Frederica Frost. *Children, Television, and Sex-Role Stereotyping.* New York: Praeger, 1981.

Williams, Frederick, Susan McRae, and Geraldine Van Wart. *Carrascolendas: Effects of a Spanish/English Television Series for Primary School Children. Second Year Evaluation.* Austin: Center for Communication Research, University of Texas, June 1972.

Williams, Frederick, and Geraldine Van Wart. *Carrascolendas: Bilingual Education through Television.* New York: Praeger, 1974.

Williams, Frederick, Geraldine Van Wart, and Monty Stanford. *Carrascolendas: National Evaluation of a Spanish/English Educational Television Series.* Austin: Center for Communication Research, University of Texas, June 1973.

Williams, Sally, and Valerie Crane. *Know Your Competition.* San Francisco: Committee on Children's Television, Inc., 1974.

Wilson, Clint C. II, and Félix Gutiérrez. *Minorities and Media: Diversity and the End of Mass Communication.* Newbury Park: Sage, 1991.

Window Dressing on the Set: Women and Minorities in Television. Washington, D.C.: U.S. Commission on Civil Rights, U.S. Government Printing Office, August 1977.

Window Dressing on the Set: An Update. Washington, D.C.: U.S. Commission on Civil Rights, U.S. Government Printing Office, January 1979.

Winick, Mariann Pezzella, and Charles Winick. *The Television Experience: What Children See.* Beverly Hills: Sage, 1979.

Winn, Marie. *The Plug-in Drug.* New York: Viking, 1977.

Woolery, George W. *Children's Television: The First Thirty-Five Years, 1946–1981. Part I: Animated Cartoon Series.* Metuchen, N.J.: Scarecrow, 1983.

———. *Children's Television: The First Thirty-Five Years, 1946–1981. Part II: Live, Film, and Tape Series.* Metuchen, N.J.: Scarecrow, 1985.

Zangwill, Israel. *The Melting Pot.* New York: Macmillan, 1925.